# The 15 Minute Mac Book
# Ventura
## 365 lessons to master the Mac in
## fifteen minutes or less

Ventura Edition
Revision v1.1

By Paul Doty

While the publisher and the author have used good faith efforts to ensure that the information and instructions contained in this work are accurate, the publisher and author disclaim all responsibility for errors or omissions, including without limitation responsibility for damages resulting from the use of or reliance on this work. The use of the information and instructions contained in this work is at your own risk.

The 15 Minute Mac Book is not associated with Apple or any product or vendor mentioned in this book. It is an independent publication and has not been authorized, sponsored, or otherwise approved by Apple, Inc. or any other entity. Portions of this work fall under the fair use copyright act in that this book may contain content not authorized by its owner, but is used by the publisher for the purpose of criticism, comment, news reporting, teaching, or research.

# About the Author

Paul Doty is a husband, father, and former CEO of West Coast Sound & Light in Northern California. He is a computer enthusiast, programmer, audio engineer, theatrical lighting designer, published author, teacher & podcaster.

Paul's computer journey started with the Commodore 64, traveled through the Windows environment from Windows 3 to Windows 11, and has taken him through ten versions of Mac OS.

# Forward by Peter Alves

I have been involved with the Macintosh since the beginning in 1984, both as a Mac sales and repair shop owner and as a consultant. The question I've been asked the most through the years has been "How did you learn all this?" My answer has always been the same, "Lots of reading." In all of that reading (Magazines, Books, and later the internet) I have found that The 15 Minute Mac Book is the best laid out and most effective source I have seen.

I say this because The 15 Minute Mac Book is very *Mac Like*. It's the perfect complement for any Apple device or computer. The Mac itself is an easy *turn-it-on-and-go* computer - and The 15 Minute Mac Book is an easy *open-it-up and read* manual.

Just like the Apple products themselves, it's an easy, well-laid-out read. 365 Short easy to understand lessons that cover everything from *Airdrop* to *Zapping the PRAM*. I've found that this is one of those rare occasions where it's beneficial to own both electronic and a paperback version of a book. I have the hard copy for reading out on the deck, and the electronic version for when I travel or need a quick searchable reference.

In 1997 Apple launched its *Think Different* campaign. They understood that Mac users were a specific breed that didn't suffer through long, tech jargon-filled manuals. We are *get to the point* people. The idea of short concise mini-lessons of about 15 minutes or less is perfectly suited to a moment of casual reading or looking up a specific problem or *how-to*.

Again, for the Apple user, The 15 Minute Mac Book is the perfect companion. My only issue with it is why didn't someone think of this concept sooner? Genius!


**-Peter Alves is a world-known Apple guru and the admin for Facebook's largest Mac community The Mac Computer Users Group.**

# 1

# Ventura

Rust, laundry, and computer technology never sleep. I began writing the original Big Sur Edition of the 15 Minute Mac Book at the end of the Mohave era and the beginning of the Catalina. It has now become a yearly project for me and at the time of the release of this edition, I'm happy to say that it has become my most successful book. I'd like to start this edition by thanking everyone who supported the previous books and if you're a first time reader, welcome!

I'm sure you've heard the question, "How do you eat an elephant?" The answer of course is one bite at a time. That's the premise of the 15 Minute Mac Book series. Each book takes 365 small bites out of the Macintosh Apple. While each book in the series is geared to a specific operating system, all will contain universal helps and hacks so in the future as the technology landscape changes, all of these books will tend to compliment each other as they sit beside one another on your bookshelf.

In writing these books it is not my intention to be exhaustive or in turn, exhausting. I have tried to focus on the features that most people use every day on their Macs. My focus is to make you more productive with the Mac operating system, not to write a 2000 page manual. Because of this, every single feature will not be covered in these books.

Each book is laid out so that the reader could choose to digest a lesson a day, thus mastering the particular Mac OS in about a year, but because the lessons are small, you may very well want to read several pages a day. You might want to read until you come across a revelation that might help you in your workflow and then stop, so you can digest that gem for the remainder of your day. However you decide to read the book, you will be able to establish your own pace, digesting the content in whichever way works best for you.

Instead of using a chapter structure, I've chosen to simply number the lessons. Each lesson or topic is titled so you can easily use the book's table of contents as a reference for specific tasks. It's also written in such a way that if you need to jump around to learn some tasks before others, you may feel free to do so.

In writing these books I didn't want them to be stuffy technical manuals. I want them to be real-world books, for real-world people using Macs. In it you'll find lessons, tricks, products, gadgets, hacks, history, and occasionally some humor.

Much of this book will remain current over time, even while operating systems change and improve. While every new release of Mac OS brings changes and improvements, you will be amazed at how much stays the same! Apple is careful to make sure that their user base never experiences a total reinvention of their operating system like we saw with Windows 8. As such, this version of this book will likely remain 95% accurate and informative to anyone who owns it, even if the operating system that you're using it with is ahead of the book!

Whether you're mastering a new task or concept in a day or taking on several, I hope you will enjoy *The 15 Minute Mac Book: Ventura.* Who knows, before too long you just might find that you've become a 15 Minute Mac Book Pro. See what I did there?

# 2
# OS Unification

For the last few years, we've seen Apple take great strides in unifying all of their operating systems. In many ways, the iPhone has been the center target for the user interface. While a computer may be quite different than a telephone, Apple has recognized that a unified operating system is a much needed step to allow people to move fluently from one device to another. As our world becomes more and more connected, we use our devices in more connected ways. With the launch of Ventura, in 2022 we have seen the biggest unification push yet between all of the operating systems with a complete redesign of System Preferences into the new app System Settings. As such this will be the biggest rewrite of the 15 minute MacBook series, in order to reflect those changes. In this new addition, we have tried to group areas of the book together better than we have in the past allowing you to browse complete sections on various topics.

Some people may not like the new System Settings app, and Apple may experience some pushback for a short period of time, but in time it will prevail as OS unification can only help as our tech world grows in complexity.

# 3

# Switching To The Dark Side

This chapter is a brief history chronicling my transition to Mac. Everyone has their own story and as my friend Peter Alves likes to point out, there are many stories out there of how people switched to Mac, but you seldom hear a story of how people switched from Mac to PC. This is my story.

About eleven years ago I was running a business that used a good number of PCs on a daily basis. My business was high tech in nature and the computers ran everything from accounting to the actual performance of my work. I had been using computers for thirty-five years at that point and I was totally immersed in the world of PC. I knew about Macs and I owned Apple gateway products like the iPhone and the iPod, but I had an aversion to anything Apple when it came to the computer itself. I shied away from the Macs because I thought that they posed a compatibility issue with my high tech world. I interacted with clients daily in programs like Word, Excel, and Outlook. My high tech world ran on PCs, so why would I be interested in learning yet another operating system that very few of my peers were using at the time? And then there was the cost. Why would I pay three or more times the amount for a computer when PCs had become so cheap over the years?

My PC world came crashing down in 2012 with the introduction of Windows 8. While Win 8 paved the way for Windows 10, 8 was a disaster for companies like mine. After updating to 8 my business was left with a confusing computer interface and an OS that lacked the solid driver support that the mature Windows 7 platform had enjoyed for so long. Add to that, viruses were multiplying at an alarming rate. In that year our computers went down on such a regular basis from viruses, I was literally unable to get most of my regular day to day work done because I was spending all my time cleaning computer viruses. It eventually reached a critical tipping point and something had to give.

It was at that point that I noticed my friends and colleagues switching to Macs like rats jumping off of a burning ship. They all universally sung the praises of the machines, but I still wasn't convinced. I had tied up so much of my life in becoming proficient on PCs, and I feared that if I went over to the dark side, I would then have two different systems that I would have to keep up and running. Later that year I was somewhat forced into the world of Mac by circumstances.

In the summer of 2012, my manager for my company was due for a new company laptop. At the same time, we had purchased a few new sound consoles with the ability to do multi-channel recording using computers. Most engineers were now using Macs as recording machines. The tide was turning. I purchased a MacBook Pro for my manager, and at the end of the year, one for myself so I could continue to support his, and so I would be compatible with our recording projects. At that time I had no real interest in going over to Mac as my personal computer, as I still had no experience at that point as to the solidness and dependability of the machine. I simply saw it as a standalone tool that would be used for recording.

That first Mac introduced me to a hardware/software ecosystem that has reshaped my technology world. I won't candy-coat the fact that the first year was a difficult learning curve. While Apple has designed a great working system free from much of the confusion that comes with other computers, I was soon to find that my decades of PC use would be my hardest hill to climb with this new system. You never really understand how entrenched your muscle memory is in a system until you break from it. In a real sense, the hardest thing you will do in learning Mac is unlearning PC.

Today, I own 10 Mac computers and 3 Windows machines running Windows 11. For me, the war is effectively over. I use the Windows machines for a few dedicated applications where PC is still king. One runs Quickbooks for my corporation and another is dedicated as a touch screen lighting console, but for all other applications, and for all of my personal and travel use, Mac is hands down the computer of choice for me and everyone at my company. My conversion has spilled over to most of my friends and family at this point as I continue to witness the mass exodus to a more reliable, virus-free, simple computing environment.

When that first Mac arrived at my office eleven years ago, I would have loved a simple book like this, with simple step by step instructions on how to accomplish tasks on the system. I hope this book becomes a handy resource for you whether you're brand new to Mac or a seasoned user. After eleven years I still learn a new trick almost daily.

# 4

# You Get What You Pay For

One of the few drawbacks of a Mac over a PC according to hardcore PC users is the initial cost. On average, a Mac can cost three times more than its PC equivalent. While it's true that you will shell out more upfront for a Mac, a case can be made that the Mac will actually cost less over the life of the machine. If you've ever bought a new car, you likely understand that the cost of ownership of that vehicle will be far greater than the $35,000 that you initially spend on it. The true cost of ownership will be the total sum of the fuel and fluids that will be required to operate it over its lifespan. You'll also spend a pretty penny on repairs, insurance, and maintenance over the lifespan of the vehicle.

A computer is no different. The cost of ownership for a computer will be the life expectancy of the unit, repair costs, and downtime of the unit. Remember, time is money. A PC might initially cost a third of its equivalent Mac but the Mac will likely outlast it at least three to one, possibly longer. This is due to a number of factors. First off, the build materials in an Apple product far outlast the materials commonly found in cheap PCs. Aluminum construction is the norm in a Mac compared to the plastics of a typical PC.

Now consider downtime of the two platforms. Macs have no virus issues for the most part. If you are a business professional who depends on their computer, you will have to consider what your downtime is worth.

The last thing to consider between the two platforms is the continued performance level over time factor. While PCs will tend to slow down over their three or so year lifespan, the Mac will tend to stay just as fast as the day you bought it throughout its six to ten-year effective life.

# 5

# Hello M2

"What do you want to do today Brain?" The same thing we do every day Pinky, try to take over the world!"

Catalina sent a clear message that Apple was going places and times where changing. The Macintosh Apple was on the roll. It brought many under the hood changes that would lay the groundwork of what was on the horizon. Yes, it broke some apps and caused their shiny new machines to slow down a bit as developers struggled to keep up with the new technology changes but all of it was necessary to lay the groundwork of what was to come.

Big Sur was a transitional release further paving the way for Apple's plans to take the Mac to the next level. At first glance, Big Sur wasn't a huge upgrade from Catalina, but make no mistake, there where major changes still going on under the hood.

Apple announced in June of 2020 that they where on a two-year track to move from their current Intel-based CPUs to their own Apple chip, the M1. We saw this change a few years back with both the iPad and the iPhone and the results where huge. The iPhone 14 Pro is now arguably the fastest and most advanced phone on Planet Earth and it will continue to improve by leaps and bounds over the decades to come unhampered by the limitations of third-party chip makers who share their technology with all of the other phones in the world. We saw the same thing happen with the introduction of the iPad Pro.

In 2022 Apple continues to push on with the M2. As the technology continues to improve we can expect more of the same in the years to come.

# 6

# Understanding the M2

Last year saw the introduction of the M1. That's a motorway in the UK right? Well yes, but it's also one of the most significant changes in computing in the last decade.

The M1 delivered a one two knock out punch to the PC world. The M1 combined all of the traditional computer circuit sections that are normally found on multiple boards in a computer onto a single chip. On an Intel based computer, the CPU, the RAM, and the video processors are all on separate boards within the computer. The advantage is that you can replace one without the others. The disadvantage is time and power.

Let's demonstrate this concept in the real world. Let's say that you have 6 people building a computer. They all live within a two block area, but all in different houses. Every day they have to walk from one house to another to assemble their computer. The advantage is that if anyone needs to be replaced, we can simply get another tech from a different house to come in.

Now, what happens if you move all 6 people into the same house? The result is two fold. First, speed. All six techs are immediately available because they have near zero travel time to their job site. Next is power saving. It takes far less energy for all of our techs to get to their workstations. This is why the M based computer is so much faster and powerful than a traditional design. M2 takes the platform to faster speeds and greater performance as the platform matures.

# 7

# The Apple Ecosystem

Apples greatest advantage may be the way that everything works seamlessly together. Every year Apple introduces new ways for all of their devices to compliment and work with each other. This is the advantage of a closed system and infrastructure. From the biggest Mac to the smallest Apple Watch, everything in the system has its overlaps and interactions. With every incarnation of the Mac OS you can see this theme of interaction touted and demonstrated with each new Apple Event.

Previously I alluded to Apple gateway devices like the iPod and the iPad, but there has likely never been a bigger Apple gateway device than the iPhone. This device is the perfect demonstration of the strength and simplicity of Apple and its ecosystem. Once iPhone is paired with another Apple device, a world of possibilities begin to open for the user, and features begin to multiply with each new device type introduced. It really is a great marketing strategy. Give people what they want, and reword them with even more functionality if more and more devices are added to the system.

# 8

# Drivers?

After buying my first Mac I bought an audio input preamp for it so I could do audio recording. The device was advertised as PC and Mac compatible. This was in the first few weeks of owning the computer, so I was anxious to find out what the installation process of a peripheral was going to be like on a Mac. My device arrived, and I set aside a Saturday afternoon to install, troubleshoot, and configure the device. I took the preamp out of its box and examined it. Hmm. It had the same USB cable for a PC or a Mac, so plugging it in was going to be identical. I grabbed the directions to see how to download and install the drivers. The directions started off on page one with a full set of instructions on how to go online, download the drivers and software from the manufactures site, how to install it and how to configure the sound card and settings to accept the new inputs and outputs. All looked very familiar. Then I went to page two of the manual to read the Mac installation instructions. On page two I read (word for word): *Mac OS installation procedure; Plug the device into the Mac via the supplied USB cable.*

Welcome to the world of Mac! I sat back in my chair for a moment in my office and stared at my new machine. *What kind of voodoo is this?* I thought to myself as I starred at the shinny new laptop on my desk. It was at that moment that I turned a corner on understanding what I had bought.

Macs do use drivers, but the driver system on a Mac is not installed into a registry like on a PC. It is overseen and distributed in updates by Apple. The disadvantage? They're fewer comparable devices out there for Mac than for PC. The advantage? Well, the advantage was huge. Full control over compatibility with the machine and ease of installation. Almost everything that you will buy for your Mac will be plug and play, as opposed to PC, which is plug and pray.

# 9

# Appearance

Appearance is where you will go in *System Settings* to set up the basic look of your computer. This is so fundamental to how your computer will look that this window will be the first displayed after upgrading to Ventura.

Here you will be able to set up the basic look and feel of your computer. Most people understand the difference between light and dark mode and will immediately set their computer up to their liking but another area that will give you a great deal of personalization is the accent color. Play with this setting and you just might end up with a new favorite look.

# 10

# System Settings

The biggest change you'll notice when firing up Ventura for the first time, besides the flashy new wallpaper, is the completely revamped System Settings. You may not remember, but this app used to be called System Preferences in previous OS versions.

Apple has been slowly merging the look and feel of IOS, Mac OS, and iPad OS to all have the same look and feel. We will go over the various functions of System Settings as we move through the book, but for anyone who has used an iPhone before, this change will be intuitive and seamless. The most notable change is that Apple has moved the update function to this area, just like an iPhone or iPad.

# 11
# About This Mac

Any time that you need to know basic information about your computer, you'll find the information in *About This Mac*. This information is found by clicking on the Apple logo in the upper left-hand corner of your screen and then clicking on *About This Mac*. When you do this an information screen will pop up with the basic information about your particular machine.

Clicking on **More Info** will take you to **System Settings**.

Throughout the book, we're going to explore the various tabs located in settings, but this is where you'll return to if you have to answer a basic question like *what's my serial number?*

# 12

# Updates

If you ask a PC user what they use their computer for the most of the time and they will probably tell you *to receive updates.* The sheer number of updates that are needed to keep a PC up and running can be staggering. The amount of time per week that the machine spends updating itself can be a hinder to productivity.

An area that Mac has PC beat is in its method of updating. PCs need updating almost daily, and those updates can sometimes take hours. While your PC updates, slowdowns are common while your resources are sucked dry by the update process. Not so with Apple. Minor OS updates happen every few months with the OS getting a major overhaul once a year. These updates usually take between five and fifteen minutes, and then you're good to go.

To check for an update for your Mac OS, click on the **System Settings** icon in the dock. That's that row of icons on the bottom of your screen. Now go to *General* and click on *Software Update,* just like on an iPhone. Click the button to see if a new version is available for your Mac. A box will appear to tell you if you need to download a new update. Many printers and external monitors will have drivers distributed through Apple's update process, so give it a minute. When updates are available, simply click them and let the machine handle everything for you.

Another location on your Mac that will occasionally need to be updated is the apps. Different programmers will update their apps at different times, but many will need to make major updates in the month following and in the few days leading up to a major OS update. To update your apps, launch the App Store, and click on the updates tab. If there are updates available, they will show up here as well as give you a history of the previous ones.

# 13

# Update Crash

The following situation is an advanced cure for a rare Mac ailment that you may encounter. Read this chapter thoroughly before attempting this fix. This is an advanced fix that requires an alteration to your machine's operating system and as such, it is carried out at your own risk. I personally have had years of experience altering Windows PCs registry's over the years to rid machines of viruses, so this type of alteration is not scary for me, but if you read this and have any hesitation, you might want to think about having a professional look at it. But, if you're adventurous, this issue can be fixed by a normal everyday computer user who is careful.

Rarely but every now and then the Mac may crash when doing an update. It will give you a message that the server could not be reached because you do not have an internet connection. You'll check your connection by launching Safari and you'll go right online. What gives? When this is happening, the computer is likely having an issue with its hosts file. This is a file that updates things like licenses when you do updates. Sometimes this file can get confused for any number of reasons. I've had this happen to me twice in seven years, so it's rare, but it does happen. When it does, pull up your computer's hosts file. To locate your hosts file go to *Finder* and click *Go/Go to Folder* and type in */private/etc*.

Before you attempt to change your host file, make a backup of it just in case something goes wrong or you delete the wrong information by mistake. Control-click the file and save a copy of it. You'll want to name the copy *hosts backup*.

Double click the hosts file and you should see the following information lines:

```
##
# Host Database
#
# localhost is used to configure the loopback interface
# when the system is booting.  Do not change this entry.
##
127.0.0.1          localhost
255.255.255.255 broadcasthost
::1                localhost
fe80::1%lo0        localhost
```

If you see additional lines like in the example below, that's what's keeping your machine from updating. In this example, an outdated version of Quickbooks that is loaded on the PC side of my machine in Parallels is trying to update and is causing issues. Take your tooltip and highlight everything below the localhost line. Double check that you have highlighted the correct text and you've not altered anything in the above text. Now hit delete.

```
##
# Host Database
#
# localhost is used to configure the loopback interface
# when the system is booting.  Do not change this entry.
##
127.0.0.1          localhost
255.255.255.255 broadcasthost
::1                localhost
fe80::1%lo0        localhost

# QuickBooks Pro 2015
127.0.0.1          entgwgtm.lb.intuit.com

127.0.0.1          activate.adobe.com
127.0.0.1          practivate.adobe.com
127.0.0.1          ereg.adobe.com
127.0.0.1          wip3.adobe.com
127.0.0.1          activate.wip3.adobe.com
127.0.0.1          3dns-3.adobe.com
127.0.0.1          3dns-2.adobe.com
127.0.0.1          adobe-dns.adobe.com
127.0.0.1          adobe-dns-2.adobe.com
127.0.0.1          adobe-dns-3.adobe.com
127.0.0.1          ereg.wip3.adobe.com
127.0.0.1          activate-sea.adobe.com
127.0.0.1          wwis-dubc1-vip60.adobe.com
127.0.0.1          activate-sjc0.adobe.com
127.0.0.1          hl2rcv.adobe.com
127.0.0.1          lm.licenses.adobe.com
127.0.0.1          na2m-pr.licenses.adobe.com

127.0.0.1          ims-na1-prprod.adobelogin.com

127.0.0.1          na4r.services.adobe.com

127.0.0.1          na1r.services.adobe.com
```

You should be looking at a corrected, clean hosts file that looks like this:

```
##
# Host Database
#
# localhost is used to configure the loopback interface
# when the system is booting.  Do not change this entry.
##
127.0.0.1       localhost
255.255.255.255 broadcasthost
::1             localhost
fe80::1%lo0     localhost
```

At this point, click the red dot in the upper left corner of the window and it will give you an option to save a duplicate copy file. Save this file to your desktop. After hitting save you will have a file on your desktop called hosts copy. Rename this file to hosts. Don't be surprised, or alarmed if your computer requires you to authenticate all of your actions during this process. This is part of the Mac's protection protocols that keeps nefarious programs from altering your machine without your authorization or knowledge. Drag the new hosts file from your desktop back into the original folder. Now restart your machine and try the update again.

# 14

# Launchpad

The Launchpad area of your Mac is one of those areas that is unique to the Mac. There isn't an equivalent in the PC world. The closest PC comes is the file structure of the start menu. For anyone who has used an iPhone, iPod, or iPad, the Launchpad will be immediately familiar. The Launchpad is that little icon with colored boxes in the lower-left portion of your dock.

Like on your iPhone or iPad, your Mac will allow you to create and store all your apps into logical groups of your own making. You can also alter the ones that come on your computer by default. It's all about allowing you to find your programs in a fast logical way.

When an application is installed on your computer, the Mac will put a launch icon into Launchpad automatically. You're then free to put that icon in any group you choose simply by dragging it into one. To create a new group, drag the icon onto another ungrouped icon and a new group will be created. You can then name the group whatever you like. I try to use the same grouping name conventions on all of my machines so there is a familiarity amongst all of them. This speeds up your workflow when moving between say your home iMac, and your laptop. My wife and I have also found it useful to group applications in similar categories between her devices and mine. Then on those occasions when I have to jump on her devices to do something, It doesn't take long to find what I'm looking for due to familiarity.

I will go one step further on my machines by sorting my groups in alphabetical order. This may seem like over the top organization, but by taking the time to do this once when your computer is new, you'll be speeding up your app launching process for the life of your machine.

# 15

# Launching & Closing Apps

Applications open and close slightly different on Mac than on a PC. While both computer formats launch an application similarly by double clicking on an icon, closing applications are very different on the Mac.

When an application opens on a PC it will have three icons available to you in the windows upper right corner. It will have an X that closes the application and it will have minimize and maximize icons as well. A Mac on the other hand will have a green, yellow, and red dot just like a stop light in the opposite corner. The most common mistake people make who are new to the Mac is to think that the red dot means *close the application*. What the red dot does is close the window that you're looking at. The application continues to run in the background.

In windows the maximize button will maximize a window but in the Mac world a green button will cause an application to take over the full screen of the computer. This is useful when you want to see something in full view like a photograph. It is not a good idea when you simply want a window bigger. When you click that green button and enlarge a window to the full size of the screen, it will take away the menu bar from the top. You can still access it by putting your tooltip up top to get your menu back temporarily, but this is not a convenient practice. The better practice is to resize the window by dragging its sides where you want the window to be.

To close an app in Mac OS you have a few options. The first thing you can do is go up to the title bar at the top of your screen where it says the name of the app, right click it by using a mouse, and select quit. The second way is to right-click on the application in your dock and again select quit. The third method involves holding the command key and tapping Q on your keyboard.

# 16

# Launchpad Customization

Other than grouping apps and moving around the order of them, the most common customization you're likely to do in Launchpad is the renaming of a group. The simplest way to do this is to click a group to open it, then double click on its title. You will then find the title editable. Type the new group name and hit enter.

I find it useful to use the same group names on all my machines. If you look at any of my computers, you'll see my categories that make logical sense for my workflow style. As such, your particular workflow might look quite different than mine. My categories include Books, Communication, Games, Graphics, Home, Internet, Mac, Music, Not Used, Other, Office, PDA, Parallels, Production, Photography, Productivity, Utilities, and Video. I have found that with these core categories, I can neatly organize my entire digital life.

With these categories, I can easily fit my entire Launchpad on a single page. This cuts the time to find and launch an app down significantly when you don't have to scroll through two, three, or more pages of loosely organized apps and groups.

Once you start the organization process, you'll likely come across a common irritation. You'll try to place an icon in a group and instead of dropping it in, the folder jumps out of the way. After you chase the group around for a few minutes, you'll start to feel like a dog or cat chasing a laser dot on the floor. This usually happens when the group is the last in line on a row. For whatever reason, the computer is just not sure what you're trying to accomplish. When this happens, you can try one of these two workarounds. Try moving the app into the group from the bottom up instead of from the side. If this doesn't work, move the group away from the edge of the row.

# 17

# Right Click

One of the hardest things to get used to on a Mac is the lack of right-click functionality. We're very used to right-clicking in the PC world when it comes time to cut, copy, paste, or delete. The right-click is also typically used for renaming files as well as a myriad of other tasks.

The good news is that there is a right-click on the Mac, it's just not called that. It's a control-click. When you click on an icon or a file if you hold the control key while you click you will get a set of alternate menu items just like on the PC. You can also use a PC style mouse that has a right-click function to get it back as well. When I bought my first Mac, I went out and bought a Microsoft mouse to use with it out of frustration. This at least gave me back a familiar feel when controlling the computer. It was a comfort to quickly get those right-click menus back in a way that was familiar to me.

There is one trick that most people, even longtime Mac users are unaware of. If you have a trackpad, you can right-click an item simply by tapping on it with two fingers. Use your single finger for select, or a double finger tap to right-click. If this doesn't work for you go to *System Settings* and select *Trackpad*. There is a dropdown to be set for this function to work. If you have a Macbook with the trackpad or a magic trackpad for your iMac, take a few minutes to start two-finger tapping on items. You will be surprised at how many new options are available to you. In a short amount of time, it will become second nature.

Throughout this book, I'll be referring to this function by the many ways that it can be done. Don't be confused if I use different terms to refer to it as right-click, control-click, and secondary-click are all interchangeable. It just depends on what input device you're using at the time.

# 18

# Moving Files

Yet another way that Windows has Mac beat six ways to Sunday is in how files are moved. With windows, you simply have two windows open, left-click the file and drag it to a new location. What could be simpler? In the Mac world, this would result in making a duplication of the original file. To move a file in the Mac environment, hold down the command key while dragging your file to the new location. This will result in an actual move instead of a duplication.

You have a few options if you wish to move several files at once. If the files are in order, that is to say adjacent to each other, you can click the first, then shift-click the last. All will be selected in between. If you wish to select all files in a folder, simply click any one, then hit command A on your keyboard to select them all. To unselect all if you've made a mistake or changed your mind, click anywhere in the folder that is a blank space in between the icons.

What if you need to select multiple files in random locations within a folder? Hold the command key and click on the individual files one at a time. After clicking the last file, release the command key.

You would think that if you needed to delete a file you'd simply click it and hit the delete key. This works in Windows, but not in Mac. Apple gives you a sort of safety latch when it comes to deleting. You do select your file or files, but then you must hold down the command key while hitting the delete key to get the job done.

Another way to select multiple files is to left-click and drag a box around your files with your mouse. This works about the same way that it does in Windows. Right-clicking at this point will give you a few options as well, but the familiar cut, paste, and delete options that you're used to in Windows are gone. You will still find these commands in the edit menu. This does take some re-training of the brain in the Mac environment.

# 19

# Saving

Saving on a Mac can be strange at first for those who come from the PC world. On the PC, saving is somewhat straight forward. The familiarity for the right-click, *save,* and *save as* works throughout all PC programs universally. In the Mac ecosystem, much of the saving process is taken for granted. In most applications, the Mac instinctively knows that you need to save, and the document is updated and saved automatically as you work, and then again as you close the application. Not all applications work and save in the same manner on the Mac and that can cause confusion at times. Some applications will use a hybrid system of both PC and Mac methods for saving.

While writing this book, I am using a professional authoring software application called Scrivener. It's an example of an application that uses both methods simultaneously. As a Mac user, you'll need to pay attention to the saving process for every new application that creates documents that you use and take note of how the application wants to save its documents on your machine. This is where the dyed in the wool PC user steps in and says, "See, this is why I can't stand Apple. It always wants to think for you." I will admit that that can be a minor frustration in the beginning, but the reason for this is that the Mac tends to automate many of the mundane housekeeping tasks for you while you work. If you simply take a moment when you're working with a new application to figure out how it wants to work, you'll save yourself any frustration with that application in the future.

Pages and Numbers in the Mac world are probably the hardest to get used to, especially Numbers. Everything is so automatic, that it just doesn't feel natural to someone entrenched in Microsoft Office.

# 20

# File Structure

Has this ever happened to you? You've created a document on your Mac and saved it. The next day you go to pull up the file to work on it, but you can't remember where your Mac saved it. This is an all-too-common occurrence for both Mac and PC users in the early going. The problem here is the phrase "you can't remember where your Mac saved it."

All computers use a file structure, much like a traditional filing cabinet. Documents or files are saved in logical groups within your filing cabinet inside folders for easy retrieving at a later date. With few exceptions, this filing cabinet does not build itself. It's up to the user to customize and build it in such a way that makes sense to them. In the world of Mac, you actually own two filing cabinets. One resides locally on your hard drive, and it's called *Documents*. The other resides in the cloud (a fancy word for another location that is reachable over the internet) and it's called *iCloud*, or *iCloud Drive*.

Both of these locations are basically a blank slate when you buy your first Mac. While both do the same thing, they both have advantages and disadvantages that will determine which one you will want to use to store a particular file. We'll look at both and talk about why you'd want to use one over the other.

First, we'll look at your local documents folder. This folder is always with your specific computer and is accessible on that machine even if it is not connected to the internet. Its size is limited to the size of your local hard drive on your Mac. As such, it is finite in size. Whatever size your local drive is, that's what you're stuck with locally, for the life of the computer unless you add an external USB hard drive. Documents are generally not shared with all of your other computers. They are local and specific to your machine. If you only own one Mac, and you always want to have all your files with you at all times, then this might be your logical choice, after all, if you enjoy working on your machine in locations like a public park without Wi-Fi, then this is a great onboard solution.

If you own multiple Macs, then iCloud Drive will be your storage location of choice. Your iCloud Drive gives you a shared storage location accessible from all of your machines. In other words, you will be able to start a document on one computer at work and access it later from your iMac at your house. Then you might take your laptop down to the coffee shop, and have full access to the same file again. Multiple computers, one storage location.

Wherever you choose to store your files, be the master of your filing cabinet. Sort your files in a way that makes sense to you, grouping documents into folders and subfolders that will speed retrieval in the future with a minimum of searching. I will tend to create folders for the particular apps that I work with. In my iCloud, you might find root folders like Word, Excel, Pixelmator Pro, or Scrivener. Inside each folder, you might find subfolders with individual projects. There are no rules other than building your cabinet in a way that works for your workflow and take the time to save your files in those logical locations without simply letting the computer pick the location for you. Be smarter than the machine!

# 21

# Finder

Finder is that blue and white happy face typically sitting in the lower-left-hand side of your dock. Finder is the only application running on your Mac that you will never be able to close. By default, it sits at the start of all of your icons on your dock. Your dock is that row of icons across the bottom of your screen that allows you too quick launch an app. You'll notice that when you open an app, there is a small dot that appears below the icon of the app that you launch. Finder will always have the dot as it is always running.

Clicking on Finder will give you access to everything on your computer, as well as everything your computer is connected to. On the left, you can customize favorite areas on your computer for easy access. You can also access other devices that you're connected to like other computers on your network, thumb drives, portable hard drives, iPhones, and CD drives. You can also customize your folders and files from here with things like colored backgrounds, or colored dots on folders to make commonly used ones stand out.

By default clicking on Finder will open one Finder window, but as you become more proficient with your computer, you'll soon need the ability to open more than one at a time. This can be accomplished a few different ways. First, click on Finder to open a window. Now control-click on the icon by holding the control key and clicking again. Choose *New Finder Window*. You can now resize your two or more windows and work within all of them simultaneously. Another way to accomplish this is while in Finder, go to File on the menu bar and choose New Finder Window.

A third way is to open Finder, and then hit *command T*. This will open a new tab. Clicking on a new location while a tab is highlighted will now take you to a new location for that tab while keeping you in another location on the other.

# 22

# I've Lost A File!

Sooner or later it happens to all of us. We're working on a file one day, and we can't find it the next. More often than not this happens because we've let the machine decide ware to save the file instead of placing the file in a specific location.

PC's are very user dependent when it comes to creating files. If you're coming from a PC world then you are ingrained in the *save as* mentality. This happens automatically in the Mac World. Unless you're using a Microsoft product like Office on a Mac, you're typically not going to see a *save as* command. In the Mac world we file our documents under the save dialog in an app or we create a document by duplicating a previous one. However it happens, for better or worse, we don't save as in the PC traditional way. This can lead to lost files as the Mac auto saves in locations of its logical choosing. The problem is that it may not be logical to us.

If you've lost a file, there are a number of ways to locate it. Take a deep breath, all hope is not lost. First go to the app you used to work in the file. Right click it and choose Show Recents. Your screen will switch to a list of recent files that you've worked on in that application.

If you know any part of the title of your document, you can search for it in Finder. Just start typing a key word into the search box in the upper right hand corner of Finder and let the computer find it for you. You can search your Mac, recent files, external drives, and iCloud.

Lastly you can always go to **Finder** and click on *Recents*.

# 23

# Customizing Favorites

When you launch Finder you will be faced with a Favorites area in the left window. This area will have some different places on your machine shown by default, but this area is totally customizable. Common areas that are shown are iCloud drive, your Downloads folder, Desktop area, and Documents, as well as Applications and others. You can also add areas to this Favorites bar like Dropbox and virtually any folder on your machine that you want to access easily. Drives, phones, and USB sticks that you plug into your computer will show up here as well.

The places in Favorites are easily rearranged by simply taking your mouse tooltip and dragging them into any priority you wish. If you want to remove an item from your Favorites simply right-click it (or control-click it) and you will find a way to do just that.

A helpful way to organize the places that you are viewing in Favorites is to color code the backgrounds of the different areas. For instance, iCloud drive could have a different color background than your desktop or your applications folder. You can color-code your areas anyway you like. To change the color of an area first click the area that you wish to change in Favorites. You will then see a window with a white background with the folders on top of it. Then go to the *View* tab on the menu bar and select *Show view options*. Here you will be allowed to change the background of the folder to a different color or picture. Select different colors for different places and you will always have a visual representation of where you are when looking at various places on your machine.

You can also customize from this window several other things about your folder such as icon size, spacing in between the icons, and the size of the font in each of the particular windows.

# 24

# Installing Apps

If you're coming from the world of PC, app installation is one of those places where the superiority of the Mac shines. I remember installing my first app off the internet on my first new Mac. I double-clicked a downloaded installation icon and a few seconds later it was done. *That's it?* I thought to myself. Surely that didn't work. Where were all the installation windows I was used to seeing when installing a program? Shouldn't there be a window with painfully slow progression bars, one after another, as the installation package wrights file after file to my machine? Shouldn't I see registry files being updated and auxiliary files being installed like Silverlight, or dot net framework, or java, or any number of the third party add ons necessary to make whatever program run on my particular machine. Nope, instead, I clicked it, a beach ball spun for a moment, and I had an app installed. I thought to myself, *man I could get used to this.* I installed app after app on my shiny new silver machine for the rest of that day and to my surprise and delight, none interfered with another. None of the installations crashed, and as Apple is fond of saying, everything just worked. *What manner of witchcraft is this?* I thought to myself as I began to get a glimpse into the *behind the scenes structure* that is the Mac operating system.

Apps are installed in three common ways on your Mac. If you're downloading from the Apple App Store the process is quite automated. Simply click purchase on an app and install it. A moment later your app will be installed automatically and ready for use. That's it.

The next method is used when you download an app from an internet location. Typically you'll click a download prompt and the file will bounce into your downloads folder (accessible from finder or by the download icon in the upper right-hand area of Safari). Double-clicking the finished download will install the app.

In some cases, an installer will give you a window with the app icon and your applications folder icon. In this scenario, you simply drag the app into the application folder.

# 25

# The Dock

The dock is that table down at the bottom of your screen where all of the applications sit that you use on a semi-regular basis. If you've never customized your dock, nows a great time to get it into shape! Did you know that the dock doesn't have to live at the bottom? It can reside on any side of the screen that you choose. Simply go to System settings/Desktop & Dock and set the dropdown for Left, Bottom, or Right. While you're there, you can also adjust the size of the dock icons. I make mine as small as I can so I have as much desktop real estate as possible, but I'm careful not to make them so small that they would be difficult to see.

You'll see some other options here as well. An important one is the Automatically hide and show the dock tic switch. This is especially useful on a laptop where screen size is at a premium. This switch will make your dock go away until you need it. Taking your tooltip to the bottom of the screen will cause the dock to pop back up and you'll be ready for action. Another adjustment here is the ability to switch between a scaling animation when you minimize an app and the cool Apple signature genie effect.

You can remove any icon from the dock that's not needed simply by left-clicking and dragging it onto your desktop, holding it for a moment until it says remove, and letting go. Don't worry, you didn't erase the app, just the icon. You can put it, or any app back on the dock simply by grabbing its icon from the launchpad and dragging it to the dock. You can also rearrange the order of your icons by left-holding the icon, and moving it to a new order location. Let go, and you've rearranged your dock!

# 26

# Cut Copy Paste

Cut-and-paste on the Mac is very similar to cut-and-paste on a PC. If you want to cut a single word out of a document highlight the word and use *command X* to cut. You can use *command C* to copy and *command V* to paste it to a new location. You'll notice that these three buttons are all grouped together in the same location on your keyboard. The C is in the middle, and C for copy is easy to remember. To the left is X. Think of X as a pair of scissors for cutting. On the right is V. Think of the V as a down arrow to paste, or to glue down.

Some applications will give you the ability to cut and paste from the edit menu as well. In some applications you may also be able to highlight what you wish to cut-and-paste and use of the control tap function or right-click on a mouse to get options for cut, copy, or paste.

When you're working with files and folders in finder you will notice that Apple does not give you the options to cut copy and paste them. This is common functionality on a PC, but Apple sees it as a redundancy. The thought here is that you can simply move files by selecting them and dragging them to another open folder. Cutting, copying, and pasting are seen as wasted time. This may be frustrating at first as you're getting used to the Mac operating system, but this frustration will eventually be replaced with the time-saving technique of simply moving the object to a different location.

What if you simply want to get rid of an item? You can do that on a Mac as well. In many situations, Apple will give you a *move to trash* option when you control-click an item. You can also delete an item by using the command delete method.

As you use cut, copy, and paste there is another command that you will need to master. Inevitably you will cut, copy, or paste something accidentally. When this happens, never fear, simply use the command Z method to go back in time.

# 27

# Sharing

One of the coolest abilities of a Mac is its ability to share content within the Apple ecosystem. Sharing works across the Apple platform between iMacs, MacBooks, iPhones, and iPads. The share function is a mix of old school and new technology methods of transferring data from one machine to the next, yours or a friend or colleague. Sharing transfers can be in the form of texts, email, messages, airdrop, or a number of other methods. Some applications even use the share function for printing.

Popular ways to share with non-Apple users are methods like email, but if you're sharing within the Apple ecosystem, this is where the magic happens! Airdrop is one of, if not the coolest method of sharing on a Mac. Unfortunately, it is an Apple exclusive technology, meaning that you won't be airdropping to a Windows PC anytime soon. Airdrop will allow you to wirelessly push a document to another Apple device if you happen to be in close proximity to it. Popular uses for this method include sharing new photos between iPhone users and transferring files quickly from your phone or computer to another.

What can be shared? Almost anything. Simply look for the share symbol in whatever environment you're working in and if it's present, you can share. Look for the square box with the pointing up arrow. While the most popular use of the ability I commonly see is sharing photos, almost anything can be shared. Documents, web pages, notes, reminders, calendar events, files, folders, you name it.

# 28

# Restarting

One of the perks of owning a Mac is the fast boot time and shut down time of the machine. Before Windows 10, the boot time difference between Macs and PCs was staggering.

Another perk is the long uptime that is possible with a Mac. My home office iMac gets a reboot about once a week. Other than that, the unit is continually on and at the ready. It sleeps when not in use but springs to life at the touch of a mouse when it's needed. My laptops are almost always on. I close the lid when I'm done using them and they instantly go to sleep only to spring back to life when I raise the lid the next day.

While a PC can sleep in a similar fashion, PCs will tend to need to be restarted more and the laptops will become glitchy if you're not refreshing the computers by continually restarting them. Now I'll admit that Windows 10 has gone a long way to improve performance in this area, but Macs still have the PC beat when it comes to uptime without issues.

Nevertheless, you will eventually have to restart a Mac. The machine will eventually run across a problem that will steal your RAM or cause a driver to get glitchy. Restarting your computer, or any Apple device for that matter will fix 90% of the day to day issues that your computer might encounter. In fact, if you're having issues with a specific app, like say your browser, you may even get away with simply restarting just the app itself.

Just remember that if ever a problem with your Mac does arise, before trying dozens of things to fix it or troubleshoot it, just try a reboot. Most of the time it will take care of the problem, and remember to refresh your computers at least once a week to give them a cleansing fresh new lease.

# 29

# Pointer Size

I'm sixty. I'm old and cranky. Get off my lawn!

As I age it seems like the Apple screens keep getting better and because they can….the objects on the screen keep getting smaller. Pretty soon our old eyes get to the point where they could use a little help.

Fortunately, there is a solution for your shrinking cursor pointer on a Mac. You can go into *Accessibility/Display* in System Settings and simply make the tooltip bigger.

Here are a few tips that will be helpful as you do this. First, you'll tend to go overboard the first time you make a change. Don't worry, you can change this setting anytime you want. Secondly, as you increase the size of your tooltip, the response of your pointer will slow down. To compensate for the size difference, go into either Trackpad or Mouse in System Settings to speed them back up.

# 30

# Scroll Bars

Recently I set my editor up with a brand-new MacBook air. She was a long time PC user and this was her first Mac. On the first night as we were setting it up and she was beginning to get used to it she looked at me and said; "Where's the scrollbars?" This took me back for a minute because I've been in the Mac environment for so long now that I totally forgot that PCs always have scrollbars in their windows. If you're on the Internet, there's always scrollbars. If you're moving from one place to another in the window, there's always scrollbars. In the Mac world they just generally assume that you know that there's more above or below what you're looking at and if you actually move your trackpad up or down, the scrollbars temporarily appear. After you're done moving, the scrollbars disappear to give you maximum viewing.

This is all fine in practice, but if you're coming from a PC environment, this can really throw you. I stopped and thought back for a moment, remembering what it was like years ago when I was in the PC world. There was a lot of comfort in knowing that I had those little bars I could grab to move up-and-down.

Fortunately, if you're a brand-new Apple user, and you really like the security of having those little scrollbars, there is a way to put them back. This can be done temporarily or permanently depending on your workflow and work style.

To put the scrollbars back, open up System Settings. Click on Appearance. There will be a place for *Shows scroll bars*. The default is *Automatically based on mouse or trackpad*. If you would like your computer to respond like a PC, click *Always*.

Once you get used to the Mac world, you will want to put this back to *Automatic*. That way when another Mac user gets on your computer they won't be frustrated by a Mac that is behaving like a PC.

# 31

# Autofill Words

With a Mac, you can set your computer up to auto-fill words automatically. What do I mean by this? Well, let's say there is a combination of letters that you type often like an email address. Let's say your email address is especially long. In our example, we'll say that your email address is: johndoe@myownwebsite.com. This can be long and tedious if you had to spell this address out time and time again in a specific document. What if there were an easy way for your computer to know what you're typing and type it out for you as soon as it had enough specific characters for it to be unique? In this example, we could set up a shortcut where if the computer sees *joh* in lowercase, it naturally assumes that you want to type *johndoe@myownwebsite.com* and then spells it out for you.

To set this up open *System Settings* and go to *Keyboard*. You will see a section that says *Text Replacements*. Hit the plus button to add the letters joh. On the right replace it with the full email address. Now every time you type in joh in lowercase, the computer will assume that you want to use the entire email address and we'll fill in for you automatically.

This is also a way you can deal with words that you miss-spell often. If you have a word that you commonly misspell, simply type the misspelled version on the *replace* side of the window and add the correct spelling on the *with* part of the window.

Within the keyboard/Edit window you can also turn Auto-correct on or off. Auto-correct is a great feature on the Mac, but there are times when it can drive you nuts. As the saying goes, auto-correct can be your worst enema.

# 32

# App Switching

The Mac environment is so easy to use that before long you'll find yourself falling into the role of a power user. Simply put a power user is a multitasker. This is a person that has multiple apps open simultaneously, bouncing back and forth between them all. My wife is a power user. On any given day I can walk into her office at work and see her in front of three monitors bouncing information back and forth between apps and operating systems. Before long you will be longing for easier ways to balance between those applications especially on systems where you may not have the ability to stretch apps out over multiple screens.

If you're using a small laptop like a MacBook, the skill of apps switching becomes paramount as desktop real estate is quite small. How then does a person with a thirteen-inch screen balance and bounce between applications like a person in an office with two or three or more external monitors? The answer is app switching.

App switching gives you a fast way on a Mac to bounce between two applications that you are using concurrently. To bounce between two apps simply do a three-finger swipe straight up on your trackpad or magic mouse and you will then get a screen with both Applications that you are working in. You can bounce back and forth between the two simply by clicking on one or the other. More than two applications open at once? Not a problem, all of the applications will show up when you do the three-finger swipe. You can now quickly switch between those applications simply by clicking.

# 33

# Desktops

Now that you've mastered app switching it's time for some real power user stuff! Did you know that OS X+ gives you the ability to run up to 16 desktops simultaneously? Each desktop can be configured exactly the way that you want to use it and see it. In other words, on one desktop you may have two applications running in windows side-by-side. On another desktop, you may simply have your browser open and nothing else, and another desktop you may have your email open alongside another application of your choosing. You can bounce between all of the desktops at will.

You set this feature up in the same way that you set up apps switching. A three-finger swipe up on your trackpad will show you all of the program options that you have open at once. You can then take any of those options and drag it to the bar up top. The bar will turn it into a preview of all of the desktops that you currently have open. You can now simply bounce from desktop to desktop by clicking the one you want to work in. A three-finger swipe will reveal the other desktops and allow you to quickly switch between them.

This skill is paramount when you are on a small screen. If you own a MacBook for instance, this skill will open an entirely new world for you. Suddenly a thirteen-inch screen does not seem to be an issue anymore when it comes to getting your work done in an efficient manner. Clicking on *no available windows* on your main desktop will bring you back to an uncluttered desktop. You can now open other programs and create new desktop workspaces. Clicking on the plus in the top bar will also open up a blank desktop allowing you to create an entirely new workspace as well.

# 34

# Dark Mode

Back in the 90s, I embraced a new advertising front called the World Wide Web. I learned how to program in HTML and put up a website for my sound company West Coast Sound and Light on the Internet. At that time it was so uncommon for a sound company to be online I was actually laughed at by my peers. At the time if you did a Yahoo search you would come up with a total of two production companies in the country, WCSL being one of them. I got on board so early that I was able to procure a four-letter URL. In the early 90s, wcsl.org was born. I went with .org at the time because wcsl.com was owned by the West Coast Soccer League.

When I built the site I did something totally different than all of the other sites were doing at the time. I programmed it in dark mode. Where all of the other websites commonly used a white background, I decided to use black. This caused my site to stand out on the web by giving it a unique look.

Today the dark mode is quite common everywhere. So much so that Apple has built it into their operating system. As of OS Mohave Apple now gives you the ability to operate your computer in dark mode.

Dark mode essentially makes a bright screen dark. Think of your computer when you're using a word processor. Almost always the page is white with a text black. This is good because it's a high-contrast look. However, it does take a lot of energy from your laptop battery because the majority of pixels that are on at any given time are running wide open bright. It doesn't take much energy to reproduce black on a laptop screen. It takes a lot of energy to reproduce white. A dark screen is also easier on the eyes if you are in a dark environment.

On all my machines, the place that I end up using dark mode the most is on laptops. As a sound engineer, I am continually using my laptop in dark environments. There's usually an audience in this environment and I do not wish to stand out as much as possible, the stealthiness of dark mode is perfect for this. I also take my laptop to places like church and when I'm taking notes I don't need a bright glaring screen disrupting those around me.

There are many reasons why you may want to operate in dark mode, and Apple makes it easy to bounce back and forth between the two modes. To put your computer in the dark mode simply go to system preferences. Under the General tab, you will have the option to change the appearance of your computer from light to dark. Select the mode that you want to run in and everything able will be in that mode. Switching back is easy, just go back to the General tab and click light again. You should know that not all programs will run in dark mode. This is not a problem as all of your programs will still run even if they're not designed for dark mode, but they will of course still be light when you are in dark mode.

# 35

# Gestures

Gestures give you an incredible amount of control on your Mac. If you've used an iPad, you're already familiar with the concept. Gestures can be used on laptops via the trackpad or on a desktop by adding a Magic Trackpad.

Many gestures by default will have to be enabled for them to work. This is done from system preferences.

*Data Look Up* is a seldom-used gesture. Most Mac users don't even know it's there, but it can be quite a powerful research tool. With this gesture enabled, try tapping on a word in any text on your machine, then once highlighted, tap the trackpad with three fingers. You will get a wealth of information about the word.

*Secondary-click* is a must. When enabled, you can perform a secondary, or control-click by highlighting, and two-finger tapping on the pad. This is a fast way to your cut, copy, and paste functions as well as all the other right-click commands.

Under the *scroll and zoom* tab, you will find more gesture abilities. Here you can change the scroll direction had and toggle whether or not you can zoom in and out by using your fingers. You can also use your fingers to rotate an image if enabled.

The *more gestures* tab brings even more functionality to your Mac. Popular options here are the ability to swipe between pages and swipe between fullscreen apps. And overlooked function by most users is the ability to look at the notification center. Notification Center will show you all of the notifications that you have configured on your machine. I t's a handy way to check them anytime.

*Launchpad* and *show desktop* are two more options that are seldom employed, but once you master them they are a quick way to get to common points of necessity, whether it be for launching a new Application or just getting to something on your desktop. Because four fingers are involved these gestures are a little on the awkward side, but with a little practice, they can be quite useful.

A good way to learn these new gestures is to take one a day. Use it as often as possible until it becomes muscle memory.

# 36

# Lock Screen

New feature as a Ventura is the *Lock Screen* tab in *System Settings*.

This is a continuation of the unification of operating systems between iPhone, iPad, and iMac. As you've already guessed this tab gives you the ability to control all of the aspects of your lock screen just like you do on your iPhone.

# 37

# Deleting Files

The other day I was watching a relatively new Mac user deleting files on her computer by dragging them one by one down to the bottom of the screen in order to dump them into the trash can. I looked over and casually said, "You know there's a faster way to do that right?" She said, "Oh I'm sure there is, but this is what I'm used to doing on my Windows machine." Now to be fair there are faster ways on a Windows machine to dump a large amount of files as well, but I'm going to tell you about a couple of ways that will speed things up for you.

You could speed up this process by taking your mouse tooltip and selecting all of the files in a single drag, then dragging that group down to the trash can to throw them away. If you're doing this within a folder instead of your desktop, you can always highlight the first file, then shift select the last file at the end and all files in between will be highlighted. This is much faster than the first method, but there are still a few methods even faster yet.

In the next method select all of the files again, but now instead of dragging and dropping, control-click the files and choose *move to trash*.

My final method is by far the fastest and if you use your Mac for any length of time you will learn this method and use it quite often. Take your tooltip once again and highlight all of the files you wish to remove. Now simply hold the command button and hit delete. Presto, all are gone!

All of these methods will delete the files from your machine and move them into the trash. In all of these methods if you need to restore one or all of these files, simply go to your trash, find the files, and restore them.

# 38

# Rename Files

Here's a lesson that many people will skip over, simply because they're sure that they know how to perform this basic task on a Mac. What could be simpler than renaming a file? Furthermore, why would I wait so long into the book to go over such a simple task? As you might have guessed, I'm not going to just show you how to rename a file in the traditional way, but I am also going to teach you a power user move that will greatly speed up your workflow.

Most of us are familiar with the standard way of changing a file name on a computer where you select the file name, right-click it on a PC or control-click it on a Mac, and choose Rename from the menu to change the files name.

This traditional way, while it works, is time-consuming and a little clunky at best. For years, this was my go-to method for changing file names. Sometimes, depending on the input device I was using, this method could be frustrating. Sometimes I wouldn't get the double-tap just right on a trackpad, or for whatever reason, it would take me more than one attempt to get it right and get a file changed. This irritation was one of those things at the beginning of learning Mac that had me saying that PC had Mac beat in this area, and then one day I learned this shortcut that changed the way I changed file names on a Mac forever.

The next time that you need to change a file name on a Mac, go to the file in Finder, click it once, and hit the Return key on your keyboard. The file will now become ready for you to replace the name. Type in the new name and hit Return again. You're done!

# 39

# Locking the Screen

There are times when you wish to get up from your computer and immediately lock the screen from other's eyes. This can be accomplished in a couple of ways. You can go up to the Apple logo in the upper left-hand corner and choose *Lock Screen*. Your screen will immediately go into the locked mode, requiring your logon code to reinter your computer.

The quickest way is to hold down the control and command keys and hit Q (for quick). Your machine will immediately lock.

A third option is to program a hot corner on your Mac to immediately go into lock screen mode.

# 40

# Clock

It's hard to believe it's taken Apple until 2022 to include the Clock app with Mac OS, but we're happy it's finally here. Clock operates the same as it does on your iPhone, so you likely already know how to use it and if you don't have an iPhone, don't worry, it's quite intuitive.

Extremely intuitive that is until you set a timer. Once the timer goes off you'll have no way to turn it off until you know how. You'll try the obvious methods like clicking Done in the app or searching through the menu items as your alarm Mocs you. Like a spy's secret handshake, here's the top secret way to turn it off. When the timer reaches its end it will display a small notification box in the upper right corner of your main screen. Now this box wont give you ANY indication this is how you turn it off at first.

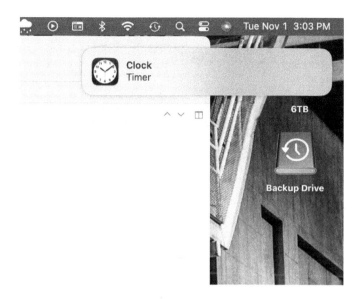

You're going to have to rest your tooltip over this display in order to get a dialog box stop it. If you're looking this chapter up franticly as your computer is blaring an alarm........You're welcome.

# 41
# Clock Options

Clock options in your menu bar are set by going to System settings/Control center/Clock/Clock Options.

Here you can adjust the date information and choose the style of clock. If you are working on a deadline you can even get your Mac to announce the passage of time over the intervals that you choose.

# 42

# Travel Time

Your Mac does a wonderful job of keeping track of time on its own via its internet connection. There are times however when you may not be able to be connected to the internet and time zones may change. A classic example of this is when you take a cruise. Unless you purchase an expensive data package, your laptop is not going to know when you pass from one time zone to another. Fortunately, the Mac gives you a way to control its time zones manually.

To set the time zone manually, go to Date & Time in System Settings. Now click general/Date & time. To take manual control of your current time zone, turn off Set time and date automatically. You can now change all aspects of time and date.

# 43

# Talking Trash

Trash is a simple concept on the Mac. If you've used any computer in the past, you'll be familiar with the feature and what it does. Almost anything you delete on your Mac will go to Trash. This gives you the ability to retrieve it if you make a mistake, or if you decide that you need a file again. When you empty your trash, the file is gone for good.

I say almost anything because there are a few exceptions to this rule. If you delete a very large file from your computer, you may be prompted that the file is too large, and it will ask you if you want to delete it instead. Another example is files deleted from your machine during a cleaning process from the *Manage storage* option in About This Mac. Files deleted in these manors will be gone for good.

Files stored in Trash will take up room in your iCloud Drive, so it's important to empty your trash lest you begin to get the dreaded out of space warning from iCloud. Your trash and storing photos in iCloud are the biggest reasons for this annoying, *and potentially costly,* warning. An easy way to remind yourself to take out the trash is to empty your computer's trash on the same day that you empty your home's trash each week. You already have a trash schedule, and it's the easiest and fastest trash bin to empty, so why not add it to your routine? To empty your trash, simply control-click the icon and choose Empty Trash.

If you find you're having a hard time remembering to empty your trash, you can set your Mac up to auto-delete every file that gets sent to trash 30 days after you throw it away. Chances are, if you don't need the file after 30 days, you don't need it. To do this, launch Finder and choose *Finder / Settings.* Click *Advanced* and tick *Remove items from the trash after 30 days.*

# 44

# Calculator

I may be pointing out the obvious but one of the most basic functions of a computer is computing. Everyone knows that there's a basic calculator built-in to every Mac and every PC for that matter. Because of this, I'm not going to spend an entire chapter teaching you how to use a basic calculator but I am going to spend an entire one teaching you about the things that you may not know about it.

For instance, did you know that your calculator on your Mac can be a paper tape calculator? All you have to do is go to *File* and click *Save Tape As*. This will give you a location in which to save a paper tape from your calculator. After naming your paper tape and telling your computer where to save it, simply start using your calculator and you will see all of your calculations printed out on the tape just like a real tape calculator. You can even come back to file to print out the tape so you have an actual physical hard copy or save it in another location for archiving.

Your calculator on your Mac is in basic mode by default but it has four other operating modes. It can function as a scientific calculator, a programmers calculator, it can be put into Reverse Polish Notation mode for those of you with propeller caps and you can even change its default decimal place.

If you go to the conversion section you'll find yet another mode. A wide list of common conversions can be done after switching the calculator to a conversion calculator.

Too lazy to launch the application yourself? Click on Siri and simply ask her an equation. She will use the Calculator app to come up with the answer for you without even launching it.

# 45

# Default Application

When you launch an application on your Mac by double-clicking on a file, you'll launch a preset application to view that file in. For example, if you double-click a Word document, the file will launch Word and open the document in it. Most of the time your Mac's automatic pick for the default application will be perfect, but now and then you might want to change the default.

Let's say your Mac automatically opens every jpg file in preview, but you wish you could always open a jpg with Pixelmator Pro instead. Changing the default is easy and easily reversible, so you can switch if you wish for a short time, and then switch back. This can be a useful feature if you're spending a week working on a specific project, and you need a certain application to open a specific file type for editing.

To change the default application of a file type, find a file in Finder of that particular type. Control-click the file and choose Get Info. In the information box click the dropdown arrow for *Open With:*. You will be presented with a box where you can choose a new default application to use every time any file of that type is double-clicked.

What if you simply want to open a file with an application other than the default once? This can be accomplished similarly without training your Mac to do it every time. To to this, control-click the file you wish to open in a non-default application and choose *Open With*. You will be presented with a number of options that can be used to open the file with on a one-off basis. The next time that you double-click the file normally, it will once again use the default.

# 46

# Emojis

Emojis have become a natural part of texting on our phones, but they can be used when texting from our iPads and macs as well. To access Emojis on the Mac click on the emoji icon in the lower-right corner of your text. It's the smiley face by the microphone. You can access a large number of emojis by selecting a category from across the bottom of the emoji window, and you can scroll down through a huge collection in each category.

It likely comes as no surprise that you can text an emoji from a Mac, but you can actually use emojis in many other apps as well. Open the Edit menu in an app like Pages for instance, and you'll find a handy option to insert an emoji.

Another quick way to drop in an emoji while you're typing is to hold the control and command keys while tapping the spacebar. This will open up a dropdown to insert an emoji in your text.

# 47

# Force Quit

I love the fact that I've gotten this far in writing this book without giving thought to writing a chapter on Force Quit. Force Quit is a way to halt or get out of a program that has frozen or has stopped working properly. If I were writing a book on PCs, I likely would have landed here on lesson two or three.

Force Quit on the Mac is the equivalent of *control/alt/delete* on a PC. It allows you to pick a program that is running or has crashed, and as the name implies, send a force quit command to shut the unresponsive app down.

When compared to the PC operating system, the Mac OS is extremely stable. It's what makes a Mac, a Mac. Because there is no registry on your computer, there is little to no interaction between applications. No drivers to conflict, and few opportunities for any type of incompatibilities. Still, you're using a computer. The stubborn fact remains that applications can and will sometimes crash. The good news is that the vast majority of situations that cause an application to crash are the aforementioned maladies that affect the PC so mercilessly. But, in those rare times that a Mac stops working, freezes up, or simply behaves unexpectedly, you do have these options.

First, try closing the application and restarting it. Because applications do not depend on a universal registry but rather run as standalone programs, you will seldom need to reboot your machine to get things happy again. If it's just frozen and you're unable to restart it, use the force quit command and restart the app. If everything is whacked and you're unable to force quit an application, simply restart your entire Mac and you'll wipe the entire slate clean, including any and all data in your RAM.

But what if your mouse is frozen and you can't get up to the Apple? You can accomplish the same thing by using the keys on your keyboard just like control alt delete on a PC. Just hold down the three keys option, command and escape.

# 48

# Apple ID

Your Apple ID is your private ID number for your entire digital life in the Apple ecosystem. Think of it as your Apple Social Security Number, or your Apple birth certificate. Wait, birth certificate? Well, in many ways it is. Your exclusive Apple ID will be used throughout your digital life with Apple to purchase apps, set up new devices, and identify and authenticate yourself with Apple. Your Apple ID will be used to set up your identity in the App Store as well as set up your free iCloud account and will be used to purchase additional iCloud storage in the future as your digital life expands and grows.

You can manage your Apple ID on your Mac by opening System Settings. Your Apple ID is so important to your Apple ownership experience, it will be the very first thing on the top of the screen.

Clicking on it will bring you to your Apple ID management screen. This is where you will see all of the Apple devices you own and if you scroll to the bottom, you will be able to sign in and out of your Apple ID.

Under Name, Phone, & Email you'll find the ability to add other locations that your Apple ID can use to get messages and notifications to you.

Under Passwords and Security, you'll find the ability to change your Apple ID password. There is no way to change an actual Apple ID name on this screen.

# 49

# Changing An Apple ID Name

Our Apple ID is generally our main email address. But what happens if you change your email address? Well, in a word, nothing. You can go on using your old email address as your Apple ID and it will work just fine. But what if you want to clean things up a bit and use your new email address as your Apple ID? Not a problem, Apple allows you to do that.

Use your Mac to open up Safari and go to your iCloud account online. If you don't already have this bookmarked in Safari go to iCloud.com. After logging into your account you're going to want to go into the drop-down menu alongside your name in the upper right hand corner. Once you're there you're going to choose *Account Settings*. Your name and ID are going to pop up on the left. In the middle, you will see a place to manage your Apple ID. Click on *Manage*. You'll be taken to your account online. You will see your old Apple ID displayed below your name. In the account section, you will see your Apple ID and the places that you are reachable. Other data will be here as well but the important thing that you're looking for is the edit button on the right-hand side.

Once you've put your Apple ID into edit mode you will be able to click *Change Apple ID*. Put in your new ID and click done. Now, remember all of your devices are still using your old Apple ID. You're going to have to log out of all of your iCloud accounts across all of your devices and log back in under the new ID.

# 50

# Double Identity

As we've talked about before, your Apple ID is your singular unique identity in the Apple ecosystem. It is your ONE ACCOUNT for everything you do with Apple. But what if you accidentally created two Apple IDs? What if you purchased an iPhone for instance, used it for a few years, and then purchased your first Mac. What if you accidentally created a second ID when you set up your new machine? The answer is bedlam.

There have been many people who have found themselves in this unfortunate circumstance with two or more Apple IDs. The problem with this situation is that you will soon find that your digital life is in a frustrating state of disarray with one ID controlling some purchases made on some machines with other IDs on others. Your calendars will not sync with other accounts, and your contacts will be spread out over multiple accounts. If you do a little research online you'll find horror story after horror story of people who in the early goings of becoming Apple addicts, created more than one Apple ID and are now trying to deal with the fallout. If you're already in this unfortunate situation, you might be wondering why Apple didn't add a nice little WARNING! to your setup screen on your shiny new Mac if it were that important. Unfortunately, Apple tends to assume that you already own other Apple products, and thus you understand how the system works. That can be a troublesome assumption for many.

# 51

# Dealing With Chernobyl

On April 26th, 1986 the number 4 nuclear reactor at the Chernobyl power plant in Russia exploded. It was the worst nuclear disaster in my lifetime. I remember the date to this day, because my wife went into labor soon after, and my daughter was born on April 27th, 1986. A few days later we brought her home from the hospital, the very day that the nuclear fallout cloud was passing over the United States. Welcome to the world, Ashley!

Ending up with two Apple IDs is a disaster. OK, not a disaster of Chernobyl proportions, but like Chernobyl, you will be dealing with the fallout for the rest of your digital life, one way or another. Once the problem is created, it will not simply go away. You can't simply merge two Apple IDs into one. Once this digital twin is born, it will follow you for the rest of your digital life.

If you find yourself in this situation, you will have a few options moving forward. If you never bought apps on the secondary account, great! It will be easy to walk away from that account. If you have, it's time to build a sarcophagus.

In the case of Chernobyl, they have built a huge sarcophagus around the destroyed building to try to contain the fallout. You will need to do the same in your digital life. First, determine which Apple ID you will be using exclusively moving forward. This will be the ID that you've purchased the majority of your App Store purchases on and the one that contains your main calendar and contacts list. Next, move anything out of the secondary iCloud account that you wish to keep in the primary. Purchase additional space on the primary account if necessary. Next, move any data out of the secondary calendar and contacts list into the primary. Lastly, set up family sharing with your secondary account so that you do not have to pay for those apps again. The last option for those who only have a few paid apps that they care about is to abandon the secondary account altogether, and re-buy the few apps again under the primary Apple ID. Then you can forget about the second account and consider the money spent on the duplicate apps as money paid for a lesson learned.

# 52

# Legacy Contact

We all know how important it is to secure our assets in a living trust. Apple recognizes that today, it's also important to secure our digital life as well. In your Apple ID it is important to set a Legacy Contact. This is someone who will have access to everything in your Apple account after your death.

You access this feature by clicking on your digital birth certificate, your Apple ID.

Under Passwords & Security you will find a way to edit your Legacy Contact.

This screen will default to a set of choices in your family sharing contacts and give you the ability to choose someone else as well. Follow the instructions and the app will give you a code that the person can you when the time comes. Your digital afterlife is now secure. Rest In Peace.

# 53

# App Store

The App Store can be found in your application Dock by default. It is the square icon with three popsicle sticks. By default, the App Store will open up to the discovery screen. This is where Apple will advertise all of its new or highlighted apps. You can change the category of what you're looking at in the left pane.

Arcade is Apple's subscription game service. Other games can be found under *Play*. These are pay per game apps.

Other major categories including utility type apps can be found in *Create*. General workplace apps are found in an area for developers. Other categories can be found under *Categories*.

If you ever notice that your App Store icon has a little red number on it, that means that you have updates that are ready to download and install, or they have been installed recently. If updates need to be manually installed, go to the updates page and you will be able to click on them individually or do them all at once by clicking *Update All*.

If you click on your name in the lower-left-hand corner you will go into your App Store account. You will see all of the apps that are either in the cloud that you've purchased in the past or are currently on your machine. If the app is on your machine already it will have a prompt to open. If you have downloaded an app on another machine or previously on the one you're looking at and it is not on the machine it will then have a cloud graphic with a download arrow.

From here you can also click on *Account settings*. This will take you to your actual account with Apple. Here you can manage subscriptions or change things about your account.

# 54

# Authorize Computers

Once you've set up an Apple account, you can share your purchased content in iTunes over five computers. At first, that number might seem odd, but if you think about it, five is a pretty good number to land on. That gives you an authorization for a home iMac, a work iMac, a laptop, and an auxiliary machine such as a media server. That's four authorizations and that will meet the needs of 90% of all Mac users with an additional authorization to spare. Setting the authorizations at five will discourage people from sharing an Apple ID across family members like husbands and wives. Apple wants everyone to have their own unique Apple ID. For a husband and wife, you now have ten authorizations available to you, so five seems to be a reasonable number.

Where people get into trouble is when they pass on a computer or sell one without deauthorizing it. Even though a computer may no longer be being used for its original owner and purpose, Apple may still have it authorized and eventually, you'll attempt to authorize a shiny new machine, only to be horrified that all of your authorizations have been used up. Don't worry, there's a fix for that and we'll get to it in a moment.

First, to authorize a new machine, launch Music, and click on *Account*. Under *Authorizations,* you will have the options to *Authorize This Computer* or *Deauthorize This Computer*. If you've reached your maximum authorizations, never fear. Go to a device that you no longer need authorized and deauthorize it. But what if you got rid of it? Oh no! Don't worry, that's easy to fix. Go to Account and Account Settings. There you will find a place to manage all your devices.

# 55

# Subscriptions

Most applications are purchased with a solitary one-time purchase price. However, some apps and services are sold by subscription. Once you have subscribed to a service you can manage it by going to the App Store. In the App Store click on your name to go to your account.

From your account click on *View Information*.

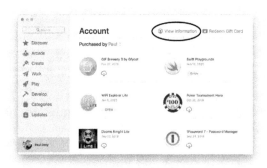

Go to the bottom of this window and you will see a category for subscriptions. Click *Manage*.

Here you will see a list of all of your current subscriptions as well as those that may have expired. To edit a subscription click on *Edit*. Here you will see a list of all of the options that you have for the selected subscription. You can also cancel the subscription.

When you are done you may either click on *Back* to work on more subscriptions or click *Done* to leave the subscription area.

# 56

# Resetting Your Passcode

So what happens if you manage to forget your passcode and lock yourself out of your Mac? You could call on the mothership's help by going down to your local Apple Store to have a genius get you back in, or you could reset your password on your own by using one of these methods.

If you've entered an incorrect password a number of times, your machine will lock up and a prompt will pop up allowing you to change the password via your Apple ID account. This will work only if you know your Apple ID and password. All you have to do here is follow the on-screen prompts and it will create a new Apple log on code for your Mac via your Apple ID.

But what if you don't remember your Apple ID either? The next method may come as quite a shock to some iMac owners. Did you know that virtually anyone can pick up a locked Apple Computer, and with a little hacking know-how, change the log on code, even if it's not their machine? I know this may come as quite a surprise to some as we have the perception that there is nothing as safe as an Apple computer. While this is absolutely true in most respects, it is still a computer, and as long as you have computers, you will have computer hackers. Use the following method to hack into your computer if you have to as a last resort.

Start with your Mac in its off state. Press and hold the command and R key while you press the power key to start the Mac. This will boot the machine in recovery mode. Let go of the two keys as soon as you see the progress bar below the Apple logo. When your machine boots up, go to *utilities* in the menu bar and choose *terminal*. When the terminal window pops up type in **resetpassword**.

# 57

# Creating Folders

Creating a folder on a Mac is an easy affair. Wherever you wish to create a folder right-click or control-click and select *New Folder*. New folders can be created anywhere on your machine. You can create a new folder on your desktop if you are collecting things that you are working on for a specific project for instance. Folders can be created and organized in your documents as well as your iCloud drive.

Once you've created a new folder the default title for it will be *untitled folder*. You can control-click the title of it and rename it anything you'd like.

Once you've created your folder you can change the background color of that folder by opening it and clicking on the drop-down menu of the box with the three dots on it. Here you will see an option for *show view options*.

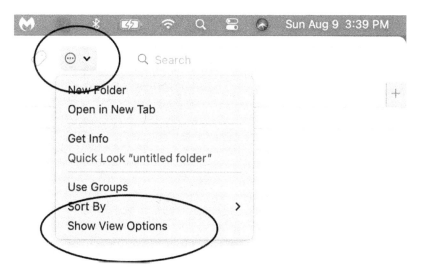

In *show view options* you will be able to change the background color of your folder. You can also use an image as the background for it, but if you do this I would caution you to use a very simple image so the screen doesn't get busy. Images with a lot of detail can make it very hard to see your files and folders within folders. If you are good at using a graphics program like Pixelmator Pro, you can take a graphic that you're going to use as your background and wash it out or change it into a pastel. This can look pretty cool.

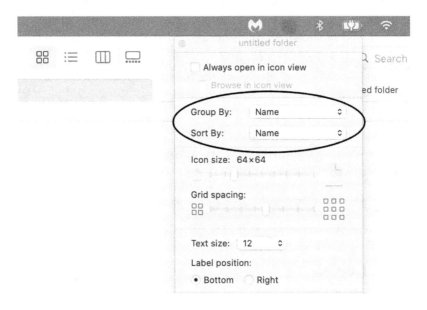

You can also set the default for the new folder sorting by name, or type.

# 58
# Changing Folder Color

We've just learned how simple it is to change the background color of a folder, however, that does nothing for you if you want to sort your folders *by* color. You would think it would be easy to do the same change on the outside of the folder, right? Well, you'd be wrong. Mac does not allow you to do this natively. However, there is some good news. You *can* do this by downloading a free little app called *Tinted Folders Lite*.

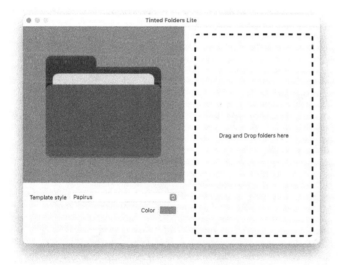

Just run the app and set a color in the color window. Let's say that you want a subfolder in a subfolder of 60 folders to stand out. Just set the color to red, or any color of your liking by clicking on the color box. Then drag the folder that you want to change into the drag area. It will permanently change to that color.

# 59

## Convert A Folder To An Emoji

A relatively easy way to customize the look of your computer is with custom folders. Many of us will keep current projects on our desk top for an amount of time organized in folders. When you create a folder on your desktop, or anywhere on your machine for that matter, Mac creates a nice uniform blue folder for you to place your documents in. Uniform, predictable, recognizable, and boring. I'm going to show you how you can spice up your desktop a bit with trendy emoji folders. First let's start by creating a blank, empty folder on your desktop by right-clicking in a blank location and clicking *New Folder*. Let's call the new folder *Test folder*.

Now go online to Google and do an image search for a smiley face emoji. Remember to click image search. You'll get a search result that looks similar to this.

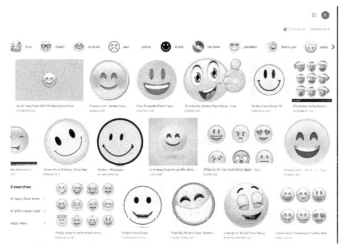

Click on the image that you want, right-click it and save it to your desktop.

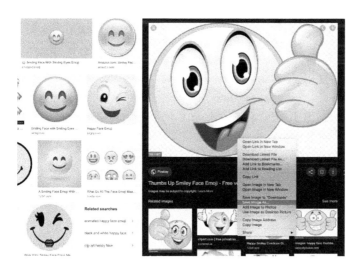

Now double-click the emoji to open it in preview. From the edit menu choose copy to copy it to your clipboard. Close the image and right-click on the test folder.

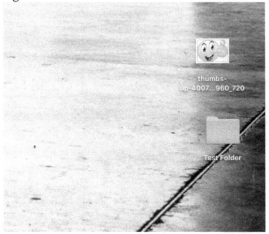

Choose Get Info from the menu. Click on the boring blue folder icon in this window and hit command V on your keyboard to paste the new image. The folder must be highlighted for this to work. You'll now have a hip cool new folder to show off. Have fun customizing!

# 60

# Metadata View

An incredibly helpful tool, especially when viewing photos, is the metadata view. When you browse for a picture in Finder you'll see some basic information about the photo. The date it was created, the dimensions, and other basic data. You'll also notice that you have the ability to *Show More*.

Clicking *Show More* will add additional data to the list. This will double or triple the information that you see along with the file, but there's more. You can actually go in and customize the data that you're presented with. To do this, click View on the Finder menu bar and select *Show Preview Options*. You can now customize your view to show only the information that is pertinent to you.

# 61

# Quick View

Here's a handy little feature that even many seasoned Mac users have no idea exists. Let's say you're working on a project and you've accumulated ten or so various files on your desktop. And let's say they all have file names that are non-descriptive of what they are. Now you're looking for a particular file and it's quickly becoming obvious that you're searching for a needle in a haystack. These files could be PDFs, JPGs, text documents, HTML pages, really any computer file that you would normally have to open up to view. You could spend five minutes or more double-clicking them all one by one to open them, or you could use this handy time saver.

Take any icon on your desktop and instead of double-clicking it, single-click it to highlight it. After the icon is highlighted, hold the space bar down. As long as your finger is on the spacebar you will get a quick view of the file on your desktop. As soon as you take your finger off the spacebar, the preview will go away.

If you open a quick view that includes more than one page, you will get an area on the side that will show you the available pages for view.

# 62

# God View

There will be times when you're sorting through your iCloud Drive or your Macs hard drive and you want to get a birds-eye view of an entire area of your file structure. Your Mac allows you to do this by changing the view from a folder or file view to a file line view. My wife renames this view God View, because it allows us to see the entire file structure from start to finish in one view, and it allows us to see the file we're looking at in relationship to others.

This view is my go-to view when I'm managing photos on my Mac. It's also great for any sorting that you're doing on your computer. You might be organizing recipes for instance and you need a fast way to see your entire file structure at once.

To invoke the mode, go to finder and click on a location such as your documents folder. If your computer is defaulting to another mode such as folder mode, click on the third mode view icon, the one with three panes.

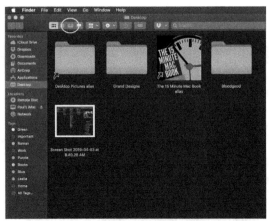

The view will switch to multiple panes, allowing you to see an overall view of the file structure. As you click through the subfolders, new panes will open up eventually reviewing the final file in the structure.

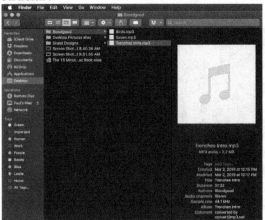

The last pane will show you all of the details about the file. Other files may be dragged and dropped into the structure now, but because of the view, you now have the option to drop them anywhere along the file structure path without clicking through a huge amount of subfolders to get where you're going.

# 63

# Smart Folders

A Smart Folder is a way of storing a smart search on your computer. Have you ever found yourself trying to remember where you've stored a file? If you're like me, you have multiple projects on your computer stored in multiple locations. Now I try to be as neat as possible, but there are times when a file location eludes me. Smart Folders, or shall we say smart searches can help greatly. To best demonstrate how they work, I'm going to set up a smart folder to help me find the latest copy of a book that I might be working on. I might have different versions in different locations, so let's create a smart folder to automatically locate books that I'm working on in Scrivener that I've modified in the last month. If I were to simply do a Spotlight search for all Scrivener files, I'd get an onslaught of information motion that would look something like this.

With Smart Folders, I can create a smart search that shows up in the favorites area of Finder, any time I want to find the latest version of a project created in Scrivener. Let's go ahead and create it. We'll start by holding down control and clicking Finder. We will now get an option to create a *New Smart Folder*. A blank smart search. We're going to press the plus symbol by the save button to open up a layer of rules to apply to the search criteria. We'll select *Kind* and *Other* so we can enter the file type for scrivener which is .scriv. Now notice that we can continue to add more rules to narrow the search even further.

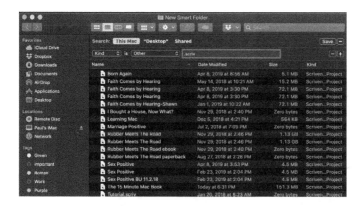

Now if we add the date last opened, and set that to the last week, we narrow the search even more.

At this point if I were looking for the correct version of the book Rubber Meets the Road, I can highlight both files and see where each is located. In this search, I can tell which file is the latest one and the one in the correct location.

When you're done with a search, click on *Save* and the search will be saved to your Finder favorites.

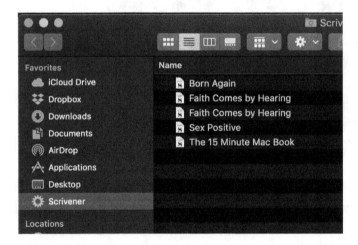

Now, know that Smart Folders are dynamic! That means that they are updated continually. They do not actually contain any files, only information on those files, so if you delete a Smart Folder, the files remain on your machine unchanged. By the way, to remove a Smart Folder, simply drag the folder out of Finder and let it go.

# 64

# The Alias

If you're familiar with the term short cut in the PC world, then you already understand what an Alias is in the world of Mac. An alias is simply an icon that you create in order to place a shortcut to an app or a folder in a convenient location like your desktop. An alias is simple to create. First find the file you'd like quick access to in a location like iCloud, or your documents. Control-click the file or folder and choose *make alias*. An alias will now be created in the same location as the original object. You can move that alias to another location such as your desktop.

An alias can come in handy if you're working on a project that you're accessing on a daily basis, or if you want quick access to a location that you go to often. Common aliases that I use on my machines offer shortcuts to my folder that contains the images that I use for my wallpaper and I also use an alias any time I'm working on a new book so I can pull it up quickly in order to write. You can even save a web location as an alias by dragging it to your desktop from your browser. I have a YouTube TV alias on the desktop of my media server for example which allows me to quickly access my TV broadcasts. Other great uses for them are business documents and templates that you may need to access on a semi-regular basis.

Aliases can be created and deleted at will. You will not lose an application or document by deleting an alias. You can also change the name of an alias to anything you wish without affecting the original document.

# 65

# Downloads

Your downloads folder is a very important part of your Mac. This folder contains all the files that you download while online. Think of it as the front room of your computer. It's also the landing folder for any file that you or someone else shares with your Mac. Because it's a popular room in your house, it will tend to become cluttered quickly. A general rule of thumb to follow is if it becomes time-consuming or frustrating to find something newly added to the folder, it's time to clean it out.

You can get to this folder via many ways. If you click on an item to download while online, you'll notice that the file will bounce up and into a little area in the upper right of Safari. You'll then see a progress bar in that area until you've completed your download. You can access the new download simply by clicking that area while still in Safari.

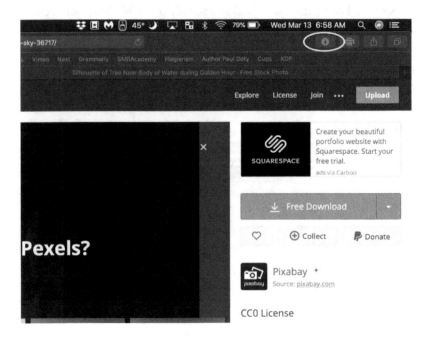

Another way to access it is by Finder. Accessing the folder this way is also the best way to do so when you wish to move items out to another location, or when you're doing housekeeping in the folder.

Any time that you airdrop an item to your machine, this is its landing place. The Downloads folder is truly Grand Central Station for your Mac. Just remember to keep it from getting cluttered, so you can continue to run efficiently.

# Keeping Downloads Clean

Isn't it amazing how fast your downloads folder gets filled with junk? Have you ever been frustrated trying to find a new download in the sea of files? What if I told you that you could program your Mac to move files in that folder over a predetermined age to the trash? Did you just cringe when you read the word program? No worries, it's relatively simple, and if you're adventurous, I'll introduce you to one of the many ways that you can program your Mac using a little utility called Automator.

Automator is a programming utility that allows you to create scripts that run in the background of your Mac to automate tasks. In this example we're going to automate our Mac to move all of the files in our Downloads folder to the trash once they've been there for 90 days.

When you first launch Automator you'll be prompted to choose what type of script you'd like to create. In this case we're going to create a Folder Action.

In the right pane you'll see an empty area in which to create your script. We will grab a few script steps from the categories and options in the left panes and drag them into the right in the logical order in which we want them to run.

The first thing we need to do is select Files and Folders and tell the script that we want to effect the Downloads folder by selecting it in the top dropdown menu.

Then we will drop over Find Finder Items, telling it to search Downloads for ALL content.

Then we will drag over Filter Finder Items to filter all by date created.

Lastly we will drag over Move Finder Item to Trash. Test your script by clicking the arrow in the upper right corner to run. It may show you an error if it did not delete ALL files because of the created date. That's fine. Once you're happy with your script, save it as delete90 or whatever creative name you wish. Congratulations, you've just taught your Mac a brand new skill.

# File Path Hack

One of the things I loved about PC was how it would always show you the path of where a file was located. One of the early frustrations for me switching to Mac was not knowing the file path of a file that I was looking at. I would go to store a word document and I would try to find it in finder but all finder would do was show me the immediate file of where it was located, which did nothing for me as far as knowing where it was. Take a look at the photo below for an example.

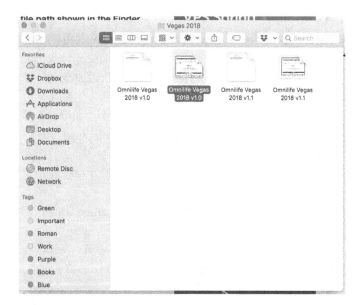

I happen to know this file is located on my iCloud Drive, but other than that I have no idea what it is a subfolder of. It could be 12 subfolders deep as far as I know. There is a hack that you can perform to add this functionality to a Mac just like you have on a PC. To do this, open a terminal window and type in the following;

**defaults write com.apple.finder _FXShowPosixPathInTitle -bool YES; killall Finder**

Now when you navigate back to the exact same file you will get something that looks like this;

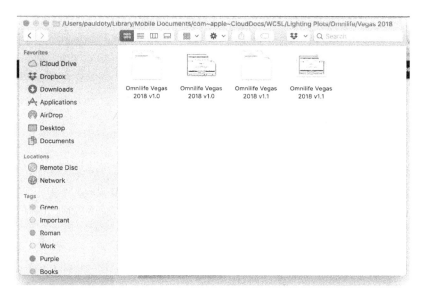

# 68

# Changing an App Icon

One complaint people have after switching to Mac is that it doesn't give you as much personal customization options as a PC. While that's true to some extent, there are actually numerous ways to customize a Mac that most people, even power users are unaware of. For instance, did you know that you can change the appearance of an app icon in Mac?

Let's say you're a writer, and you keep a number of spreadsheet aliases on your desktop for various purposes. One of those spreadsheets is what you use to track your book sales. As you know, if you have ten Excel spreadsheet icons on your desktop, they're all going to look exactly the same. Wouldn't it be great to give your book sale tracking icon a different custom look? Well, on a Mac you can, and here's how.

First, you're going to need a graphic to replace the original icon. Find an icon on the web for example, and save it to your desktop. Mac icons are typically about 400X400 pixels. Don't worry if you can't find a perfect 400-pixel graphic, I'll tell you how to shrink a larger one to 400 pixels. It's easy if you know how.

Double-click your new graphic to open it in preview. From here, use your crosshair tooltip (It will default to it) to draw a square box around your graphic so it looks square. Don't worry, it doesn't have to be perfect. Now go up to tools on the top menu and select crop. You'll now want to hit save, and your downloaded graphic will be replaced with the cropped version.

Now go to tools again and pick *Adjust Size*. You'll want to change the longest dimension to 400 pixels. You may have to change it to pixels from inches, so pay attention to all your little dialog boxes. Again, save the graphic. Copy the image to your clipboard by selecting all from the edit menu then click copy. Now close preview by clicking on the red dot in the upper left.

Here comes the magic! Go over to your generic Excel icon on your desktop and control-click it. Choose *Get Info*. Left-click the generic icon in the upper left of the box. As it's highlighted, control-click it again and select paste, or go up to edit and select paste. There! You've changed your icon!

# 69

# File Vault

FileVault gives you a way to encrypt your entire hard drive on your Mac, not just password protect it. It does this at the expense of speed and space. Because this option will slow down your machine and eat space on your hard drive, it is only recommended for someone who needs a higher level encryption on a specific machine. For most of us this added level of security is not only unnecessary, but unwanted as it will slow down your machine significantly and eat a lot more of your precious hard drive space.

This option sometimes will get turned on by mistake when someone is doing an update to the OS. Somewhere during the process it will ask you if you want to use FileVault? If you mistakenly click the button your machine will become a slow speed hi security slug.

Fortunately there is a very quick way to go check to see if this option is enabled on your machine, and if that is, turn it off, that is unless you desire the added encryption of the slower machine. Go to *system preferences* and *security & privacy*. Navigate to the *file fault* tab. Here you'll find the option that will allow you to turn it on or off. Be ready for this process to take some time as it will have to go through your entire hard drive and either encrypt or un-encrypt it. Make sure you do this during a time when you can walk away from your computer for a few hours for it to complete its task. Remember, whenever you change a security setting on your Mac you must click the little padlock in the lower-left-hand corner and enter your passcode for your computer. Don't forget to lock it again when you're done!

# 70

# Stacks

Stacks is a feature that was added with OS X Mojave. It's a great feature for those who are digital hoarders. A digital hoarder is someone who has more of their desktop covered with icons instead of wallpaper. After a certain point, it becomes difficult to find anything in the clutter. A messy desktop is like a messy room or a messy house. The Stacks feature gives the digital hoarder a way to tidy up their digital house without actually working at it. Think of it as a digital housekeeper. The first photo shows a version of a desktop with Stacks off.

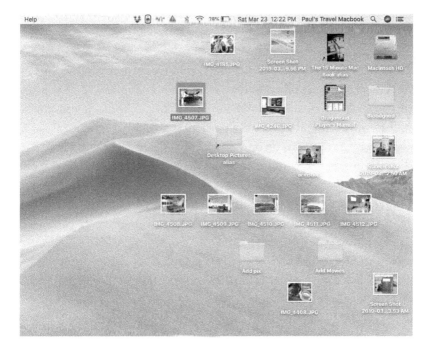

The next image is the same desktop with Stacks turned on.

When Stacks is enabled, Stacks will create a virtual stack of the same type of files on your desktop. Photos for example will be stacked until you click on a stack to find a specific photo. The stack will then unfold to show you what is in the particular stack.

Stacks is easy to turn on and off. Simple control-click on your desktop in any blank location and click Use Stacks. You can turn it off at any time in the same fashion.

You can set up Stacks to group items however you like. Stacks will usually default to a date related option but you can also sort your stacks by kind.

Who then should use Stacks? Take a look at your desktop. Is it cluttered? If it is, use the assistant. If you're a tidy housekeeper, you'll have little need for this feature.

# 71

## Sequential File Names

There are times when you might want to rename a series of files with friendlier titles. Photos are a common place where you may need to do this. You might have twenty or so files with generic titles like img_4992.jpg and you'd like all twenty to be something like new_puppy1, new_puppy2, and so on. While it's a bit hidden, you do have the ability to do a batch re-title in Mac OS. Let's look at an example.

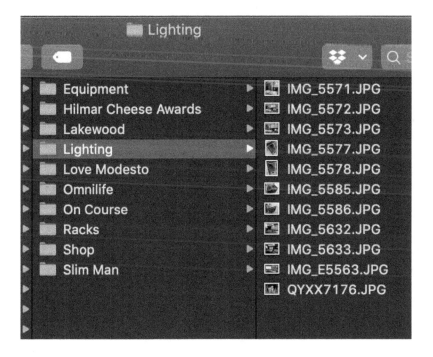

In our example, we're going to take eleven photos of theatrical lighting systems and rename them lighting1 through 11.

We select all eleven files and control-click them and select *rename 11 items*. This will give us an option window. Here we will change the format (The name) to *name and Index*. We will rename the files to Lighting, and set the start number to 1. Click Rename.

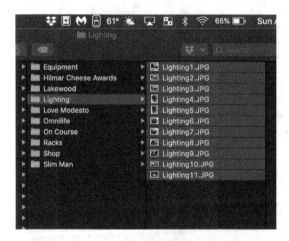

The window will process the command for a moment and return with the files renamed with the new format and number scheme.

# 72

# Interactive File Name

You've probably used your Mac to work on files that you've created and stored on your machine or in the cloud. It might be a Pages document, or an Excel spreadsheet, or like in the example that I'm about to give, a book like the very one you're reading, created in Scrivener. You may have noticed that the name of the file appears at the top of your document while it's open on your machine. Open or create any type of document and look to the top of the app. You should see an icon that represents the type of the file open, and the name of the file to its right.

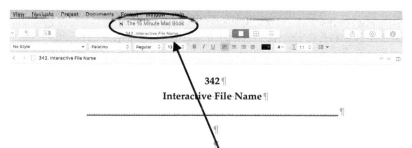

Most people think this is a simple static display of the current file you're working on but it's much more. It's actually an interactive control that will give you access to the entire hierarchy of where your file is located and access to any other files that may be stored with it. If you go up to the name and hold the command key while you click it, you'll see the entire file path of where the file is stored.

**342**

**Interactive File Name**

You've probably used your Mac to work on files that you've created and stored on your machine or in the cloud. It might be a Pages document, or an Excel spreadsheet, or like in the example that I'm about to give, a book like the very one you're reading, created in Scrivener. You may have noticed that the name of the file appears at the top of your document while it's open on your machine. Open or create any type of document and look to the top of the app. You should see an icon that represents the type of the file open, and the name of the file to its right.

In my example, you see that my file The 15 Minute Mac Book is stored in iCloud, in the Scrivener folder, in a subfolder called The 15 Minute Mac Book. I can now run my tooltip to any of these locations and open them in a new window. In my example, I will run my tooltip over to The 15 Minute Mac Book folder and click it to reveal its contents. I can now work on my cover art in another window without having to go search for it manually.

# 73

# Multiple Instance Hack

Some apps running on Mac OS will allow you to work with multiple instances at the same time. For instance, you may be working on an Excel spreadsheet, and open a completely new spreadsheet and work on both simultaneously. Some programs however may only allow you to open one document at a time. With some apps you may try this simple hack if you want two or more documents running or available at once.

I stumbled across this hack while doing a video presentation for a corporate client. They gave me two video files and asked me to run them side by side on their projection screen. On my Mac I have two different video players available to me, Quicktime and VLC media player. I told my client that I could do it thinking I'd just open one in each app, no problem. As is turned out, both videos were made on a PC and only played in VLC. Now I had a problem as VLC will only play one video at a time.

I right clicked the files, and sure enough, the only app listed in *open with* was VLC. That's when I had a revelation. What if I had two versions of VLC on my Mac? I thought to myself, no, it can't be that simple. I then went to *Finder/Applications* and found the VLC icon. I right-clicked VLC and choose *Duplicate*. My Mac made a duplicate copy of VLC called VLCcopy. I went back over to the video file and right-clicked it again. It now gave me the option to open with VLC or VLCcopy. Genius! I opened the two files in the two different copies of the same app and my client was none the wiser.

This hack will likely work with many other types of applications. Graphic apps, music apps, you name it. The bottom line is that it never hurts to try, and if you're not successful in your results, you can simply drag your copied app into the trash and say, "Oh well, I tried."

# 74

# iCloud Drive

iCloud Drive is Apple's version of an online hard drive for your Mac. You could think of it like a service comparative to Dropbox, but it's actually much more. It's also a way to sync your data over multiple devices like iPads and iPhones, not to mention other computers.

Apple starts you off with a small amount of space when you buy a Mac. To be honest, it's simply a gateway amount to get you to try the service. They offer an entry-level amount at $.99 a month that is actually a useful amount of space, and if you're a good steward of your online usage, it's really enough for most users. If you consider that a decent external hard drive costs over a hundred dollars and has a realistic life expectancy of 4 or 5 years, an online hard drive for $12 a year is actually a bargain.

Now, what do you get once you've invested in iCloud? The first big advantage is cloud-based shared storage. You get the ability to work on a document from your home computer, go to work, and log into it as if you had it saved at work all along. Head out to lunch with your laptop and work on the document there. It essentially gives you a universal place to store your work, accessible from anywhere.

Like Dropbox, as long as you have the space on your machine, the information stored in iCloud is also stored on your various computers, so you are able to work offline if an internet connection is not available. ICloud will automatically sync with your account the next time you have an internet connection.

Unlike Dropbox, iCloud is also used to sync your digital world between all of your devices, such as your calendars, contacts, and notes.

A word to the wise, your photostream, and your trash bin will eat up space in your iCloud account! Keep them all at a minimum or Apple will start nagging you to buy more space! Personally, I do not use iCloud at all for photos for this vary reason, and I'll go over my strategy for photos shortly.

# 75

# Manage iCloud

Managing your iCloud account is an important part of using your Mac. It's one of those areas where if you don't understand what's going on, it will cost you money.

Every few months I will take an inventory of my iCloud account. It takes very little time and you can catch little problems before they become big ones by doing some simple management work. To access your iCloud account go to System Settings and click on your Apple ID icon.

Next open up iCloud itself on your account. From this window, you can toggle items on and off that are stored in your iCloud Drive.

Next click on the Manage button. This manages the size of your iCloud Drive. In the left pane, you will see in descending order what applications are taking up the most space automatically on your iCloud Drive. Highlight anything that you do not want sending information to iCloud and click delete the files. Warning! This will delete all files associated with that application throughout all of your devices. Make sure that you don't want any of that information before hitting the delete. You cannot undo this!

Last is the Buy More Storage button. This allows you to select what size you want your actual iCloud Drive to be. You will find that you will run out of space quickly with the free amount of space that Apple gives you. The good news is that you can buy a 50 GB drive from Apple for $.99 a month. This is a great value. I am a power user and I still use only the 50 GB drive at $.99 a month and at that price I never feel it. If for some reason you really need 200 GB of space, the 2.99 deal is still a great deal. This is a great plan if you are using the machine as a business machine and you are storing huge amounts of data, photos, etc. in the cloud.

Now, keep an eye on things on a semi-monthly basis. Macs are notorious for doing things automatically. The computer likes to think for you. What's taking up space in your iCloud Drive is not one of the areas in which you want it to make decisions for you. Stay on top of it, know exactly how much you're using, and how much you actually need.

# 76
## iCloud File Recovery

We've all done it, sooner or later you will accidentally delete a file that you wanted to keep from your iCloud drive. When this inevitably happens, this is the procedure for getting your file back. Whenever you delete a file from your iCloud drive it gets moved to a special folder similar to the trash can on your Mac. You can access this file folder online and retrieve a file if it has been deleted within one month. After 30 days files are deleted from this folder forever.

In this example, I have an image of a shower head in my iCloud drive. I am going to select this photo and delete it. Now if I go to my trash folder on my iMac now, I will still be able to grab that photo and reinstall it to the iCloud Drive. But what if I have cleaned out my trash? You would think the file is now gone forever, but it's not.

Go to your iCloud account online and click on iCloud Drive. You will see that your photo is no longer there as well. However, if you go to the bottom right of your iCloud Drive folder, you'll see a link for Recently deleted. Click it.

Pixelmator Pro    Preview    Public Works    Published Books

Screen Shots    Scrivener    Shawn    Shipping

47 items, 12.15 GB available    Recently Deleted (1)

Here you will find a list of files deleted in the last 30 days and you'll be able to restore the file from here.

# 77

# iCloud Sharing

For years if you wanted to share an online folder with another person you would have to use a third-party service like Dropbox. As of Catalina, you can now share iCloud folders with other people.

Sharing is simple and straight forward. Right-click on a folder that you want to share in iCloud and open the share menu. Now choose Add People to add someone to a folder.

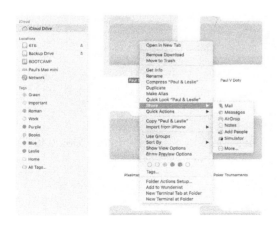

This menu will allow you to send a sharing invitation to another user in various ways. You can send an email, send a text, copy the link and send it on a service like Facebook messenger, or even airdrop it to someone in the room with you.

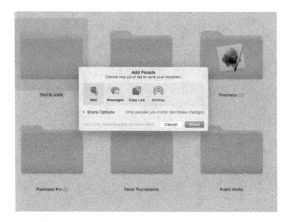

You can add as many collaborators as you like to a specific folder making this new feature excellent for business users.

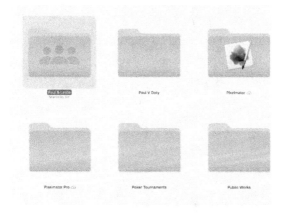

Once you've shared a folder you will see a new folder look with multiple users represented.

# 78
# Profile Pic

Your profile pic will end up being a generic picture whenever you set up a new device. But what if you want your profile picture to match across all of your devices? There's an easy way to do this.

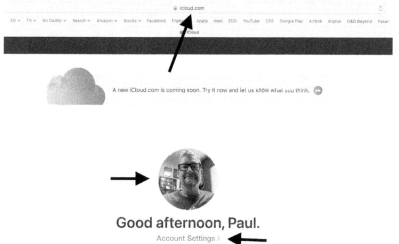

Log in to your iCloud account at icloud.com. Next click on account settings and click the edit button on your photo. There may or may not be a photo here to begin with.

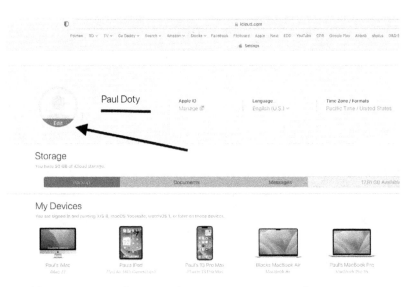

Have a master photo ready on your computer that you want to upload.

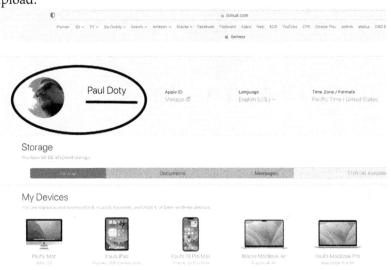

Once uploaded here, it will show up magically on all of your devices as the master photo. If you ever want to change this photo on all of your devices, simply come back here and change it. They will all update automatically.

# 79

# Manage Your Apple Devices

Whenever you register a new Apple device, that device will be listed in iCloud. It's a good idea from time to time to check your iCloud account online to check to see if your device list is up to date. Whenever you sell or pass down a device you will need to go there to remove it from your list of devices.

To access your list, go to **iCloud.com** and sign in with your Apple ID. You will need to put in a code for two-step authentication when you log in. Once your iCloud account loads, click on **Account Settings**.

Here you'll get a neat overview of all of your devices linked to your account. Clicking on any device will give you the ability to delete any device. When you're done, click on the settings dropdown arrow in the upper left corner of your window and choose *Launchpad* to return to your main icon screen.

# 80

# Put Clouds in the Sky

This one's just a fun little trick to spice up your computer. It will give you a visual reminder of when you're working in the cloud, by literally putting you, in the clouds. First, go online to a service like Google, and do an image search for the word cloud. You'll quickly be reminded that every day, God paints a sky, totally different than the day before. You'll be faced with so many cloud choices, it will be overwhelming. Go find yourself a cloud picture that you like, and is large in size. The larger, the better, as it will fill more of your iCloud window once installed.

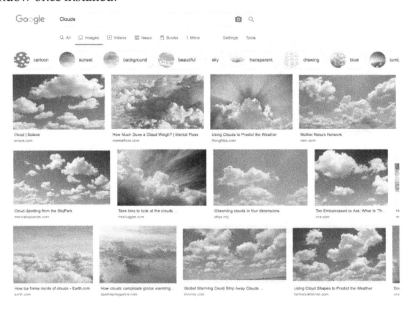

Once you've picked an image, right-click on it and save it to your desktop. This image will eventually become your background image any time that you go to iCloud in Finder. Save the image to the desktop, you will need access to it in a few moments. Now open up Finder and go to iCloud Drive. Open up *View* on the menu and select

*View options.* Here you will find a box to drag your photo from the desktop onto.

Once you've done that (and *Picture* is selected) you will see your files in the clouds every time that you go to iCloud Drive.

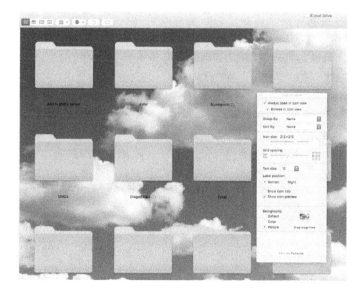

# 81

## Photos in the Cloud?

If you take a few photos a year, say under 50, then the photo streaming service on iCloud can be a wonderful thing. You snap a picture at a party on your iPhone, and later that night it's in iCloud and accessible while you're working on your laptop. But what if you're a person like me who actually uses his awesome camera on his iPhone all the time, almost daily. For a person like me, I'm going to start seeing those annoying nags to buy more iCloud space in a very short amount of time.

My solution is to manage my photos outside of iCloud (and Dropbox for that matter) with an external photo server hard drive. 4TB and larger drives have become relatively cheap these days and they provide an excellent place for storing huge amounts of data, like a photo collection. Some people will use the Photos app on their Mac to manage their collection, but I'm a little more hands-on, storing my photos in a way that makes it easy for me to find what I'm looking for. On my photo server drive (a simple USB external 5TB drive I picked up for just over $100) I have my photos organized in the following folder structure; Photo Server/Years/Events. If you opened my drive on my machine at home you'd see a folder called Photo Server. Open that folder and you'd see a number of folders laid out by year. 2015, 2016, 2017, 2018, 2019, etc. Once I've completed a decade, I create a folder for that decade and move the 10 folders into it. Within each year, I break down the events of the year into separate folders as well. It now becomes quite easy to pull up Christmas photos from 2016, or photos from work in 2009.

It's a little work to keep it organized, but my photos are worth it. I also have a second identical drive that serves as my onsite backup via Time Machine. As a third redundant backup, I have a third hard drive offsite that I physically back the last year up to every year just after New Years'. I keep this backup at my work, thus giving me the added advantage of having my photo library there as well.

The above method does take some commitment and work to keep it up, and Apple knows this. They also know that most people won't take the time to organize their own photos. That's why they offer to do it for you and at a premium price. The question that you have to answer is whether or not your photo collection is important enough for you to manage, or are you OK with continually throwing apple more and more money every month to deal with it for you, as your data expands.

# 82

# Sync Desktops

The iCloud experience is great! It gives you the ability to save something to your computer at work, and retrieve it at home. But wouldn't it be great is you could do that with all aspects of your computer? Wouldn't it be great to save a folder on your desktop and have it show up on another computer? Or how about a shared documents folder as well as a shared iCloud drive? All of these things are possible with Mac if you want it.

Personally, I'm not the person who's going to use this feature. I want my work computer to be just that, and I want my home computer to be just that. If I need access to a shared file, I'll put it in iCloud, but that's as much as I want all my machines talking to one another. You may be the complete opposite. You may only have an iMac at home for instance, and a MacBook Air for use as a mobile extension of it. In other words, you want your home experience, and files to follow you when you step out. If this is you, then turning on the sync desktop feature is what you want to do!

To turn this feature on, go to System Settings and click on Apple ID. In iCloud, you will find a button for iCloud Drive. Click Options. Here you will want to turn on *Desktop & Documents Folders*. This will share these folders with any computers in your account that have the box checked.

# 83

# Sync Issues

The wonderful thing about the Apple ecosystem is the way that everything talks to everything else throughout it. Update a calendar event on your phone and it populates on all of your computer screens just like magic. Put a new contact into your Mac and go out into the field and find it on your phone moments later. No other place in the apple ecosystem demonstrates the Apple mantra of *It Just Works* like iCloud and syncing across all of your devices. That is until it just doesn't.

If you're having syncing problems with your Apple devices, the first thing you're going to want to do is to be a detective. Ask yourself some logical questions. What has changed? Did the problem arise when a new device was added, or a new operating system was placed on a computer? Is the problem localized to one device? With a little detective work, you should be able to isolate the problem or at least narrow down the issue. If nothing has changed on your end at all, the problem may be on the server and with Apple. A telephone call to Apple support could confirm that iCloud is having some issues on a given day.

If your detective work leads you to the conclusion that the problem is one particular machine in the system and to the best of your knowledge nothing has changed on that system, then the place to start is to log out of your iCloud account and then log back in. This will reset a number of files on your machine. If there is a corrupt file that is causing issues, that file will usually be rewritten at this point and the problem fixed. If the issues seem to be systemwide, try logging out of your iCloud account on all of your devices and then back in. If you've tried all of this and your syncing world is still sunk, then it's time to call the mothership.

# 84

# Desktop & Dock

This is where you will go to adjust all of the settings pertaining to these in *System Settings*.

Dock size and location is managed here as well as the animation effects. You can choose what happens when you double click a title bar as well. What's that you might ask? Go to Desktop & Dock in System Settings. Set Double-click a windows title bar too: Do Nothing. Now double click Desktop & Dock in the top of the open System settings window. Nothing should happen. Now switch to Zoom and try it again.

# 85
# Menu Bar

The menu bar at the top of your Mac gives you all kinds of useful information, but did you know that you can pick and choose what to show and how to show it? Simply open up *Control Center* in *System Settings* and you will all of your items with drop downs. You can use the drop-down's to decide how you want them displayed.

# 86

# Hide Menu Bar

The small screen Apple laptops are great for travel but when you give up size for portability and weight, you also give up screen real estate. Apple gives you a great way to combat this by allowing you to hide your big menu bar when you're not using it. Just go to Desktop & Dock in System settings and adjust the Menu bar to your liking.

# Control Center

Anyone who has an iPhone or an iPad is familiar with Control Center. This is an area that brings all of the control buttons of your device into one place. In the past, most of these have taken up space on your menu bar across the top of your machine. Now they are all neat in one place just like they are on your iPhone or iPad.

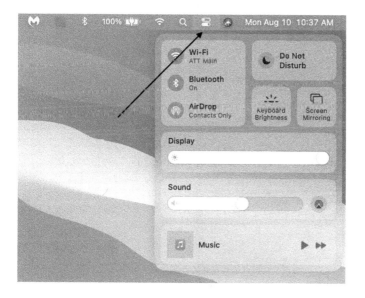

Here you will find all of the basics like your display intensity and volume control. You can also adjust keyboard brightness and set your do not disturb options. If you are playing an album in Music, you will have controls here to start and stop as well.

# 88

# Focus

Focus is a new feature in Monterey that allows you to concentrate on your work. It's used to tune out the distractions that come at inopportune times while we're trying to get work done.

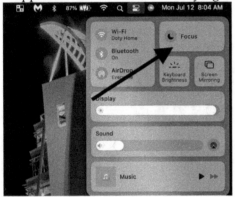

Focus is found in the control center. It operates like Do Not Disturb, but it's much more customizable.

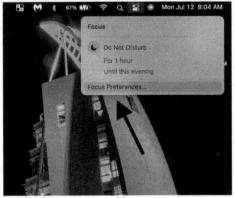

In Focus, click on Focus Preferences to get started. Here you will find all the ways that you can customize your personal Focus experience.

# 89

# Siri

A few years ago Siri came to the Mac. Even though Siri has been on the Mac for a few years now I have noticed that not many people are using her on the Mac as compared to their iPhone. There's good reason for this. Siri has had many years on the iPhone to mature and when paired with the iPhone, Siri is a very powerful tool.

Siri on the Mac however is still in her infancy. More commands are being added all the time so she continues to become more powerful, but as of the writing of this chapter, I will be the first to admit that Siri can be somewhat frustrating on a Mac. This will change as months go by, but for the time being there are some pretty cool things you can do with Siri on the Mac.

Some older Macs will simply not have enough resources to run Siri, but if you have a newer Mac, try a few of these commands. Note that Siri does need to be enabled in your system preferences.

Hey Siri;

Open my calendar.

Who was the fifth president of United States?

What is the square root of 4000?

What time is it in Atlanta?

How do I boil an egg?

How is the weather today?

What time is sunset?

What is the first day of spring?

When is daylight savings time?

Send a text message to (say the name of a recipient in your contacts)

Open the documents folder.

Open iCloud drive.

Show me what I was working on Monday.

Remind me to leave for work in one hour.

Play (song name) in Apple Music.

Make my screen brighter.

Find podcasts about photography.

How many ounces are in a liter?

What is the population of Modesto California?

How much iCloud storage space do I have left?

Find coffee near me.

Tell me about the band Bloodgood.

If you want to have some fun with Siri, she can be entertaining as well. Try some of these fun questions;

Do you believe in God?

And lastly everyone has to try this at least once in their life, Hey Siri, "I see a little silhouetto of a man."

# 90
# Touch ID

Touch ID first appeared on the iPhone and it's now available Mac laptops and the new iMacs. It allows you to use a series of fingerprints to unlock your machine. You likely set up Touch ID the first time you set up your Mac Book Pro, but you can alter and add to that initial setup by going to *Touch ID & Password* in System Settings.

In Touch ID you can add another print by clicking on the *Add A Fingerprint* icon.  This comes in handy if you wish to add another user to your computer.  Once you add more than one fingerprint to your system, you'll want to name them to keep them straight.  You can do so by clicking on the generic Finger # and typing in a new name.  Your Mac can store up to 5 different prints.

# 91
# Users

You may be the only person using your computer but if you have multiple users, you can manage those users by clicking *Users & Groups* in System Settings.

Here you will see your name listed as the administrator on the computer as well as other guests and people that you have added to your machine. A husband and wife for example may share the same universal computer at a house. You can then manage your calendars and contacts by creating different users on that computer.

To create another user simply press Add Account. Clicking on the information circle will allow you to change the password for a user.

# 92

# Login Items

This area of your Mac allows you to sign apps to auto run whenever you start your Mac. Access this area by going to system settings / General / Login items.

Here you will see the apps that are auto running on login. To add an app just click the + button.

Like an iPhone, you can allow or disallow apps to run in the background by switching them on or off from this window.

# 93

# Anywhere Checkbox

Sometimes you'll want to download or install an application from a source that is not affiliated with Apple. While Apple allows you to do this, they do not make it easy. You will have to go to the Privacy & Security section of System Settings and allow it every time you wish to install something that is not from a recognized developer. Apple used to have an option you could click to allow installs from anywhere, but they took that option away years ago. Now the only two options you have are allowing downloads from the App Store or identified developers.

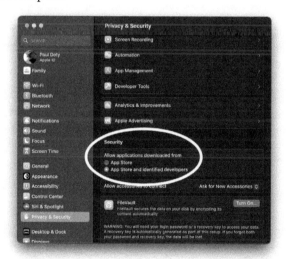

If you install apps from non recognized developers on a semi-regular basis, here's a hack that will restore that option so you're not continually going in and giving your computer the OK to install. Open up an app on your machine called Terminal. It comes on every Mac and it allows you to input programming commands into your computer. A window will open up similar to the one below. The terminal window will be waiting for text input from you. Enter the following code:

**sudo spctl --master-disable**

and hit return.

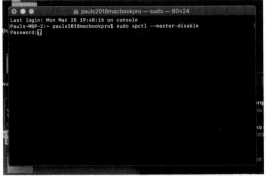

The window will now be waiting for your Mac's password to enter the code and this is where it gets a little weird. Enter your passcode for your Mac. You will NOT see it as you type, but your computer does. This is normal. Hit enter and go back to Privacy & Security. You should now see a new option that will allow the installs without the nagging.

You'll want to create a note on your Mac with this line of code because every time your machine does an operating system update, this option will be overwritten and you'll need to put it back.

# 94

# Touch Bar

The touch bar on the MacBook Pro is kind of like an iPad. Most people really don't need it but it looks really cool and you want one. Before I get totally flamed, let's make it through the rest of the chapter and we'll see if you will agree with me in the end.

Apple needed a new whiz-bang feature that no other computer had when they launched the completely redesigned MacBook Pro. They needed something that would aw people and make them want to go out and buy one even if they already owned a previous MacBook Pro. You see, that's one of the problems from a marketing standpoint with Apple products is that they tend to last forever. At the time that I bought my MacBook Pro, I had already been using my previous MacBook Pro for about seven years. In fact it took nine years for my original MacBook Pro to finally die, and I still could have fixed it if I had wanted to spend money on a new battery. With this kind of longevity, Apple needed something to make this new machine stand out and the Touch Bar certainly fills the bill.

I know that there are those out there that love their iPad and use them every day. I am a professional and I use two iPads professionally to control consoles. This is something that I cannot do with the laptop unless I want to carry a laptop around on a stage, which is not very effective or convenient. So these devices do have a place, but most people using them for everyday use could get along just fine without them. That's all I'm saying.

Does the Touch Bar bring new functionality to a MacBook Pro? Yes and no. Most people can get along just fine with a regular MacBook Pro without the newfangled gadget. There are going to be those that work in music production for instance that will love the ability to scroll and scrub on the Touch Bar. But for the most part, if I'm being honest, most of these functions can be done just fine on a trackpad. In the end, it looks cool, and you want it. Apple knows this and so the feature exists.

Can I justify saying that it exists solely to sell MacBook Pros? Well, think about it this way. If professionals loved this feature so much, and it changed their workflow to a huge degree, isn't it funny that the feature is not showing up on desktop keyboards in the Apple lineup? One has to assume that it is there for its main purpose. To sell a product. Is that a bad thing? I don't think so. I love my MacBook Pro with my Touch Bar, but if I'm being honest, I would tell 90% of people out there that they can get by without it.

# 95

# Special Characters

At the risk of sounding cliché, sooner or later you're going to need to type a special character.

See what I did there? I came up with a sentence specifically so I can use the word cliché, so I could have to type a special character. But seriously, now and then while composing an email or writing in general, you're going to need to type a special character. You can do this in one of a couple ways. First you could use the voice recognition feature built into your Mac and simply say the word. Your Mac will recognize the need for the special character and type it for you with the special character. You can also manually type in a special character simply by holding the letter that needs the accent. In this case I would type out cliché and when I got to the *e* I would hold my finger down on the E key until I got a menu of special characters. I would then select the number of the special character I wanted and the computer would automatically put it in for me.

# 96

# Direct Download

Every once in a while, for whatever reason, you may experience a frozen update. You will go to update your machine as always and you will get to a certain point during the update and it will just sit there. It will show you how you've got but it won't advance any further. You can get out of the update and go back and try again, but it will just sit there in the same spot.

There are many reasons why this may occur. Regardless of the reason, the important thing here is and how to fix it. The best method for getting by this circumstance is to go directly to Apple's website and download the update from their update page. You can find this page at **https://support.apple.com/en_US/downloads/macos**. Once you are on this page simply find the current download and double-click it. Download the file to your downloads folder and install it the same way you would any other downloaded a program. This will bypass the automatic mechanism on your computer and it should allow you to download your new OS without any issues.

# 97

# App Autostart

My wife is a casual computer user at home but at work, she is a power user. At work, she has several apps that she uses every time she turns her machine on. At any given moment at work, my wife will be running Thunderbird for her email on her monitor one. She will be running Parallels with QuickBooks open on her monitor two, and she will have the Internet open in Safari on monitor three. She has set her machine up to autoload this configuration every time the computer reboots. When she comes in in the morning she simply turns on her machine and all three of these monitors will be populated in this way as part of the computer's normal boot-up process. If you find yourself in similar circumstances and want the exact same working environment to pop up in the exact same way every time you reboot your machine, do the following.

Launch *System settings* and go to *General*. Next click on *Logon Items*. This controls which apps load every time you fire up your machine. Items can be removed from the list by highlighting them and hitting the minus button. An application like mail or Safari for instance can be started automatically by hitting the plus button and then selecting the proper application. If you have multiple monitors, drag the applications to the monitors you wish them to come up on every time your computer boots. Make sure the windows are properly sized or running full-screen, and then shut your computer down. You should now be able to turn your computer on and the applications that you have chosen should preload on their own in their proper place, on their proper monitors. This configuration can be tweaked anytime simply by going back to this screen in system settings.

# 98

# Notifications

On your Mac, you can get to your notifications by clicking on the time in the upper right-hand corner. Mac will group your notifications in the way it sees fit unless you intervene and customize it.

To customize how you see your notifications go to *Notifications* in *System Settings*. You'll see all of the things that are capable of giving you notifications in the pane on the right. Select any app and adjust how you want to see its notification delivered. You can even turn a notification off that you never want to see by sliding *Allow notifications*.

# 99

# AirDrop

AirDrop allows you to send files to and from your iMac to any other Apple device that has AirDrop is turned on.  To enable this you're going to go to *General* in *System Settings* and set up AirDrop. The *Everyone* setting will allow you to AirDrop to any iPhone or computer that comes into your home.  You  will also need Wi-Fi turned on in order to use this feature.

# 100

# Hot Corners

Wouldn't it be nice if you could tell your Mac that you're walking away and please go to sleep? Well, you actually can, and you can do it in a number of ways. If you're on a MacBook Pro with Touch Bar, you can touch Siri in the upper right corner and say go to sleep and your laptop will immediately go into sleep mode. If you're on a Siri enabled iMac, MacBook, or MacBook Air, you can click the Siri button and give the command, or you can always do it old school by using a hot corner.

Hot corners give you the ability to send commands to your machine by moving your tooltip to any one of the four corners. They are independently configurable, so you can have a single hot corner, four hot corners that do the same thing, or four totally different commands, one for each corner.

Hot corners are configured by going to *System Settings* and clicking *Desktop and Doc*. There you will find the hot corners button.

# 101

# Video

The stock video app on your Mac is QuickTime. Think of it as the equivalent of Microsoft's Windows Media Player. It's bundled with your machine and serves as the systems default player. On the Mac, it also serves as the recording app if you choose to make a screenshot video. It's quite powerful, robust, and will handle a good amount of different formats out there, however, it is limited when it comes to many movie codecs that are available on the internet. Soon, you'll find a movie on the net that you want to watch and you'll get the dreaded message that QuickTime cannot play the particular format.

Enter VLC Media Player. VLC is a free open source media player that will allow you to watch many more video formats than are available in QuickTime. While QuickTime focuses on Apple formats primarily, VLC is a cross-platform app, so it has a much higher compatibility rate by default. I have come across very few movie codecs that VLC is not capable of playing. You can download VLC for Mac by going to their website at **www.videolan.org**.

The native app for editing video on the Mac is iMovie. It's a full-function basic editor great for home movies but if you're going to want to do serious videos of length, you're going to want a pro editor like Final Cut Pro or one of the other third-party professional editors. You're also going to need a Mac with much more ram than a standard machine that's doing little more than reading email and surfing the web. 16GB of ram is really your starting point if you're going to be movie editing and the more the merrier. Another item that will speed up video editing on a Mac is an SSD drive as opposed to a mechanical one.

# 102

# Handbrake

If you plan on using your Mac for anything having to do with video, you need Handbrake. Handbrake is a free application that will compress almost any video file. This tool is a must if you plan on uploading videos to YouTube or Vimeo. It will also help you compress a video if you wish to share it on social media or send it to another person.

To download HandBrake go directly to the makers URL. Do not attempt to do a Google search for it because there are many manufacturers out there that like to fake this product's name in order to draw attention to their own product. You may think you were on a HandBrake website but you won't be. Go directly to **handbrake.fr**. Once there, click the download HandBrake box to download it. If you are on any site that says it wants to charge you money for this product, you are on the wrong site!

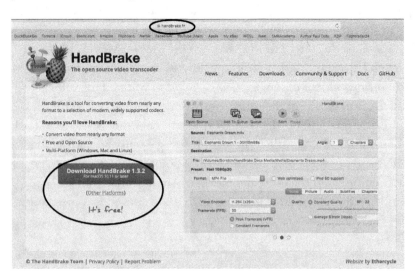

Once you launch the app there will be an icon in the upper left-

hand corner that says *Open Source*. This is where you click to load a
video into the app. Here is an example of a video that I compressed. I
loaded a MOV file into HandBrake that came in at 38.59 GB. That's
much too large for YouTube.

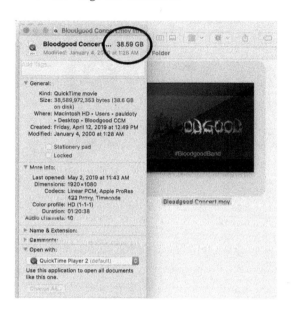

Once in HandBrake, I have many options in which to process the
file and save it as. I have chosen to compress it into an MP4 file. On
the top bar, you will see the original name of the file and the original
file type. In format, I have changed this to an MP4 file. In the middle,
you can see that I can go in and further alter video settings and audio
settings if I wish it to compress even more. In my example, I left those
settings as is. On the bottom, there is a place that you can change the
title and it will show you the format extension after it saves, in this
case, MP4.

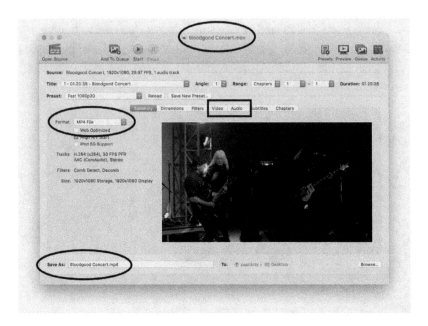

After clicking start the program will chew on the video for a while. The longer your video, the longer the conversion will take. When this video is finished you can see that it is now 4.63 GB instead of almost 40.

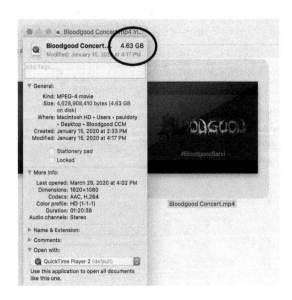

# 103

# Media Server

Throughout the '70s and '80s, I enjoyed many incarnations of high-fidelity stereo systems and multimedia systems in my home. As technology changed, the components in my system changed with it. My first stereo system had cool innovations like eight-track tape recorders and reel to reel tape decks. As the years went by the technologies changed. Cassette decks replaced eight-track recorders and real to reel. CD players replaced turntables.

Today's entertainment systems are driven by digital content. That content can be in the form of movies that we watch and stream, to music that we playback for our listening pleasure. Today more than ever, the integration of a media server computer is one of the best things that you can do for your at-home entertainment experience.

What exactly do I mean by *media server*? The media server is simply a dedicated computer that lives in your entertainment system that provides it with Internet access, movies to stream, and your audio collection.

In the history of computers, there's probably never been a computer more suited for this task than the Mac Mini. The Mac Mini's size allows it to sit anywhere in a home entertainment system. Even old original Mac Minis still have enough RAM and hard drive space to allow them to function as a simple media server. Now that the new Mac Minis are out, old Mac Minis are readily available on platforms like eBay and Offer Up and often can be had at an incredible price. Simply look for a unit with at least 8 GB of RAM and as large of a hard drive as you can find.

To integrate your computer into your multimedia system, hook its HDMI output up to a multimedia receiver or television monitor. This can be a regular TV with HDMI input or a projector for big-screen projection. HDMI output will also carry audio to your receiver or television set.

If you can't afford a dedicated computer, you can use a laptop as a media server, but you'll soon tire of plugging it in every time you want to access it. A dedicated machine is by far the way to go. Can a normal iMac be used as a media server? Of course. In this scenario, you simply hook it up to your stereo or TV in the same way that you would add an external second monitor.

My media server is my television tuner accessing services like YouTube TV for my day to day over the air television broadcasts and DVR service as well as providing an easy way to access Amazon Prime and Netflix as well as others. My entire music library also resides on the computer allowing me to create playlists.

Once you pull the trigger and integrate a computer system into your home entertainment set up, you will wonder how you did without it, and you'll never go back.

# 104

# Cord Cutting

Looking back now, it's hard for me to fathom that there was a time when I paid over $200 a month for cable services into my home which included three feeds to three TV sets with DVR services on each of them. In those days the customers rented the tuner boxes which included the DVR recorders.

Today, the majority of people have cut the cord in one way or another and the home computer has become a central player in that process. Today it has become possible to stream live television over the internet to computers via a multitude of services. My current personal choice is Youtube TV, but it's by no means the end-all when it comes to the many available services.

One of the many benefits of streaming TV content is that the personal computer can now be used as the personal TV. The laptop can now be used as a wireless portable TV that can be used in any room inside the house, or outside for that matter. With the case of my provider of choice, Youtube TV, I can also take my TV with me as I travel, and that was an important factor in my decision in picking a provider.

Cord cutters enjoy the ability to custom tailor their TV experience to the way that they watch. Some people watch mostly sports, while others watch mostly premium movie channels. Others may primarily watch network television. Cord cutters may pick and choose their best solutions for their particular needs and viewing habits without paying for services that they might not use.

There is no single right package to recommend for everyone. My best advice to cord cutters is to do your research online and explore the many services available. Then make your choice. Whichever way you go, the retina screen of a MacBook Pro will likely be one of the best looking TV's inside, *or outside* your home!

# 105

# Printers

The printers that are installed on your Mac are available for you to see and adjust in *System Settings*. Open System Settings and find the icon for Printers & Scanners.

Apple has chosen to put both printers and scanners under the same icon in system preferences because most scanners today are part of an all in one printer. However, if you do happen to have a specific flatbed scanner installed on your machine it will show up here as well.

In the right area, you will see a list of all of your printers. You may have a number of printers here because you may have multiple printers at your home or you may have a laptop that you routinely print from home and from the office on. The different printers from the different locations will be displayed in this panel.

Adding printers can be done by clicking *Add Printer*. Deleting a printer may be done by clicking *Remove Printer*.

An important box to check on a home or office machine in which you want to make a printer connected available to other computers on your network is the *Open Sharing Settings* box & switch. If this switch is not in the On position you will not be able to access that printer from another computer.

# 106

# Installing A Printer

Installing a printer on a Mac is fairly straightforward. First, go to your installed printers by clicking the *printers and scanners* icon in System Settings to make sure that there are no old printers that you are no longer using and delete them. You can delete a printer by clicking on it and clicking the Remove Printer button.

The next step is to install the actual printer. To do this go to the manufacturer's website and download the current printer drivers. Do not use the printer drivers that came with your printer! They are likely outdated by six months or so. You will save yourself an update step by simply going to the manufacturer and downloading the latest update from there.

Go to the support section and search for your printer by name. When you get to the printers page look for the downloads page and download all of its drivers and utilities. The download will go into the downloads folder and you can access it by clicking the downloads icon in your browser or by going directly to your downloads folder. Double click the installation package to install the printer. Now follow the instructions step-by-step for your particular printer. Every printer will be a little different in its set up procedure, so just follow the directions for each individual one.

When your set up completes always remember to first print a test page. This will ensure that your printer is working perfectly.

# 107
# Rename Printers

This year I moved my wife's office from our off-site business location into our home. One of the issues this created was multiple printers residing on our home network. Both of our printers are the same brand and it quickly became confusing any time we printed something.

The solution was to give each of our printers a  personal name on our individual computers. You do this by opening your *Printers & Scanners* window in *System Settings* and click on the printer to be renamed. Then simply give it a new name and click done.

# 108

# Print Command

Printing is straight-forward on a Mac. Depending on your application, you usually just go to file on the menu bar and choose Print. There is another way that will allow you to access the print screen from anywhere, and do it with lightning speed. Anytime that you want to print something out that's in front of you, use the Command P shortcut to instantly access the print menu.

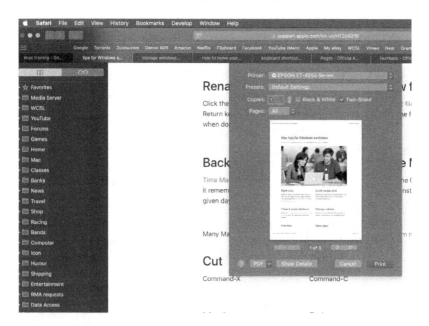

This works especially well while you're surfing the web. This command will also give you the ability to save a document as a PDF instead of printing it out to a hard copy. Just click the PDF dropdown menu in the lower-left of the print box.

# 109
# Print Single Sided

If your using a printer that will print on both sides of your paper, it's fairly easy to set your printer driver to print single sided by unchecking the double sided box in the print screen, however, if your using a non-Apple app like Microsofts Word, you'll notice that the dialogue box does not give you that option. That is because Microsoft uses its own print driver.

To print on a single page from Word or another Microsoft product, click print as you normally would. Then open the *Copies & Pages* drop down box and select *Layout*. Next set Two-Sided to Off. Yes….it's just that simple.

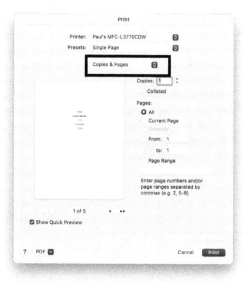

# 110

# Print Scaling

I discovered print scaling one day out of necessity. I had been shipping some eBay items and I came across a very small item that I needed to ship in a very small package. The problem was that the pre-printed USPS labels that I was printing out were twice as big as was needed to fit on the package. That's when I discovered a marvelous box in the print window called Scale.

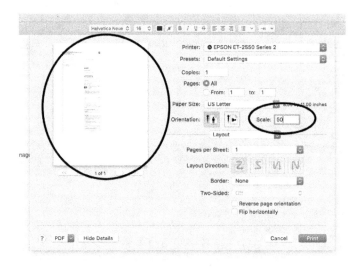

Scale will allow you to print an image at any scale you choose. If something's too big, like my label example, simply scale it to the size that you need and print.

Working in conjunction with the scale box is the preview window. As you change the number in the scale box, the preview window on the left will show you what your printed document will look like. This takes the guess work out of finding the proper scale amount.

# 111
# Scanning

If you're running the latest versions of Mac OS and IOS 12 or later on your iPhone, you can use the pair to scan a document or photo directly into an application. Not all applications support this, but most Apple apps do and many third-party as well. To set this ability up on your Mac, make sure that both devices have Bluetooth turned on. Both devices must also be using the same iCloud account and be signed in. Open an app that is compatible with the process. You'll know your app is compatible if you control-click in a place where you'd like to insert a picture, and you get the ability to import from icon or iPad.

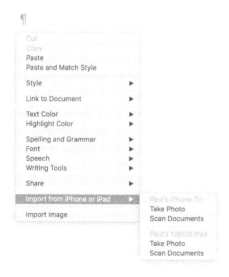

The menu will show you all of the devices available to you. In this example, simply select take a photo from your phone, and use your phone camera as you normally would. The picture will appear in your document where your cursor is.

# 112

# iPhone Scanner

Flatbed scanners are a great addition to your Mac and you may have one simply because you own an all-in-one printer. They have their uses to be sure, but what you may not know is that if you own an iPhone, you also have a handheld travel scanner! Your phone will allow you to scan any object into a file and then later insert that file into a document on your computer.

To scan a document, open Notes on your phone and go to a new blank note. Tap the camera icon at the bottom of the note. Line the phone up with the document using the screen as your viewfinder. Your phone will take a scan of the document. Now save the result for insertion later into a document on your Mac.

Later, you can open the note on your phone that contains the scanned image and share it with your Mac over airdrop. The scan will now be in your downloads folder and can be imported into just about any document that you might be working on.

As this technology develops, more and more apps will likely start to be able to access the iPhone directly as an import source from the app natively, but until that happens, you can simply import scans from your downloads folder.

# 113

# 3D Printers

Paper printers have been a staple of computing, almost since the beginning. There's a large variety of 2D printers available for Macs. In recent years 3-D printers have become much more affordable. It wasn't that many years ago that it would've cost you between $1000 and $5000 to get into a 3-D printer. Today anyone with an Amazon account can buy a good quality 3-D printer for under $200. Today it's almost unthinkable to have a computer in your house without a printer hooked up to it. Almost daily we have the need to print out something whether it be tickets to a show or a recipe. I foresee a time in the future that we will feel the same way about 3-D printers. They are a bit of a novelty today, but after owning a few for sometime, I have found that like the 2D printer, you will start developing daily needs for 3-D printing.

First started looking for 3-D printer. The first thing I noticed was that it was very difficult to find one that was Mac compatible. In time, I learned that 3-D printers are not Mac or PC compatible per se. They are standalone devices. The Mac or PC compatibility part comes into play in the software that you're using to design your 3-D prints, not in the printer itself. Many 3-D printers will come with their own design software, but there is a software package called PrusaSlicer that is PC or Mac compatible, and it works great. Essentially the software will allow you to design your print on your Mac and then transfer it to your printer via an SD card.

# 114

# TinkerCAD

When you buy your first 3-D printer you will quickly become acquainted with a website called thingiverse.com. This site will provide you with all of the STL files that you will need in order to print something. Think of it as the worlds largest depository of three dimensional files.

Eventually, you will want to start designing your own. In order to do that you are going to need a CAD program. Now you can spend a lot of money on a program like AutoCAD, which was developed in the 60s during the Apollo missions and now is the worlds largest and most used CAD program, or you can use a great starter cad online application for free. The program I am referring to resides on a website called tinkercad. Almost anyone can spend a day on tinkercad and learn how to design something for 3-D printers. It is built from the ground up to be simple and intuitive. It will not take you long to learn its basic controls, and in short order, you'll be printing your first STL file designed by you.

Tinkercad of course can be used for many other applications besides 3-D printing. Essentially anything you need to design in a CAD program can be done in tinkercad. The difference between the free CAD program and the spendy ones? Flexibility and power. However, if you're just learning a brand new craft and you're looking for simplicity, tinkercad.com is the place to go.

# 115

# The History of Windows

In January of 1984, Apple began beta testing a revolutionary new operating system with an icon-based graphical interface. While IBM was still using the code input system known as DOS, Apple conceived a new system that would allow the user to interact with the computer visually, and environmentally. The graphic environment would be broken up into workspaces called windows.

Wait a second, hold the iPhone! Am I telling you that Microsoft didn't invent the very operating system that its flagship product is named after? That's exactly what I'm telling you as it's simply a matter of tech history. While we're at it, we can give Apple the credit for the invention of the mouse as well.

Microsoft would release a proximity of Macs OS in November of 1985 called Windows 1. By that time Mac had already released System 2, and the copycat game was afoot between the two companies. By 1987 Microsoft had released Windows 2 and Apple was already on System 5. During this period in computer history, I was busy programming on various Commodore systems that used a similar icon-based graphical user interface but lacked the power of the windows environment.

In 1990, Microsoft brought Windows 3 to market, and shortly after, I made the switch to my first PC. Apple was still in the lead with its System 6, and Microsoft understood the obvious public perception problem with the numbering method of operating systems. In 1995 Microsoft released Windows 95, a colorful take on the Windows-based system, and it turned out to be a great marketing strategy. First-time computer buyers were now choosing between the outdated sounding System 7 and the new flashy modern-sounding Windows 95. At first, Apple went on, business as usual releasing System 8 in 1998, but the tide was turning. Later that year Microsoft released Windows 98 and Apple changed its name to Mac OS 8. OS 9 followed in 1999 and

Microsoft released the futuristic-sounding Windows 2000.

Now Win 2K stumbled with driver and compatibly issues and Microsoft effectively entered a time of hit and miss with their operating systems. Computers were becoming more complex. Microsoft had had the advantage when it came to price as everybody was building cheap hardware to run the system. Apple on the other hand kept everything in-house, banking on the fact that people would pay more for a more stable, reliable system. In the new millennium, Microsoft would bank on mass-market saturation at the cost of compatibility issues, and Apple would thumb its nose at everyone and focus on complete control of every aspect of hardware and software system integration. Later that year Windows tried to bounce back from its Win2K debacle with Windows ME, but it too suffered from the same compatibility frustrations with many users.

In 2001 Apple released OSX and taking advantage of PCs stumbling, it was game on. Microsoft fired back in that same year with an OS that addressed many of the issues that plagued the past two operating systems with what I consider to be their first stable, widely used, and arguably world standard operating system, Windows XP.

Apple would continue its OSX system throughout the decades, giving each incarnation of OSX a themed subname. Microsoft would go on with a string of hits and misses. While Windows 7 was a stable hit for the company, the next two misses, Vista & Windows 8 drove many of us to the Mac ecosystem, and I'm guessing many people who are reading this book can relate to that. As time marches on, few people took notice that the Mac OS switched from OS10 to OS11 as now the company is fully invested in its popular California themed names. Microsoft seems to be enjoying a time of rebuilding now in this decade with the fairly stable Windows 11, but Apple is enjoying a renaissance period and coming of age of its product and design philosophies.

# 116
# Working With Windows

Lest anyone accuse me of being an Apple fanboy, I will endeavor to give PC credit where credit is due throughout this book. When it comes to working with windows on a Mac, I must concede that this is an area where Microsoft has Apple beat, at least for the time being. With each new incarnation of the Mac operating system, updates keep getting better when it comes to handling windows, so in the future, we can only hope that some of the window handling functionality will eventually trickle over to the Apple side. The good news is that there are some third-party apps out there that will restore much of the function that you are used to when working with windows on the PC. In the next few lessons, I will tell you of one such application. For now, I'm going to go over the simple basics of how to move Windows around your screen and work within them on your stock Mac.

The first area to understand when working with windows on your Mac is the three little dots in the upper left corner. The first thing that you need to do is get PC out of your head when it comes to these three dots as they have almost nothing in common with a PC when it comes to functionality. For instance, the red dot will not close your application. This is one of the basic beginner mistakes people make when they switch from PC to Mac. The red dot will simply close the window that you're currently working on, leaving the application running in the background. The second, the yellow one, will not make your window smaller. This dot will take the entire window and minimize it to the dock. The green dot Will toggle your window between window view and full-screen view. Bear in mind that when you go full screen, you will not have access to the menu bar unless you run your tooltip up to the top.

To move a window on your screen, place your tooltip anywhere in the top bar of the window that is free of elements, click your mouse and drag the window to the new location. This is one of those frustrations for new Mac users because unlike a PC you can't simply drag it to the right of your screen and have it fill the right side automatically. More on that as promised in the next two chapters.

Dragging on a side or corner of your window will resize it. Doing this while holding the option key will resize both sides at once. In other words, if you hold the option key and drag the right side of a window the left side of your window will drag proportionally. This can be a hard trick to accomplish without a mouse.

# 117

# The Green Dot

Resting your tooltip on the green dot in the upper left corner of your window will reveal additional functionality by opening a small menu of choices. You can enlarge this window to full screen or tile the window to left or right. You can also move the window to other screens if available.

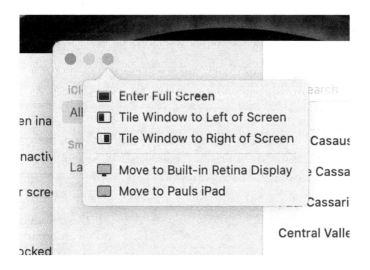

While I applaud Apple for this feature, it still falls short in a number of areas. There is no way to resize your window quickly to fill the screen while leaving the menu up top for example as enter FULL screen, will do just that, taking away your vital top menu. You are also left on your own dragging and resizing if you want to open say four windows in the four corners of the machine. Because of these reasons, I recommend installing an app called Better Snap Tool. Apple is getting closer to PC, but it still has a way to go and at this time, it still requires a little third party help to get there, which brings us to our next chapter...

# 118

# Better Snap Tool

On a PC it's easy to snap a window to half screen by simply dragging it off to a side, or to a corner to get a corner window, and so on. A stock Mac can't do the same trick, but the OS does give you the simple ability to run two applications side by side by snapping windows left and right. To do this, first, have two applications open on your Mac. In the first window, place your tooltip over the green dot in the upper left-hand corner. A menu option will appear giving you the ability to snap the window to the left of the screen. Now hover over the green dot of the second window and choose to send it to the right of your screen. This power-user move will greatly enhance your productivity, and once you use it for a day, you'll wonder how you used your computer without it.

The above ability is free with the Mac OS operating system, but what if you still want your Mac to be as versatile as a PC when it comes to window snapping? The good news is that at the present time there are around eight different third party applications out there for mimicking a PC. The app I use personally is called *Better Snap Tool* and it's available in the App Store for a few dollars. I use and recommend this one because it most closely mimics the windows control that I'm used to on a PC. There's no holding the green button, just grab and drag a window to the top, bottom, side, or corner and it will snap into place just like you're used to on your Windows PC.

# 119
# Stage Manager

Over the years, Apple has tried to come up with ways to unclutter your desktop.  Its latest offering is stage manager.  Stage manager is off by default and you must turn it on by going to the switches in the upper right hand corner of your Mac.

There you will find stage manager, and when you click it for the first time it will turn stage manager on.  Now, anytime you have a cluster of windows open on your desktop you can simply go up and hit the stage manager button.  This will move your top window to the forefront and park all of your other windows to the left.

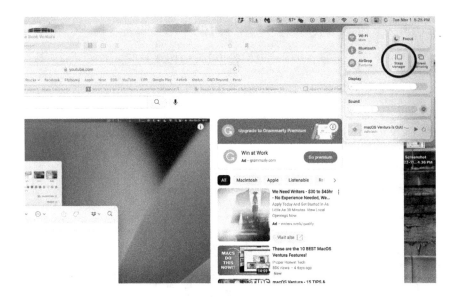

When you click on any of the parked windows, it will become the forefront and the window. Your head centered will become parked on the left. This will help many situations, however, it is not for *all* situations. You do give up some functionality when you use stage manager.

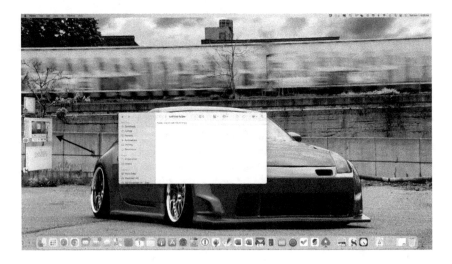

For instance, you will no longer have any icons that are saved on the desktop. Any drives that are normally there will not be shown as well. Don't worry, they're not gone. All you have to do is turn off stage manager and everything will be back the way that it was.

# 120

# Window Go Away

As you're working on your computer, there will be times when you need a window to go away. You'll still be working in that application, so you don't want to put the app away, but you need the desk space, and you just need the window to go away for a while.

In this example, I'll have Microsoft Word open, but I'll want to get it out of the way for a few minutes to be able to use my screen for something else. While Word is on the top of my other windows, I'll hold down the Command key and click W.

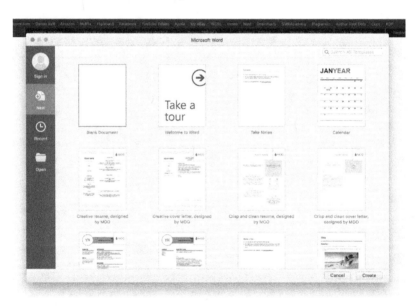

Word instantly disappears! Oh no! Is it gone? Did I lose what I was working on? Fear not, the window has simply been placed into a protected space of RAM memory on your machine. If you look at your dock, you'll see that the app is still running, it's just not showing on your screen.

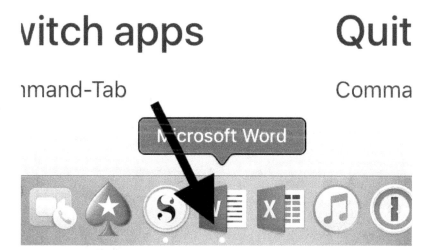

Clicking on the Word icon in your dock will restore the app to the screen in the same condition as when you left it.

# 121

## Close Multiple Windows

This one is a simple trick, but it just might be a game-changer for you if you routinely work with multiple windows open at once. This can be especially true for anyone working with photographs. If you're opening a bunch of photos, before you know it you can have twenty or thirty open windows. When it comes time to Close your project, it can be a real pain to go through each one of those windows, closing them one by one by clicking the red dots. Before long you're seeing red dots, even with your eyes closed.

Wouldn't it be easier if there was one quick short cut to close literally every window that you have open at any given time on your desktop? As you've already guessed, there is. To accomplish this simply go to the window that is on the very top of your stack, hold down your Option key and click the red dot. All of your windows throughout your entire stack will close. Note that this only works with files, not applications.

# 122

# Running Windows

A great feature of owning a mac is that you can run OS X and Windows on the same machine. This is something exclusive to the Mac, you will not be able to do the same thing on a PC. In order to do this you'll need a third-party application like Parallels.

Parallels allows you to have multiple operating systems open and operating at the same time, sharing information between the two. You will be able to move between machines simply by swiping back and forth on your trackpad.

Parallels partitions off a section of your computer to use as a Windows Computer. You can assign the amount of RAM and hard drive space available to it. While it's running, your RAM will be allocated between the two machines. I say two machines because it is actually like running two separate machines on a shared network, sharing printers and network connections between the two. What the machines will have in common are the keyboard and mouse. Whenever you plug in a new USB device you'll be prompted as to which machine you'll want to use it on. When you close parallels, your machine will return to its normal Mac state will all resources dedicated to Mac.

If you are wanting to run Parallels on a machine, it's important to buy that machine with enough RAM to do so. I recommend a minimum of 16GB of RAM on any machine that will be used to run Parallels as you'll want to use between 4 and 8 GB of RAM or more on the Windows side.

# 123

# Sound

I am a sound engineer by trade, so it's only fitting that we talk about Mac sound in chapter 1 2 3. 1 2 3. 1 2 3.

That's a sound engineer joke.

The various aspects of your sound on your Mac computer are controlled by the sound section in System Settings. Opening this area will give you access to the computer's default sound effects, as well as its input and output devices.

The default alert sound on all Ventura Macs is Submerge by default. If you click the arrow of this in the alert sound you will hear the familiar tone. But you can change and customize your computer to sound different than everyone else's simply by choosing a different sound from the drop down.

Back in the old days, the volume control on your Mac had a nice little sound every time you change the volume up or down. For some reason, Apple decided that this was no longer cool and took that feature away. The good news is that if you like that feature you can add it back by clicking play feedback when the volume is changed. Doing so will put your Mac back to the way it used to be.

In the output section, you can choose between different outputs for your sound. This can come in handy if you have a media server in another room and you want to throw its sound to a device like an Apple TV in another room.

The input screen gives you the ability to adjust the volume of your internal microphone. Come here if you are having problems with a program that uses this microphone. You'll be able to adjust the volume louder or drop it down if it is distorting.

# 124

# Dictation

Did you know that your Mac can be your secretary? If you use your computer to do a lot of writing (like I do), you can simply dictate to your computer and let it do the work.

Dictation is not something that is on by default when you buy a Mac, you must enable it. To enable dictation go to *System Settings* and click *Keyboard*. Now switch on *dictation*. You'll see a graphic of an internal microphone and if you did everything right, You will begin to see a meter moving up-and-down on the microphone as you talk. The default trigger for turning dictation on and off is to press the function key on your keyboard twice. There is a place on this page where you can change it to other shortcuts if you wish, but I would advise leaving it set at its factory default. That way if you begin to use multiple Mac computers, they will all function in the same way.

Dictation can be used almost anywhere on your Mac. You can use it in a word document or a pages document, you can use it when you're sending a text to someone or use it in composing an email. After a while using dictation will become second nature to you on a Mac.

The quality and accuracy of dictation is affected by the microphone you are using to dictate. The best and most accurate way to dictate is to wear a headset, however most Mac computers have excellent microphones built into them that can be used. Just be forewarned, if you are in a noisy environment, you will be met with mediocre results. If you are in a quiet environment, the accuracy is astonishing.

# 125

# Speech

We've just learned that you can talk to your Mac. Your Mac can also talk back! Mac OS has a built in speech synthesizer that will work in many applications and environments. Many websites for instance will give you the ability for your Mac to read an article to you. Pages and other documents are also speech ready. Many ebooks can be heard as an audio book even if they were not specifically designed as one. Once you become accustomed to using dictation and speech on your Mac, you just might find yourself using these useful features almost every day.

To enable speech on a Mac, open System Settings and click on Accessibility. Now click the Spoken Content tab on the right. Select a voice and set your playback speed preference. My personal preference here is the Nicky voice.

To make your Mac talk in most apps, highlight the area of text that you want to hear and control-click the area. Now select Speech and then Start Speaking. Your Mac should now be reading to you. A fast way to select an entire page for speech is to place your curser in the middle of the text you wish to hear and use *command A* to select the entire body of text. This is a helpful function when reading a book, or listening to an ebook or pdf file, but be forewarned, it doesn't do very well on websites as it will grab all text on the page including links, picture descriptions, and any other formatting in the html of the page that your looking at. The best way to read back a website is to grab a small section at a time such as paragraph by paragraph.

# 126

# Voice Memos

Voice and meeting recordings are really easy on the Mac. All you need to do is launch Voice Memos and hit the record button. Your Mac will use its onboard microphone and set all your levels automatically.

There's no hard limit to how long or how short a recording can be. You can record anything from a quick note to a full-on hour-long business meeting or classroom session with surprisingly good results and clarity.

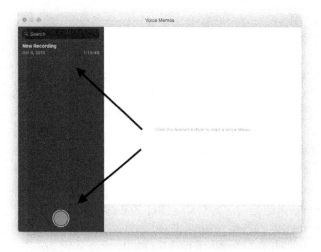

Your new recording will be automatically titled, New Recording. When you're done, click it off and it will show you the running time of the recording. You can then highlight the title and rename it anything you like so you can keep multiple recordings organized.

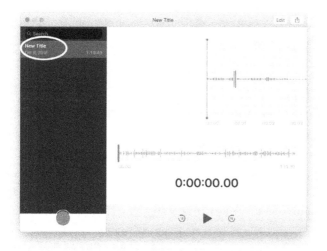

Playback happens within the recorder with a set of simple navigation tools allowing you to jump ahead or go back fifteen seconds at a time. You can also grab the playback bar and scrub to anywhere in the file. Old recordings can be selected and deleted when no longer needed.

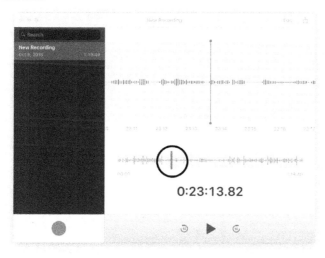

# 127

## Bluetooth Headphones

A few years ago I bought a little rose gold MacBook for travel. Yes, real men have rose gold computers. The plan was to hand it down to my wife a year later as I was waiting for it to be released in a 16MB version, and she wanted rose gold, so I got the rose gold. A year later I bought a space gray with twice the memory for hundreds less. What a deal! Although a bigger surprise came when I went to check out online. It seems that I was just in time to get in on an Apple promotion, and they gave me a free pair of $200 Beats headphones with it! That's cool I thought, although I couldn't see myself actually using them for the laptop. I'm a traveling sound engineer by trade, so I could see myself using them for listening to music with my iPhone outside of California while on the road doing long drives in headphone legal states.

My assessment of how I would use these headphones could not have been more wrong. My precious Beats Bluetooth headphones have become an invaluable part of how I use all my computers, not just my trusty travel MacBook.

First, a bit of praise for the product itself. I am an audio engineer. Over the years I have owned many headsets that cost far north of the $200 price tag of the Beats. In my closet, you'll find $500 Sennheiser studio sets, Shure in-ear monitors, and a host of various wired and wireless units. All well worth their respective price tags. But at $200, none come close to the sound quality and comfort of the Beats and if that wasn't enough to cause me to totally fall in love with them, there was the battery life. Unbelievable. I could go out on a four-week tour in a truck and only need to charge them once the whole time I was gone. I know, this sounds like a paid endorsement, and I wish it was, but it's not. It's an actual honest endorsement of a product.

So how did I end up using them? There's plenty of times when I'm writing early in the morning when I need to be doing research online. That includes listening to online videos. These headphones give me the ability to isolate my work into an outwardly silent environment. Plus, because they can be used to take calls with their built-in microphone, they make the perfect headset for dictation. And in the end, yes, I still use them for listening to music in my truck. Well done Apple.

# 128

# Google

The Internet is a huge place. It is as vast and diverse as the physical world itself and your Mac is the doorway to it. In this chapter, we'll be taking an overview look at Google.

Google was not the first search engine and it's by no means the only search engine on the net. What it is, is the biggest and most popular search engine with a vast array of features. Some of those features I have even dedicated specific chapters too in this book. Think of Google as a cross between a digital road map of the world wide web, and an index to the largest book anyone has ever, and will ever write. As such, you'll likely use Google almost daily. Need Google's address? Google it.

That joke works because we have become so familiar with Google, that it seems almost a waste of a chapter to spend time talking about it, but Google has become one of the most powerful tools that your Mac, or any computer for that matter, has at its disposal.

With great power comes great responsibility. It's important to note that Google is still a non-governed, and for the most part, non-regulated company like your grocery store on the corner. Its owners have their own agendas and political views just like every business out there. Google understands that they have ability to shape public opinion and direct search results as they see fit. Am I insinuating that Google is evil or manipulative? Not at all. I'm a big fan of Google and what they've built, but at the same time I understand that they are just another company with their own ideas, values, and agendas that will have an impact and influence on how the company works and I must be a discerning adult when using their services.

Google has expanded its product over the years to include many powerful utilities for computer users. No longer simply a search engine, Google has a great array of services offered for Mac and PC owners alike to explore.

# 129

# Google Drive

When it comes to online storage there's many providers. The most popular for Mac users of course is going to be iCloud Drive. Because iCloud is a part of your operating system native on your Mac, it will tend to be the easiest to use, however it will lack some of the functionality of other services. Not that it is better or worse, it is simply different.

Google Drive is similar to Dropbox in the sense that it will give you an amount of online storage for free and then you will pay after you exceed it. At the time of this writing, Google Drive will give you 15 GB of free storage. You will need a Google account to set up a Google Drive. 15 GB is a good amount of space. The maximum amount of free space that you can get with Dropbox is 16 GB, but they will only give you 2 GB to begin with and you must acquire the rest through referrals.

Google Drive is different from the others in the fact that it works hand-in-hand with all of the Google applications that are available in your Google account. Google Drive is also a little bit better when compared to Dropbox as far as bang for the buck, although Dropbox has Google Drive beat in other areas like file sharing.

Google Drive will map to your finders folder just like iCloud Drive and Dropbox making it quite convenient when it comes to dropping files into it from Mac OS. All three of these seem to be on the forefront today in cloud storage with a plethora of other services out there that are up and comers.

To access Google Drive and get started, simply go to Google and click on the little squares in the upper right-hand corner of the webpage. There you'll find an icon for Google Drive.

# 130

# Google Translate

Unlike in the Star Trek universe, Mac does not have a built-in universal translator. You can take a foreign website in Safari and go to *View* and click *Translation* to see the page in your native language and you can ask Siri how to say Yes in Spanish, but what if you want to do more than that. What if you want to translate sentences to other languages other than your own? There are a number of paid third-party apps that you can buy for this purpose, or, you can visit our friends at Google and use their universal translator for free.

When you go to google.com in Safari you'll notice a group of squares in the upper right-hand corner of the site. If you click on those squares, you'll see an icon for Translate. When you launch the app you'll see a screen with two windows. You can set these two windows to translate between languages. As you type in one window, you'll see the translation in the other. You can even copy and paste text into one of the windows. When you're finished, you can even secondary click either of the text to copy it into a document on your Mac. You'll now have a universal translator as long as you have an internet connection, and it's free. Live long and prosper!

# 131
# Safari Home Page

Safari's home page is what you see by default when you launch your Safari web browser. It has a great deal of information on it and it is quite customizable.

Once launched you can scroll down to see a wealth of information including your favorite sites and the ones that you visit most often. You will also have an opportunity to view your privacy report to see who's tracking you online.

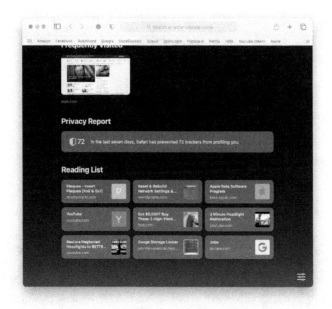

You can also see your reading list on this page. If you click on your privacy report you will get another dropdown box that will go in-depth into all of your trackers. This homepage is quite configurable by going to the slider icon in the lower-right hand corner of Safari. Here you can check or uncheck the things that you want to see. You can also add backgrounds to this page from here.

# 132

# New Safari Window

Tabs are a great function in Safari but there will be times when you will want to completely different windows open simultaneously. You might want to compare information on two sites side by side for instance.

You have two quick ways to do this. While in Safari, control-click on the app's icon and choose New Window.

Another quick way is to hold Command and click N for New. Multiple instances of Safari work great with two monitors, or you can throw the two windows left and right on a single.

# 133

# Privacy Report

Safari has added a Privacy Report badge to allow you to see what online trackers the browser is blocking. This feature is a great way for the average user with little to no computer savvy to protect themselves from trackers.

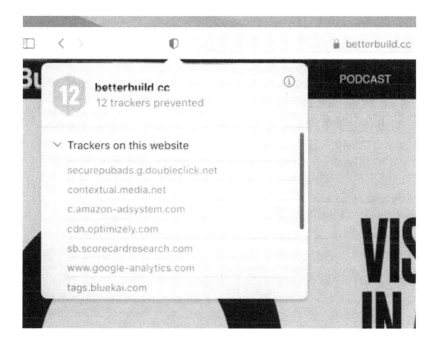

While this is a great feature to have, if you need more control you might want to consider a paid product like Little Snitch.

# 134

# Private Web Browsing

Safari is like a snotty little brother. It always watches where you go, and writes down where you've been. Sometimes you want a little privacy. Let's say it's your wife's birthday and you want to surprise her with roses. You go online and order them from **webesellingflowersandjunk.com**, and when she gets home she goes online and for some reason looks at the browsing history. Great! That surprise was ruined. Thanks a lot, Safari!

Fortunately, Apple has given you a way to sit your little brother down in a chair in the basement and secure him to it with duct tape, so to speak. It's called private browsing. To enter this mode while in Safari, click on File in the top menu and choose open *New Private Window*. A second window will appear allowing you to browse any site without recording your history in the browser. The URL window will change from a light color to a dark color to let you know that you are in privacy mode. Your history will now be private as long as you are browsing in this window. Closing the window will end your private browsing session.

Now, go in privacy, don't use this tip for anything nefarious, and don't forget to eventually let your little brother free.

# 135
# Safari Autoplay

You're surfing the web, perhaps browsing news articles or scrolling through your favorite blog, and out of nowhere comes an annoying video or commercial. Now you've been distracted from your enjoyable online experience and you're scrambling to find the mute or the stop for the video. You've become a victim of autoplay.

Autoplay is a "feature" built into Safari that will allow the browser to autoplay video content as soon as it encounters it on a website. It sounds like a fun useful tool, and it is, or should I say it was until the advertising community got wind of it. "You mean we can force people to watch our ads? Hmmm. We shouldn't do that to people, that wouldn't be ethical"....said no advertiser, ever.

Fortunately, there is a way to shut most of this feature off in Safari. To do so, while in Safari, click on *Safari* and choose *Settings*. Choose *Websites* on the top of the window and *Auto-play* on the left.

From this window you can set up your autoplay preferences for individual sites, but you can also set preferences for all other sites by adjusting the dropdown in the lower right-hand corner.

From this menu select Never Auto-Play to disable the function on all sites. If you want a particular site to auto-play, go to it in the website list menu, while it's currently open in your browser, and click a specific preference for that particular site.

Congratulations. You've just taken control of your browser back.

# 136
# Safari Extensions

As the name implies, Safari extensions allow you to extend the capabilities of the Safari web browser. It gives third-parties the ability to develop customization tools for the web. These tools can be anything from ad blockers to shopping tools for sites like Amazon. You can find a number of these extensions, approved by Apple by clicking on Safari/Safari extensions while surfing the web. This will open up a gallery in the App Store to browse. You'll find that not all, but most of the extensions are free, so feel free to browse for ones that will truly help your browsing experience.

Approved by Apple is important because when you install an extension, you are trusting the developer by granting them permission to affect your browsing experience. You don't want to install an extension only to find out that it had nefarious intentions, and now it's spying on your browsing history, or hijacking your search results with products that it's paid by.

# Permissions For Websites

If you're worried about a website accessing your WebCam, there's a better way to handle permissions for each website you visit then putting tape over your camera on your computer. In Safari, you can set specific permissions for every single website that you visit on a regular basis. If you are curious to see what a particular website has as far as permissions on your computer, go to the website and click on *Settings for this website* in your Safari dropdown menu.

Here you will be able to adjust all types of access specific to that particular website. You can turn parts of your computer like the WebCam on and off, and adjust many other aspects like whether or not you allow videos to play automatically. Explore the menu to see all of the things available for a particular website.

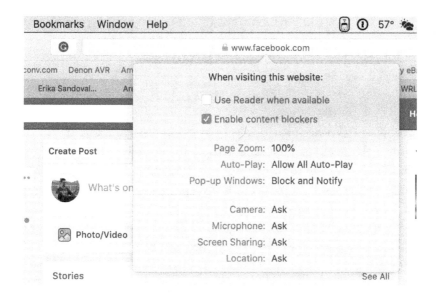

Clicking on any of these values will open up other options and permissions.

# 138

# Browser Favorites

Browser Favorites provide a simple way to bookmark your favorite web pages so you can get back to them easily. There are essentially two places to store a favorite. You can store them in your favorite bar across the top of your browser. This area is a great place to store favorites that you visit on a semi-regular basis. Favorites that are only visited on occasion can be organized and stored in a file structure in the favorites area on the left of your browser.

If your screen is too small to fit your favorites, they will spill over into an overflow area that is accessible by clicking on the dropdown on the right of the favorites bar.

Your favorites are shared across all of your computers over iCloud, so it's possible that you might have plenty of room for all of your favorites on your large screen iMac, but you might have to use the dropdown when you're viewing them on a small screened MacBook.

Favorites are easily organized into folders by dragging the favorites from one location to another.

# 139

# Tab Preview

Safari made some great improvements back in Big Sur when it came to tab management. Previously when you opened a lot of tabs you'd just get lost because there was no room on the tabs to see the names of the websites. Now the tabs show the small favicons which take up far less room.

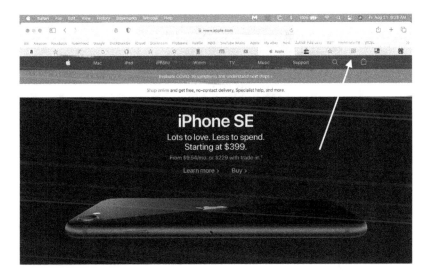

And now If you have a number of tabs open you can preview each one by resting your tooltip on it.

# 140

# Tab Groups

Tab groups gives you the ability to store all of the particular tabs that you're viewing on your web browser in one folder for a later session. This feature is great for doing research such as shopping for a particular product. In our example I have 18 tabs open, more tabs than my browser can show at one time.

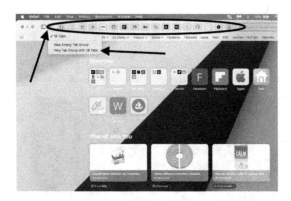

All I have to do to store them is click on the drop-down arrow by the icon I would normally use to open up my favorites. Here I will have the option to start a new tab group with the 18 tabs that I have open. After assigning a name to them I can go to any other favorite and leave the group of 18 tabs. I can shut my browser down and come back in a week and continue where I left off just by opening my favorites and clicking on the group that I created. Every website will load into the tabs just as before.

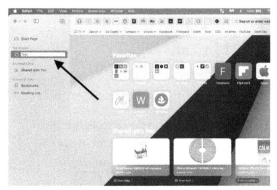

If you right click the first tab in your browser you can close all tabs by clicking *Close tabs to the right*.

# 141

# Pin Tabs

Tabs in Safari are great. Especially when you're researching a particular topic. But what happens when you get too many open? Well if your screen is small, or your window for that matter, you're going to start losing the titles of the tabs because they become too small.

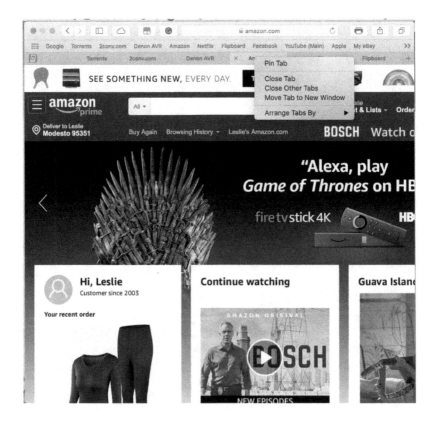

In the screenshot above, you can see that I've opened too many tabs and the first two can no longer be read. Let's say that the sixth tab I opened is the most important to me. Let's say that I always want to be able to find it, no matter how many tabs I have open at any given time. I can control-click that tab and pin it.

The tab will always be available to me now until I close it. It will show up as a pinned icon with a mini logo from the site at the beginning of your tabs. You'll never lose a tab again.

# 142

# Clear History

From time to time you'll likely want to delete Safari's browsing history. In previous lessons we've gone over browsing in privacy mode but what if you simply want to delete your history for a short time? What if you're not in privacy mode and you want to delete just the last website information.

Safari gives you the ability to delete its browsing history in both the short and long term. Begin by clicking on the *Safari* tab and select *Clear History*. You will find that you have a number of choices. Clicking the *last hour* will delete only your most recent websites. Today will take out everything in your history recorded in the last 24 hours. *All history* will completely clear your entire history file on your machine.

Be aware, clearing your history will take out everything in the file in the selected time. This means automatic logons the websites as well. Don't be surprised if you clear your history and then find yourself having to log back into your Facebook account manually.

# 143
# Hijacked!

One of the perks of owning a Mac is freedom from viruses. It's so nice not to have to worry about cyber criminals trying to break into my machine with key loggers in attempts to gain access to my bank accounts and personal information.

While the above is true, Macs are not impervious to many forms of hijacking. Hijacking occurs when an individual is able to get a plugin running in your browser that will redirect it to websites that it wants you to go to rather than the ones you intend. It's fairly obvious when you've been hijacked. Your web experience begins to slow down, you're plagued with pop-ups and ads. In short, nothing behaves as it once did and your online experience becomes miserable.

If you suspect that you've been hijacked, there's a number of steps that you can do to break free. Let's start with some good news, you're on a Mac! Because you're on a Mac your hijacker has only been able to affect your browser. Your computer has no universal registry system like a PC so your malware infection is likely isolated to the browser by design. When you close your browser, it will close the malware in most cases.

More good news. Malware is fairly easy to get rid of using free readily available apps like Malware Bytes. If you think you might have gone to a site that put malware on your machine, run a scan to see if you're infected. If your normal browser of choice is locking up to the point that it is unusable, try to load another browser onto your machine like Chrome or Firefox. It's always wise to have multiple browsers available to you on your machine at any given time. If you have a second unaffected browser available, you can use it to download an anti-malware app like Malwarebytes to clean your issue.

# 144

# Website Notifications

Have you ever had a website ask you if it can send you notifications?  This is a really handy feature on information-rich websites that you might visit often.  Perhaps a website that is updated routinely with recipes or tech information or a myriad of other things that you might have a legitimate interest in.  But after a time, you may lose interest in some of those sites and now you're being annoyed with notification pop up messages.  From time to time, you will want to go in and manage these notifications by doing the following.

While in Safari, click on Safari in the menu bar and choose Settings.

Choose Websites from the top bar and click on notifications on the left.  On the right you, will see all of the websites that you've visited that want to send you notifications.  Here you can allow or deny them individually.

# 145
# Reading List

Most people know that you can bookmark any website that you wish to return to on the Internet. All of your bookmarks will show up if you click the pane icon in the upper left-hand corner of your browser.

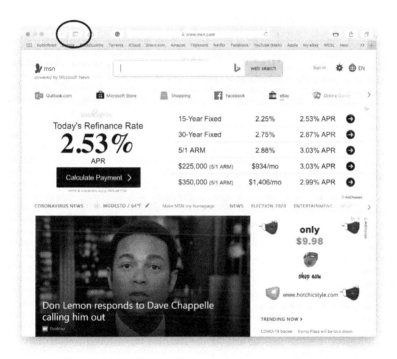

But what if you simply want to read something at a later date. You're not interested in making a favorite of it for all time. You just don't have enough time to read it right now and you need quick access to it later. Once the pane is open you can change it from its default favorites setting to the reading list setting by clicking on the glasses icon.

The article or webpage is now saved as a reading list item that can be read at a later date. Simply go back to the reading list pane to see your saved reading list. When you're finished reading an article, right-click it, and remove the item. You can also clear all items if you're done with all of them.

209

# 146
# Private Relay

Private Relay is a feature built into your Mac that has some similarities to a VPN but also some major differences. Private Relay will hide your DNS from the websites you visit making it virtually impossible to track you over the internet. This effectively ends companies from developing online profiles of you and your surfing and buying habits. It will still give the websites that you visit a basic idea of your location so things like weather reports are still accurate, but it won't allow exact computer locations to be logged.

The service is included with any paid iCloud account. Turn the service on by going to your Apple ID in System Settings and clicking on iCloud.

You can now toggle this service on or off. Remember, this service does NOT replace a VPN. If you want a site like Netflix to think you're in the UK when you're actually in the U.S. you're still going to need a traditional VPN. Using the service may also slow your web browsing experience.

# 147

# Cookies

If you're like me you're very particular about your cookies. I like chocolate chip and a few others. There's a lot I just don't care for. When it comes to cookies on my computer I'm no different.

Cookies can be good and cookies can be bad. The cookies that I like on my computer are the ones that allow me to enter into a frequently visited website without having to type in my login credentials every time. The cookies that I don't like are the nefarious ones that track me across the Internet, telling their owners everywhere I go. They're the ones that are targeting ads in my browser.

One day ago I was on Amazon searching for brother printers. The very next day when I pulled up my MSN news website guess what I was getting ads for? I know I'm preaching to the choir and I know that this has happened to you countless times. There is a way that you can get rid of the cookies that you don't want while keeping the ones that you do.

To manage your cookies on a Mac go to the Safari menu and choose *Settings.* In Settings, you're going to go to the privacy icon and click on *Manage Website Data.*

This is going to show you all of the cookies that are stored on your machine, and you are probably going to be amazed. You will have cookies that date back to the very beginning of your machine if you haven't cleaned them out recently. The trick here is to keep the cookies that you want and get rid of the cookies you don't. Generally, the only cookies that you want to keep our cookies that you recognize from sites that you visit often like Facebook or your bank account. The other cookies can be highlighted and deleted. You can highlight them individually and hit remove or you can highlight the first one that you don't want, scroll to the last, hold the shift key and click. Now you can remove all of them that are highlighted.

What you don't want to do here in most cases is hit *Remove All*. This will remove all cookies from your machine including all of your logins and you'll find yourself having to put your information back every time you go to one of these sites again.

# 148

# Browser Wars

There are currently ten or more internet browsers available for your Mac, but if the truth be known, there are only a small handful of these that are major players. Each of them has strengths and weaknesses. In this chapter, we'll look at these and discuss why you might want to use one over another. While I will offer my opinion, I must also say that I have no horse in this race. I currently use all three of these, depending on what I'm doing at the time.

The internet is one of those few areas where PC has an advantage over Mac. The vast majority of websites on the world wide web have been coded to be viewed by Microsofts old browser Internet Explorer. As such, that is still your most compatible web browser to date, and unfortunately, you can't run it on a Mac. In fact, every PC I own is still running Internet Explorer instead of Microsofts relatively new Edge browser, simply for compatibility reasons. For this reason, Internet Explorer still ships with every Windows 10 machine, though it be hidden. You have to actually go make a shortcut for it on your desktop in order to use it. Microsoft is also launching Edge for Mac, so we'll have to see if this browser eventually wins the compatibility war, but currently, these three are in my opinion, your best bets.

**Firefox**

I have found that Firefox is the closest browser compatibility wise with Internet Explorer. It also has the closest look and feel to it. This is my goto browser anytime I encounter a website with a script that is behaving strangely on the Mac.

**Google Chrome**

Chrome is a developing app from Google with fairly strong compatibility and speed. It also looks a bit streamlined to the other players. If you subscribe to a Google service like YouTube TV, you will be forced to use Google's browser when you watch the service.

**Safari**

Safari is of course Apple's own brand web browser and as such is my personal recommendation for day to day surfing. I use Safari until I encounter an issue. When an issue arises such as a logon script that won't work on a banking or government site, I will attempt to open the same page in Firefox. Nine times out of ten, it will then open.

Because it's an Apple product, it has the same programmers writing code for it who write for the Mac operating system itself, therefore it tends to be the most solid, fastest experience on the web for Mac, and it is improving with every update.

# 149

# Malware

I have been an avid Mac user now for eleven years. During that time I have contracted exactly zero viruses. While the lack of viruses on a Mac may not be the number one reason for owning Mac, it *is* one of the major reasons.

While Macs are mostly impervious to common computer viruses, they are just as vulnerable as a PC to malware & adware. You may be asking, "What's the difference?" A virus infects a computer at its operating core. On a PC a virus writes itself into the background of its registry and continually runs in the background using the computer's resources for its own evil programming such as logging your keystrokes for the purpose of hacking into your various accounts. A virus is an evil, illegal attack on your security. Some viruses will give the perpetrator access to your computer to use it as an attack zombie on other systems to bring them down in what's called a *denial of service attack.*

Malware and adware on the other hand are far less nefarious and far less damaging. These are annoying third-party programs that push ads at the unassuming user, or at worst, slow down a machine by using up its resources with pop up ads. On the malicious side, some even go as far as redirecting search results and links in your web browser. On a Mac, however, these programs do not reside in the machines sole as viruses do on a PC. They instead attach themselves within apps like browsers, executing their malicious code only after the app has been opened. Because of this, they are easy to prevent and are easy to get rid of once you have one on your machine.

Be forewarned, there are many free downloadable apps out there that claim to clean your Mac of malware, only to be instruments of malware themselves. Never put any Mac cleaner software on your machine without Googling the particular software first to see if it has a nefarious reputation.

My favorite piece of Mac protection software is an app called Malware Bytes. It comes in two versions, a free version, and a paid version that works automatically behind the scenes. If you choose to use the paid version, it will watch your computer continually. If you opt for the free version, you will have to run it manually every few weeks or so to make sure nothing is amiss. Other than that, you'll never need virus protection on a Mac.

# 150

# Malware Bytes

There are a few malware apps available today to choose from for your Mac. My preference is Malware Bytes for a few reasons. First, it's fast. If you're used to running virus scans in the PC world, the idea of a malware scanner taking 30 seconds to do its job can be unsettling at first, but remember, on a Mac, you don't have a registry to sift through. On a PC, looking for a virus can be like looking for a needle in a haystack. A Mac is like playing hide and seek in a one-room apartment.

The second thing I like is that it's free. Sure, you can pay for the deluxe edition if you want it to check for adware automatically, but honestly, I just run mine every week or so, or whenever I might suspect that something might have been put on my machine from a questionable website.

You'll find the companies website at **www.malwarebytes.com** and you'll be asked if you're looking for the home or the business version. Clicking the home version will allow you to install it for free. Once installed, it will occasionally nag you...I mean ask you if you'd like to upgrade to the paid version. You do not have to do this, you may use the free version as long as you wish. You may want to upgrade to the paid version to take advantage of the automatic checking by the app.

Once installed, run the app and do a scan of your system by clicking the scan now button. That's really all there is to it. Most of the time the app will come up with nothing and happily report that you are clean after 30 seconds or so. If it does catch something, it will quarantine it for you.

# 151

# Duck Duck Go

There is no doubt that Google remains the largest search engine on the web. The upside to Google? It's arguably the best at what it does. The downside? Google makes money off of its ability to track you across the web. If you're looking for a Google alternative, try Duck Duck Go.

Duck Duck Go prides itself on not tracking you, nor letting others. You'll be able to verify the difference by clicking on the privacy shield in Safari, or by using a third-party app like Little Snitch. Clicking on the three lines in the upper right-hand corner of Duck Duck Go will allow you to set up your preferences. You can even save your preferences in the cloud anonymously so you don't have to change them every time you search.

# 152

# Speedtest

**Speedtest.net** is a simple single page site that will allow you to test the connection speed of your Mac from any location you happen to be. It shows you your provider and IP address and gives you one control option. A big button that says go. To use the website, press go. After contacting a remote server location (that you can change if you wish) it will analyze your connection and return your upload and download speed. Use the site to see if you're getting all the speed that you're paying for or check the speed of a hotel room internet service. It's good to keep a log at home or at work of your speeds once a month or so to be sure that your provider is not throttling back your service so you can complain if they are.

Internet speed is an easy place for a provider to take advantage of an end-user, as end-users tend to be tech-illiterate for the most part. Most people have no idea what internet speed really means, other than bigger numbers are faster, and faster is better. Providers know this and some will, unfortunately, take advantage.

Why would they do this? Well, to put it simply, bandwidth is not infinite. There's only so much available in your particular area. Think of internet data as water flowing through a pipe into your house, and bandwidth as the size of your delivery pipe. The pipe size will determine how many customers get high-speed. If you are an unscrupulous greedy company, you're going to sell as many high-speed services to as many customers as you can. When the bandwidth runs out, the speeds slow down. So it's the tech-savvy customer who complains that gets their full service back. As the saying goes, *the noisy wheel gets the grease.*

# 153

# Saving Graphics Off the Web

Did you know that it's easy to grab virtually any graphic or picture off of the web with a Mac? Before I tell you the secrets and methods of doing this, let me preface this chapter with the fact that almost any graphic on the world wide web is a copyrighted item. Graphics should not be used for any commercial venture without permission to do so. Having said that, there's plenty of times when you might want a graphic for your own personal private use. One example I can think of offhand is perhaps an album cover for artwork in Music.

Google is probably the best resource for finding specific graphics on the web. Let's say that you need a good picture of a dog. Go to Google and do a search for Dog. After Google returns the results for the initial search, you'll see an option at the top of the search for other types of searches including images. Click *images*. Your results are now populated specifically by dog images. You can even narrow the results even further by breed if you wish. Each image also contains the image size information that can aid you in picking an appropriate image for your particular use.

Find an image that you want and click on it. You now have options going to the original image on its original page, seeing more images like that image, or grabbing the image itself. You can place your tooltip over the image and control-click in order to *save image as*. I will usually save an image directly to my desktop as I'm usually downloading it for an immediate purpose, but you can download it anywhere including to your downloads folder if you wish. You can even click the share option to airdrop it to your iPhone.

What if you come across a graphic on the web that will not allow you to save it? Hold down command/shift and tap 5 to invoke the screen capture options to grab the image.

# 154

# Dropbox

The oldest and in many ways, still the best third-party online storage solution is Dropbox. This service doesn't have a ton of bells and whistles like others, but what it does, it does very well. Dropbox gives you a hard drive in the cloud where you can sync files between computers. They give you a small starting amount of 2GB and allow you to add to it in 500MB increments for getting others to sign up as well. Of course, you can always just pay for more storage.

You can store a document in Dropbox and simply right-click it and get a sharable link if you need to share information with others. Send that link to someone and they will have instant access to the file.

It's important to note that with services like Dropbox you're not getting a hard drive that can be used separately from your computer. In other words, don't think that if you have a laptop with a very small hard drive that you can purchase a 1TB Dropbox to store your photos off-site instead of on your computer.

Dropbox syncs files from your computer, so essentially if you have 50GB stored in Dropbox, it's going to take up 50GB on every machine that you have Dropbox installed on as well, so you might want to consider that if you have a 1TB machine at work, a 1TB machine at home and a 256MB laptop and you have a huge amount of information stored in Dropbox, you might not want to install it on the laptop. However, the laptop could still access Dropbox anytime it needed to as long as you had an internet connection by simply going to your Dropbox account on the web.

# 155

# VPN

There's a lot of talk today about VPNs. But what is a VPN and who needs to use one?

A VPN is a Virtual Private Network. At its core, it provides a way to trick the internet into thinking that you are in another location. They can be used to hide your current location from others and prying eyes on the web. They are popular for anyone who is downloading content that might be illegal in a certain area.

I recently traveled to an area of the United States where online poker is forbidden. It is controlled locally by casino owners who do not want people using the internet to play online poker, even though the games that I play are points-based games as opposed to real money. They want to control the local access to sites like Poker Stars, forcing people to come into their casinos to play. In this case, I used a VPN to route my internet signal through San Francisco California instead of the state and city I was actually in. I was then able to access the site because the local internet provider was none the wiser that I was going through it as all of my signatures were coming from San Francisco.

A VPN service operates by creating a direct, hidden path to a remote server location around the world. Think of it as a secret tunnel dug under the actual internet. The tunnel comes up in a remote location, then uses that server to trick the internet into thinking that it is the location of origin. Your local internet provider may frown on your use of their service for downloading torrent files on the web, but you may have no issue at all if you were doing the same thing in Denmark.

# 156

# Ransom Where?

In 2020 ransomware was on the rise affecting PC and Mac computers alike. In many ways it was the golden age (although it lasted only a year) for people plotting ransomware attack's. At this point people were generally not on their guard for this form of cyber-attack and as a result many people were vulnerable to it.

In 2021 cyber attacks on major US infrastructure brought the reality of ransomware to the forefront of public attention. Oil pipelines and similar infrastructure were brought down in the United States by persons executing cyber-attacks. In many ways it was the worst thing that the criminals could've done because up to that point the general public and corporate world was generally unprepared due to ignorance.

A ransomware attack generally hijacks your computer system and locks you out of your data. In order to get your data back you generally have two choices. One, wipe out your systems hard drive and start over from scratch, or pay a ransom, usually in bitcoin to the cyber criminals.

As of 2021 there are still few anti-ransomware apps out there. However there is one that works pretty good, and it's free. A company called Objective-See makes a product called Ransom Where? It works by monitoring your system and reports to you when any application is trying to encrypt and move files.

Now the application is basically dumb. That is to say it's not specifically looking for a ransomware application running, but rather for the result of one on your computer. The downside of this is that there are a lot of false positives. Having said that, I use the application on all of my machines and I have never found it to be a problem. Yes, once a month or so I will get a false positive but it is usually an obvious one. It will usually be Google Calendar compressing files or a similar service going on on my machine. What you're looking for with

Ransom Where? is for the screen to pop up with a process that you do not recognize. When that happens you have the ability to either allow or terminate the process. When in doubt, terminate. This will not harm your machine in any way. It will simply stop whatever process is going on. If you have a particular process that you are continually having to stop, or if you have the Ransom Where? dialog box pop up after installing some questionable software, you may have just saved yourself from a ransomware attack. Again, did I mention it's free? You can download Ransom Where? from objective-see.com.

# 157

# Skype

When I was a kid growing up in the 60s the space program was up and running full-tilt. The Vietnam war was raging and everyone was looking to the future to be our hope for things that were amazing. The future promised us flying cars, telephones where we could see people, and Dick Tracy talked to people on his watch.

Now in the 2020s hovercraft taxis are just starting to go into production. I can make a call to anyone on my Apple Watch, and the visual telephone is called Skype.

Conferencing software like Zoom is quite popular on our machines today. They allow us to conduct meetings online. But when you just want to make a simple phone call to someone and want to see them face-to-face, Skype is the answer. Currently, an app loader for Skype comes on every new Apple computer, but if one is not present you can always go to the Skype website and download it directly for your Mac. It's relatively easy to set up a Skype account and start using it right away. The caveat for using Skype is, of course, both parties on a Skype call must have Skype installed on a machine. The beauty of it however is that Skype is also available for your smartphone. A Skype call can take place from any location anywhere in the world as long as each participant has access to the Internet. This could be by using cellular data or by using a router in a hotel room.

Is Skype the final fulfillment of the visual telephone? Microsoft thinks so. That's why they spent big money to buy it from Skype to develop it as their own. Who knows though, technology comes and goes. In the 60s Captain Kirk routinely called Scotty and Spock on his flip phone. Flip phones came and went. The future of Skype remains to be seen as well.

# 158

# Online Storage

We covered the big three online storage services in previous chapters, iCloud Drive, Google Drive, and Dropbox. Now I would like to spend just a bit talking about the strategies for using these services. All of them give you a small amount of Storage space initially. At the time of this writing, iCloud provides 5 GB, Dropbox provides 2 GB, and Google Drive provides 15 GB of free storage.

Your iCloud drive will fill almost immediately with only 5 GB of storage but the good news is that you can expand it to 50 GB for as little as $.99 per month. If you consider the cost of a hard drive, that's a bargain. I'm willing to bet just about everyone reading this book can afford $12 a year for a 50 GB hard drive and the convenience thereof.

2 GB of Dropbox is ridiculously small. Dropbox is also the most expensive when it comes to adding additional space. If you are a good salesman for them, you can add to your space, up to 16 GB by referring others to the service.

If you have 50 GB of iCloud storage, 15 GB of Google Drive storage, and 15 or so gigabytes of Dropbox storage, you can actually do a lot if you have a strategy for organizing it without spending additional money. The secret is to use each one of the services for specific tasks.

In my iCloud I will store all of the things that I would have normally stored in documents. It is my online documents folder. This way I have access across the Internet on all of my machines to all of my files. As for the other two services, I will use each one of them for a specific task. Currently, Dropbox is where I store any files that I will want to share with others as it has the easiest file sharing capability. You might use Google Drive specifically for documents created in Google docs for instance, and only store that type of file there. Another use for an online drive would be an archive drive. Files that you want access to, but not necessarily ones that you're working in on a day-to-day basis.

However you decide to organize your various drives, with a little planning you can make the minimum amounts of storage go a long way, and stay organized in the process.

# 159

# Using Articles & Pictures

Importing news articles or pictures off of the web into Facebook is easy on your Mac. Let's tackle sharing an article off of a website. First, determine if you are free to share it. Many news-oriented websites might have an actual Facebook share button allowing you to share it from the website itself. If not, you can still share a site by highlighting the site's URL at the top of Safari and copying it by the Command C method. Now it's a simple matter of going to your Facebook page and using the Command V keystroke to paste it into a new post.

Photos are just as easy. Let's say you're heading down to the movie theater to see the latest summer blockbuster and you want to set a picture of the movie poster as your banner. Find a picture on the web large enough to cover the area and secondary click it. Here you'll have the option to *Save As*. Save the photo to your desktop and upload it as you would any photo into Facebook.

Facebook does do an amount of auto-cropping, so you usually don't have to worry about getting the perfect picture size. If you're using a photo as a header of a post, you might want to look for pictures that are close to a square, simply because they look the best.

# 160

# File Sharing

Love it or hate it, file sharing over the world wide web has become commonplace amongst computer users. As the name implies file-sharing programs allow you to share files over the web with others. These files can be virtually any type of computer file imaginable. File sharing programs in and of themselves are not illegal. Sharing certain files with other users is a slippery slope. Record companies and movie houses are in a constant war with online sites that either host copy-written files, or search for them. These sites are incredibly hard to stop because searching for a file is not illegal. Downloading the file could be. I am not a law expert and this chapter is not going to be about law, it will be about educating you on the subject.

Go to any search engine and do a search for torrent search engines and you will find a plethora of sites out there for searching torrent files. A torrent file is a file that will tell an app where to download a file. The reason it is called a torrent is because the program does not have to be located in one specific place. A torrent program can go out on the World Wide Web and grab bits of a program from 100 different sources and reassemble them on your machine into a complete file.

Contrary to popular belief, although there is a lot of pirated software and movies out there, the world is not simply filled with illegal torrents in totality. There are many torrents out there of bundled public domain works such as fonts and graphics to be shared and downloaded. There is also a large number of open-source programs that are readily shared via torrents. In order to find and download a torrent, you are going to need a torrent application. Up until Catalina, Micro Torrent, known as utorrent, was the application of choice for most people using torrents. Catalina somewhat broke that application, but there are many other applications out there that are rock-solid. One such application is FOLX. It's by no means the only one available, but it's likely one of the easiest to use.

# 161
## Save Web Page as PDF

Yes you can save a viewable portion of a website as a png by simply taking a screen shot, but what if you want to save an entire page?  You would think that you would simply open the **Save as** command on the file menu in Safari, but you'd be wrong.  This method will only allow you to save an HTML version of the page.

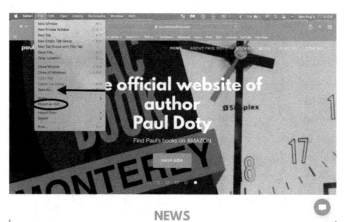

Safari will however allow you to export the current page as a PDF. The command works with varying results depending on the particular page and how it's coded.  If you need an entire page rather than just a snippet, try experimenting with this option.  If it doesn't work for you, you can always take a screenshot and convert it into a PDF.  I should also note that all of the other major browsers allow you to do this as well.

# 162

# Default Browser

Your Mac comes with its default web browser set as Safari. For many reasons, I recommend leaving Safari as your default web browser, however you may set your default to any browser that you may have loaded on your machine.

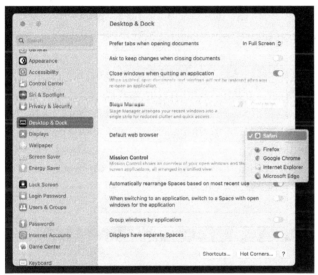

If you go to *Desktop & Dock* in *System Settings*, you will find that all of your browsers have been loaded into an option that you can set manually under *Default web browser*. Once you set an alternate default Mac will default to that application anytime you click on a link that takes you to the Internet.

# 163

# Track Air Traffic On Your Mac

Our house is located in Northern California in the flight path of the San Francisco Airport. It's also in the Mediflight flight path to Highway 132, an infamous two-lane highway that local residents refer to as "Blood Alley". On any weekend you can hear Mediflight helicopters above our house heading out to a head-on collision on Highway 132. Many nights my wife and I would wonder who was actually flying over our house as we sat out in our back yard on a hot summer night.

A good friend of ours is a Mediflight EMT at one of our local hospitals and on one given night the air traffic was especially heavy. So much so that we sent a text to our friend to see if he was on a flight overhead. He responded back and though he wasn't active on that particular night, he did turn us on to a really cool way to track air traffic on a Mac (or any computer for that matter). As it turns out, there is a website for those in the know that tracks all flights overhead.

The website is called **flightradar24.com** and it will allow you to track any flight currently over your location. Find flight numbers, aircraft type, follow flight paths, and more from this easy to use website. There's even an iPhone app that gives you additional information.

Now if you hear something overhead, you'll have an easy way to identify what it is on your Mac.

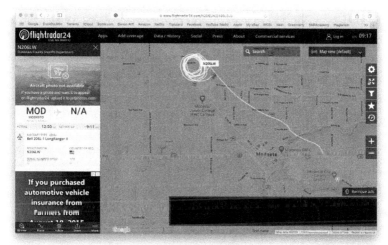

If you have a loved one taking an international trip, you can even track its flight in real-time across the ocean.

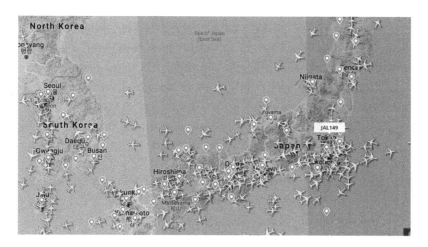

# 164

# Throttling

Throttling is the practice of an internet provider slowing down a customers service by limiting the bandwidth that they've paid for. Let's say you've paid for 30Mbps of service, but your internet is still too slow at times to watch a YouTube video or stream a show. Does this sound a bit nefarious on the part of your provider? Well, it is, and it's also illegal in the sense that you've paid for a service that they are purposely not providing.

Now there's many reasons why your service might slow down and throttling may not be the cause. There could be net traffic out of there control, or there could be a defect in equipment. But if you're noticing that your service is slowing down at the same time every day for no explainable reason, then you may be the victim of throttling.

Why would a provider stoop to an illegal practice like throttling? The short answer is profit. Every area or section of a city has a finite amount of bandwidth that can be sold because the cables and infrastructure can only transmit so much. To demonstrate this, lets throw out all of the tech terms like megabytes and bandwidth and let's just substitute basic numbers for our illustration. Let's say you have a section of town that is capable of the number 100. Now let's say every person that buys your service is sold 10. Simple math says that I can sell 10 people 10 before my service has reached its maximum of 100. Logic says that I can sell my service a maximum of 10 times. But greed says that not all of those people are going to use my service at the same time, so why not sell a few more. The problem is that greed by its nature never stops at a little more. Soon, you've oversold an area by two, three, or more times and you simply cannot provide what the people are paying for. Here's where it goes from nefarious, to evil. When the customers complain, you convince them that they just need a faster service and you upsell them to a higher priced product.

Now the provider is making money hand over fist by selling

235

product that doesn't really exist, or more accurately is unavailable under peak usage times, so what do they do to get by? They limit your service by cutting it back by a percentage during the peak times. This is throttling.

This practice works because it is incredibly difficult for the average computer Joe to prove when they are being throttled. The companies also know that the average computer user is oblivious to these practices, let alone possess the knowledge of how to detect it, and if they manage to detect it, they can't prove it. In this next section I'm going to tell you how to detect it, and what to do about it if it's happening to you.

The first thing that you need to do is to run a speed test to determine your base internet speed. Let's say that you're paying for thirty megabytes of bandwidth or 30Mbps. Go to **speedtest.com** and run a test. You should be getting within 5% of 30Mbps on the download side. Now run a VPN (VPNs are covered in previous chapters) and set your location to a nearby city. In my case here, I've set my connection to San Francisco about 70 miles away.

Relaunch your web browser and rerun the test. Because your location DNS address must be targeted by your provider in order to throttle you, you're fooling them into thinking that you're not who you are by using a VPN. If your bandwidth goes up significantly, 10% or more, you're likely being throttled.

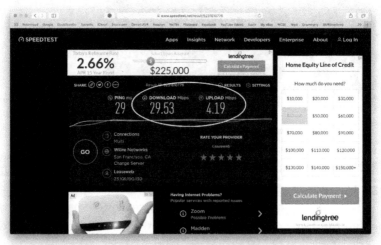

In my case, no throttling was detected. In theory, you should see a small drop in Mbps when using a VPN. That's normal because you're using a small bit of your available bandwidth to piggyback through another server, but if it's significantly higher, then something is cutting

237

back your computers specific address.

Calling your provider and going off on them will likely get you nowhere. Neither will accusing them of throttling. The best way to deal with the situation is to become a squeaky wheel. Be the customer that complains every time that the bandwidth goes away, insisting that a person comes out to repair or troubleshoot the line. Before too long, you'll be the customer that gets the full bandwidth while your uneducated neighbor pays the price. As the saying goes, it's the squeaky wheel that gets the grease. I know that sounds harsh, but you're not the one overselling the service. Your only other option is to drop the carrier for another.

# 165

# Podcasts

This lesson will be a very basic overview of the Podcasts app. We will go over functionality and a little more history in greater detail in later chapters.

Podcasts have always been an afterthought in iTunes. It was one of those areas that was added long after iTunes was an original app. This was a shame because the Holy Grail in podcasting has always been to have your podcast listed in the iTunes store. Podcasts have always taken a backseat to music in iTunes, so it's great to see them finally get their own application.

When you open the Podcasts app the first thing you're going to notice is that it looks a lot like the music app. Using this universal look throughout all of the media applications is intentional. Apple always tries to give the customer a universal user experience. In other words, they don't try to reinvent the wheel that often. This concept can be seen throughout apple's design. Most notably in the operating system changes. They will typically give you enough changes to make everything look bright, shiny, and new, but they never change anything so much as to confuse the user or cause you to learn something all over again.

In the right pane of the application, you will find all of your podcasts that you're currently subscribed to under *Up Next*. Click *See All* will show you all of them in the window. Scrolling to the right will take you through all of your subscribed to podcasts. Below that the application tries to predict other podcasts that you might like based on ones that you've already subscribed too, and recently played will show you the ones that you've listened to recently.

In the left pane, you can search the podcast store for a specific podcast or browse particular topics that might be of interest to you. All of the controls are relatively straightforward. The player at the top works exactly the way the player works in the Music app.

# 166
# Podcast Settings

In this lesson, I'll take a quick look at the controls available to you in *Settings* in the Podcast app. You get to preferences by clicking on *Podcasts* in the upper left-hand corner of the application menu and selecting *Settings*. Under *General,* you will be able to tell your computer to download new episodes automatically. This gives you a way to manage your computer's resources.

Under *Playback,* you will be able to have control over the forward and reverse buttons. Depending on the type of podcast you listen to, you may want to jump ahead or back a small amount or large amount in time. You can adjust your player to give you precise increments in this window.

Under the *Advanced* tab, you will get boxes to tick that will control how your library works for your podcasts. Here you can set up the player to automatically delete episodes and control other syncing functions.

# 167

# Podcasts, Past, Present, and Future

I wrote my first book in the early 90s. 25 years went by before my second book came out and I've put out a book roughly every year or so sense. During those 25 years, I had a number of other creative outlets that I invested my time into one of which was a brand new budding media called podcasting. Over the years I produced four different podcasts. In the early years, your podcast could be found on many of the new and upcoming services out there. But the Holy Grail of visibility was to have it excepted by iTunes. Once Apple excepted your podcast you were instantly thrust in front of millions of potential listeners. Today apple podcasts are the premier place in the world that you want your podcast to be listed in.

In 2019 podcasts received their own standalone app simply called *Podcasts*. No longer would podcasts be lost in the bloat of iTunes. One could argue that Apple pulled them out of iTunes and gave them their own app simply so they would not interfere with other entertainment streams that actually make money for Apple, but Apple has been supportive of artists and producers since the very beginning of podcasting.

Why would Apple pour time, money, and effort into an area that doesn't make revenue? Well, I think the answer is that Apple has always been pretty good at doubling down on future technologies. That is to say, at the time you may not be able to figure out how something is going to be a revenue stream, but Apple has always had the ability to look ten to twenty years or more down the road and not only try to predict that future but steer it as well. In light of that, who knows what the future of podcasting may hold for Apple. Time will tell and in the meantime, podcasters have a new home in the Apple ecosystem.

# 168

# I've Been Hacked!

Over the next few chapters, we'll spend some time exploring Facebook. You may not be on Facebook, so these chapters may not pertain to your personal computer usage, but plainly, many of us are. In fact, many people use their computer for little more than web surfing, email, and social media, so I would be remiss not to cover it in some detail.

People generally get hacked in one of two ways on Facebook. In the first method, a hacker infects a machine with a key logger virus that grabs the user's password and logon credentials to the site. The hacker then goes into the site and takes control of it. Because this is a virus-driven attack, it is not the preferred method of attack if you are using a Mac instead of a PC, because the Mac OS is not prone to the same vulnerabilities.

The second method of attack is how most Mac users get hacked on Facebook, as this method could care less as to what computer you're using. In this method, the hacker simply takes the time to create a bogus Facebook account under your name and tries to get the people on your friend list to join it.

If you become a victim of either form of attack, do the following two things immediately. First, change your password. Time is of the essence on this one. If your hacker changes it before you you'll be locked out of your own account. If you change it before them, you'll effectively lock them out. Next, report the attack to Facebook. If a fake has been created, report the account so Facebook can shut it down. Avoid starting over with a new account as this will cause more problems in the long run as it will cause even more confusion for all of your friends.

# 169

# Changing Your Password

In the previous chapter, we talked about how important it is after you have been hacked to change your Facebook password as soon as you can. While the hacker has access to your password, he has access to your account. Changing your password will take your account back from him immediately. If the hacker gets to your password before you do and changes it you will have lost your ability to control your account so time is of the essence. This is how you change your password on Facebook.

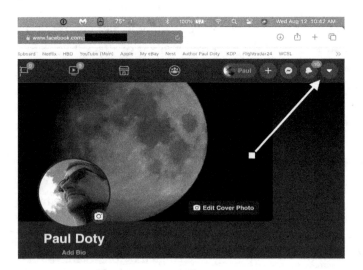

From your normal page (the one that has your name on it) or from your homepage, click the dropdown arrow on the far right of the menu bar. This area may simply be a your profile picture. You will see a selection for Settings & Privacy. Click it.

Now click on Settings.

Click Security and login.

You will now be able to change your password.

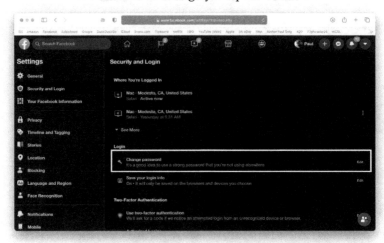

Note that after you do this any third-party application that is using your Facebook account will now effectively be locked out until you give permission for it to access it again. My wife recently changed her Facebook password because she feared that she had been hacked. The next day she was wondering why her Echo Show device in the kitchen was no longer showing pictures on its home screen from Facebook. After thinking about it for a few moments she realized that she had changed her Facebook password and now her Echo had to be updated and redirected to those folders.

# 170

# I'm Listening to You

Creepy as a Stephen King novel is seeing something pop up on Facebook that absolutely and obviously relates to a conversation that you had in private, perhaps with your spouse. If you're on Facebook long enough, you will begin to feel like your computer and phone are listening to you. To the best of my knowledge, Facebook has never admitted that their advertisers are tapping your microphone or camera on your laptop, and I am not a conspiracy theorist. However, I also cannot deny the creepiness of having a two or three-day breakfast conversation about retirement, only to see ads about retirement popping up on my Facebook account after three or four days.

On the upside, there are some steps that you can take that may be able to help the situation. There are preferences within Facebook that you can turn off that may or may not help this scenario. I say may or may not, because Facebook does not make it easy to completely disable anything having to do with their ads as that is how they make their money. Also, I say may or may not because for everything that you will want to turn off having to do with ads on Facebook, there are multiple places where it has to be turned off not just one.

Unfortunately, the most likely place that Facebook is able to listen to your conversations (if they in fact are) is via your smartphone. If you go to the permissions on your smartphone you will see a list of things that you can either turn on or off or only allow when you are using the app. An interesting thing happens when you get to the microphone and camera settings. There are only two choices for these functions. On and off. So essentially, if you are going to use your microphone for Facebook to say, dictate a post on your iPhone, you are essentially giving the application permission to listen via that microphone anytime they wish, as there is no option for permission only when the application is being used.

By the way, a half-hour after writing this chapter and discussing it with my wife verbally, the following ad popped up on my Facebook page. Probably a coincidence.

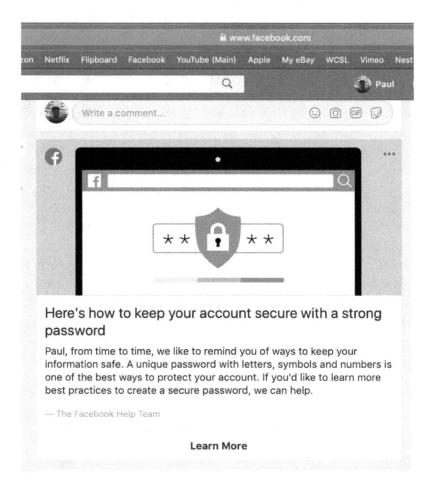

# 171

# Facebook and Contacts

Facebook is an awesome resource for finding profile pictures for people in your contacts list. If you're on Facebook then chances are that a good amount of your friends are there as well. In contacts, you can always use the camera on your phone to snap a picture of someone when you enter them into contacts, but you're not always with the person when you enter them in. Plus, many people have an aversion to someone taking a picture of them for their phone and computer. The perfect solution is profile photos on Facebook. This method has two big advantages. The first is that the person does not have to be present when you put their photo into your contact list, and the second is that you're using a photo that they themselves like as it's already their public profile picture on another platform.

Grabbing a profile picture is relatively easy. In Safari open the person's Facebook page and their contact page in contacts. You can either drag the photo from one to another and drag and drop, or you can copy and paste. Contacts will give you the basic edit to enlarge or shrink the area of the photo that you want to use, and it will remember your edit. Once you've edited contacts on your Mac with the new picture, it will update to all of your other Apple devices over iCloud.

This method will work with other pictures as well. You may wish to add a profile picture for the contacts page for your auto repair shop for example. If your shop does not have a Facebook page, check to see if they have a website. You can grab a logo from either location and drag it into contacts. If a website does not have a graphic of appropriate size or does not give you the ability to copy and paste, take a screenshot.

# 172

# Contacts

Build into every Apple device is a wonderful contact manager called Contacts. Contacts uses iCloud to sync your contacts list across all of your Apple devices. This means that you'll only have to enter a contact once to get it to show up on all of them. Most native apps on your Mac will recognize the contacts database and will pull information from it when necessary. Here are a few tips to follow when using contacts.

First, it's a good idea to have one person per contact. In other words, don't create a single contact for both a husband and a wife. The reason that this is important is because your Mac will use this database to get phone numbers for things like texting in iMessage and multiple names and numbers in a contact will become confusing for both you and your computer. The best method here is to create a contact for every separate member of a household, and if you want to make note of kids name or a spouse, do so in the notes of the contact, but keep separate contacts.

Contacts allows you to store general information on a contact in an area called notes. Any information can be stored here. Notes is a great area for things like directions to a contacts house, or a gate code to get to their front door. You can even store the likes and dislikes a person might have for Christmas gifts, or virtually any information you wish to access about them. You can add or alter this information any time you like, on any of your devices, and the information will be updated across all of them automatically.

When you create a contact you can either enter in all the information that you have for them manually or copy and paste the information in from another source like the web.

# 173
# Sharing Contacts

Sharing a contact with someone else is easy on your Mac. From your contacts app pull up the contact that you want to share. In the lower-right-hand corner click on the share icon. It's the square box with the arrow pointing up.

From the share icon you are going to be able to send the contact in an email to another Apple user, text message the contact, or airdrop the contact to another Apple device in your proximity. MacOS may even try and anticipate your needs by suggesting a person that you text often.

You can also send a copy of the contact to local applications on your Mac. You can send it into your Notes application for example or if you are a developer you could send it directly into an OS simulator like Xcode.

# Adding Contacts

There are many ways to add contacts to your contact list from your Mac or iPhone. The most basic method is to simply pull up contacts and enter in one by hand. As you work with your Mac however you will find that anytime you come across contact information, Mac will give you a way to import that information into Contacts. One great way of importing contacts or updating contact information is to look at all of your past information at a glance in Mail. Mail allows you to do this by clicking Window at the top of the page, and then go to Previous Recipients.

Here you will see a complete list of previous recipients of the emails that you have sent or received. You can then choose any recipient and click *add to contacts* to add them instantly. You may already have one of the recipients in contacts and you may be able to find further information like secondary email addresses or telephone numbers here as well. Checking back every six months or so to this location in Mail will give you a huge resource for updating your contacts.

# 175

# Calendar

No where does the apple ecosystem shine as bright as in the calendar app. Calendar will use iCloud and it will sync across all of your Apple devices. Update an appointment on your iPhone and it will appear on your iPad, iMac, and MacBook. However, if you do want to update immediately, go to *View* and click *Refresh Calendars*.

A new event can be added to the calendar by double-clicking in any days square. You'll be prompted to supply an event name. The event will automatically be stored to your default calendar but you can change that by clicking on the dropdown box in the upper right-hand area. Now fill in the other bits of information such as the time location and tell your calendar if you want to add reminders in the form of alarms.

You can also add notes to your events. Notes can be almost any kind of attachment including Internet URLs. Sadly the one thing that you still can't do in Calendar is add a photograph to the background of a day. This would be a great feature for children and people with special needs. Hopefully, Apple will add this feature in a future update.

If you want to get rid of any event on your calendar click on it and hit the delete key on your keyboard. It will be deleted from all of your devices.

You will likely find that your default view for Calendar is the month view, but you can also view by day, week, or year. You will find that the day and week view will come in handy if there is more information on a day then is able to be displayed in the month view. The week view will also give you a good overview of the week you're about to go into.

Navigate throughout your calendar by clicking the forward and backward arrow in the upper right-hand corner and when you need to get back to the view for today, click *Today*.

# 176
# Reoccurring events

Reoccurring events are relatively easy to set up in Calendar. When an event is created, click on the date and time field to set up a *repeat*.

Below the start and end times, you will see a field for repeat. The default is None. Click on *None* to change the field.

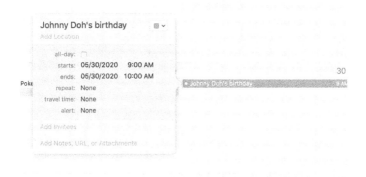

Once this field is open you will have a variety of types of repeats to choose from. You can set things to reoccur every day, week, month, or year. One feature that you may not have used before is the *Custom* option. Use this option if you need a complicated repeat. There is almost an infinite number of ways you can customize a repeat.

In this example, I have set a repeat to change my HVAC filters every three months on the first Sunday of the month.

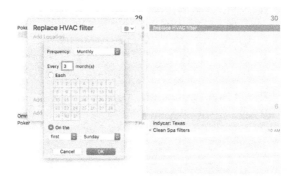

# Multiple Calendars

The calendar app makes it easy to create and manage multiple calendars between all of your machines. I personally have separate calendars for work, my own private calendar, and a shared calendar with my wife. You may want to set up a calendar that you share with your entire family for events that affect everyone in your household. That way when you update an event on that calendar it updates on all of the calendars for your various family members.

A work calendar could be shared with all of your employees. Multiple calendars come in handy for a business that handles multiple clients that might need to schedule and track different events. A good example of this would be a booking agent who has six different clients. They could have a shared calendar using a third-party vendor like Google for instance. The booking agent could have a separate calendar for each one of his clients that they book for. Updating an event on a particular client's calendar would also update it on the shared calendar on the client's machine.

The easiest way to make a new calendar is to go to the calendar pane on the left and right-click and choose *New Calendar*.

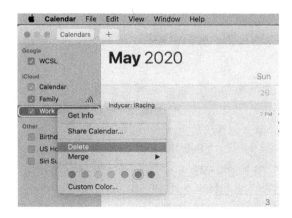

Once the calendar has been created it can be deleted in a similar fashion. Go to the calendar and right-click it and choose *Delete*. This will delete the calendar from all of your machines. This will delete all data. If you want to save the data before deleting the calendar, merge that data with another calendar before deletion.

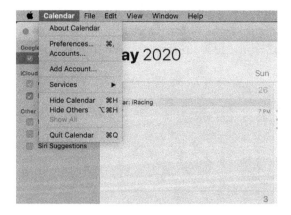

Google calendars can be added to your calendar app by going up to *Add Accounts*. Google calendars are great because they can be shared with other people for collaboration outside of the Apple ecosystem.

# 178
# Pete & Repeat

Have you ever had your contacts or calendar events duplicate?

Have you ever had your contacts or calendar events duplicate?

The next two lessons will deal with an annoyance that everyone will likely eventually face. That syncing feeling you get when either your contacts or calendar events begin to duplicate. Syncing with iCloud is awesome..until it isn't. There's a lot of reasons that can lead to iCloud sync issues but the end result is the same. Duplication of data. First we'll look at your contact list.

When you first notice duplications, you'll want to find out if you're looking at a glitch, or something permanent. Our devices can sometimes glitch and momentarily duplicate information. To confirm that this is an issue that needs your intervention, sign out of your iCloud account and sign back in. This will refresh the sync and let you know if you have a continuing issue. If the duplicates are still there, you have two ways to correct it.

In the first method you can go to Card in your Contacts app on your Mac and choose Look for Duplicates. This will tell you how many duplicates that it found and allow you to merge data between them this eliminating the duplicates. This method is automatic and while it's the faster way to affect your entire contact list, it also makes its own decisions as to what it combines.

In the second method you will go to your iCloud account on the internet at iCloud.com and pull up your contact list. There you will see what's duplicated and what's not. When you fix this one location, all of your contacts across all your devices will be repaired.

# 179

# Pete & Repeat Again

In this lesson we'll look at your calendars. Again, sign out of your iCloud account and back in to see if this clears up the duplications. If not, you may have confused your calendar app at some point into thinking that the calendar on your local machine is different than the one in iCloud. Open Calendar and look at the calendars in the left pane. Do you see a duplicate local calendar AND an iCloud calendar? If so, that's your problem. You can uncheck the box of the local calendar to see what would happen if that calendar went away. If that restores your Mac to perfection, you can delete that calendar by right clicking it and deleting it. DO NOT delete your iCloud calendar!

If you still have birthday's repeating, that's another story. Birthdays do not use a local calendar on your Mac like the other calendars that you see. They come from your contacts list. If you have a duplicate contact for a person, you'll have a duplicate calendar entry until you eliminate the duplicate contact.

# 180

# Notes

Your Mac comes with a simple, underrated little app called Notes. So underrated in fact that we'll spend a few lessons looking at different ways to use it. This little app got a facelift a few years ago and is now a handy little app for those who embrace it and use it regularly. In its most basic task, it is a simple note pad for jotting down notes, but this little guy has some features that push its usefulness well beyond that. I'll be the first to point out that there are currently no less than 30 note apps out there on the market, but Notes is included for free with Mac OS and has a lot going for it. When Apple revamped Notes in 2015, the competition was stiff. Giants like Evernote and One Note had functionality way beyond simple note-taking, so if Apple was going to bring a competitor to the table, they were going to need to completely rethink the product, and that they did.

First off, Notes is connected to iCloud. That means you have a place in your digital life to make a quick note of important information that will follow you throughout your devices. Any little piece of information that I might want to keep and reference at a later date, goes in notes.

Casual users are probably unaware that you can save much more than text. You can drag and drop pictures, videos, and links just to name a few of your options.

What you don't want to keep in Notes is any information that should be encrypted as notes is not a secure app. Meaning that anyone with access to your open computer can pull up all your notes, so it's not the place that you want to store things like passwords and access codes.

# 181

# Collaboration in Notes

Notes gives you a built-in collaboration tool within the Apple ecosystem. If you need to share information with friends, family, or co-workers, Notes can handle it. From sharing a grocery list with your husband to managing a project to-do list with someone at work, the possibilities are endless.

To collaborate on a note, double-click the one you want to collaborate on and click on the add people icon in the upper right. You can now mail it, message it, airdrop it, or send a link. You can add and remove individuals to the note at will.

What if you simply want to share a note instead of giving people the ability to change it? You can do that as well by choosing the share button instead of the add people button.

# 182

# Notes with iPad

When the iPad Pro came out I was only slightly interested in the notion of Apple's new Apple Pencil. I thought it was a cute idea, and I was sure that there where a few people in the world of art and graphics that would get some use out of it, but what would it offer for the casual day to day iPad user. Then Apple revamped Notes to take advantage of the new technology.

Notes is one of those applications that really starts to shine when you pair your Mac with an iPad. Remember, the two are connected through iCloud, so in a sense, the iPad can be an input device for getting notes into your Mac. Pair the two with an Apple Pencil, and you can do the following.

Take your iPad and turn it on. While on the lock screen, tap anywhere with your Apple Pencil. Immediately the iPad will spring to life in Notes, and you're ready for a new note creation. Now, know that this is a feature that you have to turn on in notes, but once it's configured, it's pretty cool and incredibly convenient.

The iPad can be configured to always create a new note when you tap on the lock screen or continue working on the last note that you opened. A third option will bring up the last note viewed on the iPad. You'll choose one of these three options depending on how you use notes. If you are a continual note-taker, you'll likely default to the new note option. If you have many notes on your system that tell you how to do things, or configure things, then you might default to the last viewed option. The last created option is a convenient place in between.

# 183

# Quick Launch Notes

New in Monterey is the ability to quick launch the notes application.  After adding this feature to the iPad it only seemed fare to add this ability to Mac.

To invoke Notes at any time on your Mac, in any application, just take your tooltip down to the lower right hand corner of your screen. You will get a pop-up note.

You can now simply start typing your note.  This is a really handy feature to take notes while internet browsing.

# 184

# Tables in Notes

Notes allows you to create spreadsheet-style cells within a note. Within a note select *Format* and click *table*. You will get a four-cell table in your note. It will have pulldowns for both rows and columns. Use the pulldowns to create a note with the appropriate number of cells for your purpose. Obviously, you're not going to want to create a huge multi-cell note, because a spreadsheet would be much more suited for that application. But if you need a quick note with say, four columns and eight or so rows, this will get the job done fast.

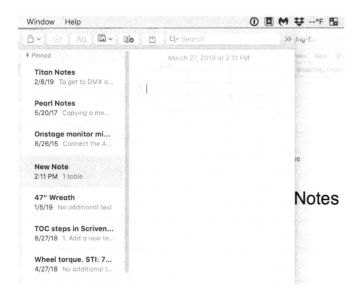

Need to delete a row? No problem, just highlight the row or column and hit delete.

# 185

# Scan Into Notes

Notes is another place in the Apple ecosystem where it is
wonderful to use multiple Apple products simultaneously. Notes will
allow you to use your iPhone as a handheld scanner to scan any
document photo into a pre-existing note.

To use this feature, put your cursor anywhere that you want an
imported photo in your note. Go up to file on the menu and choose
insert from iPhone. This will allow you to either take a photo or scan a
document directly into your note. Make sure that your notes are
shared everywhere through iCloud.

# 186

# Organizing Notes

Soon you'll want to start organizing your notes better. If you only
have four notes pertaining to a certain subject, it can be hard to find
them fast amongst a hundred or more notes. The best way to keep
organized is to create folders by topic. In the example below, I've
organized two lighting specific notes into a folder called *Lighting*. Now
if I'm looking for one of the two specific notes, I can click on the
Lighting folder and sift through the two notes instead of a hundred.

To create a sub folder, control-click on *All iCloud* and create a new
folder. Next select all the notes that you want to move to the new
folder and control-click them. Follow the path in *Move to* to place the
items where you can easily find them in the future. Now if you click
on the new folder, you should only see the notes that you want.
Returning to All iCloud will once again give you a list of all your
stored notes.

# Searching In Notes

Eventually you're going to have so many notes that it will be difficult to find something in them unless you're good at sorting. Inevitably they'll be something that gets lost that you'll want to find. That's where the search feature comes in. Located in the upper right-hand corner is a magnifying glass that will allow you to search all of your notes to find a keyword.

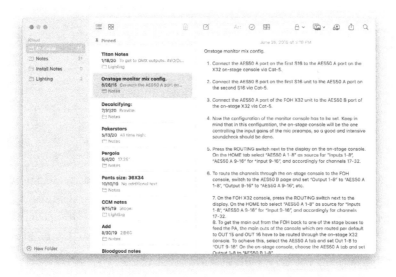

In this example you can see that I have twenty-three notes in iCloud. I want to find the note that specifically tells me what to set my torque wrench at in order to tighten the bolts on car's wheels. I have gone up to the search feature and typed in wheel. That's all it took, and the top hit shows me all of the notes that contain the word wheel. Now all I have to do is click on the right note and I'm off to the races.

# 188

# Import and Export Notes

Notes will allow you to import a wide variety of file types from many different note and text type applications. To import a document simply go to file and select import. If notes is able to import the file, it will show up as a normal-looking file, if not, it will be grayed out. Notes will want to import an entire folder when you choose it, so if you have a single document that you wish to import, it's oftentimes helpful to save it by itself on your desktop before the attempt. If you have a format that Notes does not recognize, oftentimes you can simply use the cut and paste function to import.

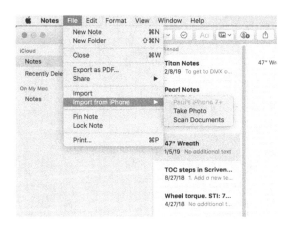

If you use the import from iPhone option, you will be able to add a picture or scan directly from your phone.

There are two ways to export from Notes. You can use the export command and Notes will produce a PDF version of the note, or you can simply copy the content of a note and paste it into another document.

# 189

# Getting Deleted Notes Back

Sooner or later you're going to delete a note on your Mac by mistake. No problem, it's in the trash, right? Wrong! Don't panic, here's how to get it back.

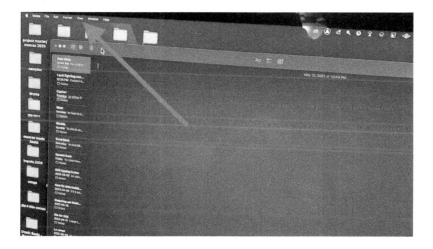

Go up to your view menu and click *View*, then *Show Folders*.

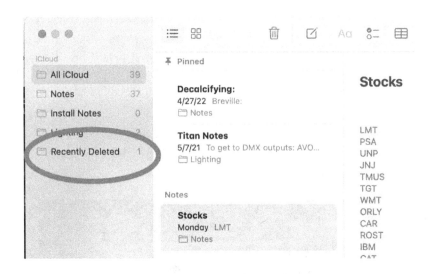

You'll find your deleted notes in *Recently Deleted*.

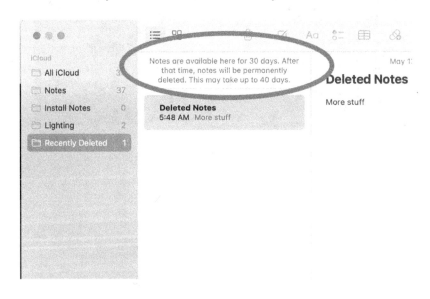

# 190

# The Fear of God

I was working in my shop yesterday and a phone call came in from a friend. "P Doty, you're never going to believe what happened. I've been on the phone with Apple support for four hours followed by a trip to the Genius Bar, and I'm still screwed." "What's the issue?" I asked. "Today I turned on my phone and every contact was gone. I mean, totally gone, everything blank. They had me open iCloud online and everything was gone there as well. I've lost all of my contacts. Contacts that took years to acquire. They're all gone."

Now if the story above strikes a level of fear into you, congratulations. It should. We seldom contemplate what would happen if our digital life was suddenly gone. After all, Apple makes it so darn easy these days with multiple backups of our data over multiple devices. We update our phone, and the information updates over the cloud to our iMac, our iPad, our laptop, our work computer, and so on. With all of this duplication of our data in multiple locations, we are lulled into a false sense of security when it comes to our precious data. We know if our phone crashes or dies, we can simply sync a new phone and bingo! We have all of our contacts back!

On another day, I walked into a friend's business to pick up a piece of rental gear. I asked what day he wanted me to bring it back and he answered with frustration; "I don't know. The office is in a bit of crisis right now. I came in this morning and all of our booking calendar was blank, and I can't get it back."

Here's the lesson in a nutshell: While it's amazing that you can have all of these data streams backed up over multiple devices because you're syncing to the cloud, never forget that you're *syncing* to the cloud. Meaning, that if any device for whatever reason decides to dump all of your calendar or all of your contacts, that *new nothing* is going to sync with the cloud. Then every time a new device logs on and syncs, it will be updated with the new data. Which is…..*nothing*.

Now, did that get your attention? Let's move on and talk about how we can protect ourselves from this happening to us.

# 191

# Contacts Backup

We'll cover an overall data backup plan in later lessons, but over the course of the next few chapters, we're going to look at two specific areas of great importance. The first of which is your contacts.

Before we make a backup, let's do something that is equally important. Let's go into Calendar and set a reminder to ourselves to actually do a backup the first of every month, because the knowledge of how to do a backup will do you little good if you don't remember to do it on a regular basis. Set your event to do a backup on a set day of the month, and then use the repeat every month feature to remind yourself every month.

Next, open your Documents folder and create a new folder called *Backups*. You will save your snapshots of your Calendar and your Contacts here every month.

Apple makes it quite easy to save a snapshot of your contacts at any time. With Contacts open, click on *File* and go to *Export/Contacts Archive*. You will be prompted as to where you'd like to save your export. Choose the new folder that you created in your Documents folder. Now if disaster strikes in the future, you will always have a restoration point here as a fallback in case you don't have a Time Machine backup for whatever reason. Think of it as cheap insurance and peace of mind. The calendar is backed up in the same way, and we'll go over it later in the book in detail so it serves as a refresher course.

# Calendar Backup

The Mac OS is robust, to say the least. It can spoil you with how bulletproof it is, especially after working for any number of years within the PC ecosystem. However, you can be extremely bulletproof and still have someone throw you a grenade. Never forget that you're still working with a computer, and computers, all computers, will eventually have an issue.

You may feel confident that you're immune to corruption and sync failures with your Calendar, and you may not feel the need to do a specific secondary backup of it if you're routinely using a backup plan like Time Machine, but trust me when I say, you still need it. You can't have too many backup strategies when it comes to computers, and backing up your calendar is far too easy not to do it on a regular basis.

I recommend using Time Machine for your daily backups and creating a backup folder in each machines documents folder specifically for snapshot backups of both Calendar and Contacts.

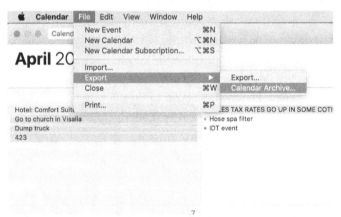

Your calendar is backed up in the same way that your contacts are backed up. In Calendar, go to *File/Export/Calendar Archive* and save a backup to your backups folder. Now if disaster strikes, you can restore from that file using Import.

# 193
# Time Machine

I could spend an entire page preaching the need for backups at this point in the book, but right now we'll assume that everyone understands the importance of regular backups and we'll move on to spend a moment talking about the built-in backup program that comes native on every Mac.

Time Machine is far more than a simple backup program. As the name implies it is an app that allows you to time travel on your Mac. It accomplishes this by taking snapshots of the state of your computer at various points in time. It stores these snapshots on an external drive and later allows you to go back through your timeline to find a specific file or folder that may need to be replaced on your machine.

You will need an external hard drive attached to your computer in order to use Time Machine. Almost any external hard drive can be configured to be used as a Time Machine hard drive.

You can enter Time Machine by clicking on its small icon in the top menu bar.

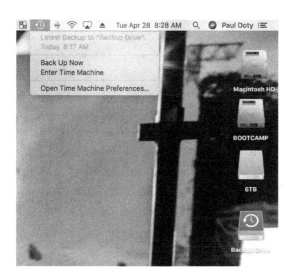

The initial menu dropdown will show you the last time that your machine performed a back up of your system. It will also allow you to make a current backup of your system at that moment. The other two options will allow you to select the Time Machine drive, or enter Time Machine it's self.

The first important checkbox to be checked in Time Machine settings is *Back Up Automatically*. Essentially when this box is checked, Time Machine will do everything for you. This screen will also allow you to select a specific drive on which to store your Time Machine backups. Show Time Machine in the menu bar will give you the small icon that we saw in the first photo. If this site box is not checked you will have to go fishing for the application in Launchpad or the applications folder in order to launch it.

In *Options*, you can choose which external drives back up and which ones do not. In my application, you can see that I have chosen not to make a backup of the backup drive for obvious reasons. You could also choose whether or not you want Time Machine to back up applications. The thought here is that if you have a small drive you can save space by not backing up things that you can simply re-download from the App Store. I suggest buying a backup drive that is large enough to back up your entire machine and simply back up everything.

Once you enter Time Machine that's where the real magic begins. You will see a window that takes you back to a virtual snapshot of your machine at any given point in time. There will be a timeline on the right where you can click on to go to any day in the past where a back up exists. Once you find the file that needs to be restored from the past, simply click on it and restore that file.

# 194

# Numbers

Numbers is Apple's spreadsheet application. It's a large one and it could literally use a book of its own, so this is simply an overview. It is the direct Mac alternative to Microsoft Excel.

Now it's no secret that the business world operates on Excel. It's by far the most popular spreadsheet and if you are a business professional on an Apple product you're probably using Excel along with the rest of the business world. However, if you are an occasional home user, you may have no interest in paying money to get on board with the world standard. Apple offers an excellent alternative that's built into every Mac operating system.

Don't get me wrong, Numbers is a powerful tool and can be used for business just like Excel. One of the powerful features of Numbers is its extensive template offerings. When you first launch Numbers you can quickly go to any of the tasks in the supplied templates to get up and running with the application with little to no knowledge of how to program it specifically. A background in Excel or basic spreadsheets is always a plus.

One of the hardest things that you're going to have to get used to if you've used Excel in the past is how Numbers autosaves. All of the saving and printing process is a little different and a lot more of an Apple mentality than Microsoft. If you've used both you will know what I mean. One of the big advantages of using Numbers over Excel is auto-saving to iCloud. Numbers works seamlessly with iCloud.

Need a template that is not found in the stock application? There's a website out there called iworkcommunity.com that has a large number of free templates that you can use with Numbers.

# 195
# Pages

Take everything I just told you about Numbers in the previous chapter and apply it to Pages. Pages is the apple alternative to Word. Apple will argue that fact and probably say that it is simply a word processor, and Word is simply another word processor. But the fact of the matter is the business world revolves around Word when it comes to word processing. Word is like Kleenex. It is a product that is so prevalent it has become synonymous with the type of application.

Probably the biggest disadvantage of using Apple's versions of Word and Excel are the compatibility issues with the rest of the world. The advantages however are great as well. Because both save to iCloud Drive, your documents are always available on all of your Apple devices. You can start typing a Page document on your Mac and finish it later on your iPhone or iPad. Because these documents are stored in iCloud you can even open them from a non-Apple product like a Chrome Book over the Internet.

Another reason you may choose Pages over Word on your Mac is compatibility within the Apple ecosystem. If you are already using Keynote and Numbers, it probably makes little sense to use Word over Pages. All of these applications will talk to each other seamlessly. You can still get information from one application to another if you're using Microsoft and Apple products together, but you will probably be doing so by importing, exporting, cutting, and pasting.

# 196

# Keynote

Keynote is the last piece of the iWorks puzzle, although Apple dropped the iWork moniker some years back. The three of them, Numbers, Pages, and Keynote make up the equivalent of Microsoft Office. The only disappointment in this is that Apple has no alternative for Publisher in its lineup. Those of us who are used to the Microsoft ecosystem and then switch over to Mac will miss this. Fortunately, there are some substitutions for Publisher which I will go over in other chapters.

Keynote of course is the Apple equivalent of Microsoft Powerpoint. Both are a drag and drop application for putting together presentations for school or business. Use Keynote anywhere you need to get a point across and you need a visual representation to do it. Board meetings, zoom meetings, the uses for Keynote are really endless and really up to your imagination. Think of Keynote as a slideshow on steroids. It's the perfect application to use if you need a slideshow and you want a little more information on all of the slides. You could use Keynote to assemble a slideshow for a memorial or wedding for example.

# 197

# Microsoft Office

In the world of Mac, you'll have two major choices when it comes to your day to day word processing and spreadsheet needs. Apple gives you Pages and Numbers (as well as Keynote) for free when you buy an Apple computer. The problem is that the computer world and business world in general use Microsoft Word and Excel. The good news is that Microsoft Office is available on the Mac. The bad news is that it is not free, and not complete.

Back in my PC days, my go-to graphics program was Microsoft Publisher. One of the disappointments that Mac users are faced with when they make the switch is that Microsoft has chosen not to make Publisher available to Mac users. There are however some workarounds for this.

First, you can always run Microsoft Publisher in Windows on your Mac by using Bootcamp or Parallels. This is not my method of choice for convenience reasons and I try to avoid running a Windows environment whenever possible.

The second workaround is to use a copy cat application. I use an application called Publisher Plus. While these applications may not have all of the bells and whistles of the Original Publisher, they just might be able to get the job done for you.

The third workaround is to use multiple applications geared for specific tasks. I have found that I can get 100% of the functionality that I once enjoyed with Publisher by using a combination of Publisher Plus and OmniGraffle.

The fourth workaround is to use an online Publisher style website. These sites offer subscription-based services to do what Publisher does, more or less, and the advantage to them is that because they are web-based, they don't care if you're on a Mac or a PC.

If you choose to use a Mac version of Office, compatibility and familiarity will be your two biggest pros. The biggest con will be the continual annoyance of Microsoft's constant updates. Because of those relentless updates, you will be reminded almost daily why you switched from PC to Mac to begin with.

# 198
# LibreOffice

Now we're going to look at another alternative to Microsoft Office. LibreOffice is an open-source project that has been around for a while under the name OpenOffice. Recently it has made the change to its new title and it has become a contender for those who do not want to spend the money on Microsoft.

LibreOffice differs from Microsoft Office and Mac's version of the Office products by combining all of its modules into one application. It features *Writer*, a word processor, *Calc*, a spreadsheet, *Impress*, a presentation package, *Draw* for diagrams and graphics, *Base*, for database management, *Math*, for formula editing and *Charts*, for you guessed it, making charts. All of these modules are accessible by simply installing the master LibreOffice application.

One of the big pluses here is that you do get a graphics program with LibreOffice. The biggest pro for LibreOffice is the fact that it is free. It is an open-source application meaning that it is built by hundreds of people around the world collaborating to make the project. This also means that it is continually updated and continually gets better as time goes on.

Whether or not LibreOffice will work for you is a matter you will have to decide for yourself, but the download is free and there's no risk in trying it out. If just one of these modules becomes a go-to tool for you, then it is well worth installing on your Mac. I have LibreOffice on my Mac as well as the Mac version of Office and Microsoft's version as well. I will use different modules and applications for different things. They can all coexist on your machine and many of them will be able to open each other's files. You can download LibreOffice by going to libreoffice.org.

# 199

# Dictionary

Every Mac computer comes with a built-in Dictionary app. The app can be accessed as a standalone application by going to Launchpad and launching Dictionary. It's also available in many other apps working behind the scenes as a utility. The app that I am using to write this book uses Dictionary as one of its options for checking spelling.

Once you launch the application you have the choice to find a word in the Oxford dictionary or thesaurus or use Apple's built-in dictionary, or Wikipedia online. Find a word by using the search bar in the upper right-hand corner of the window.

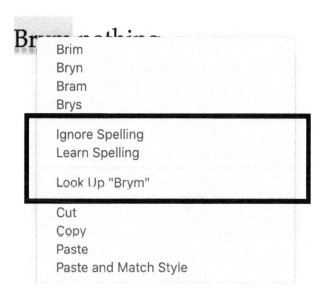

If you commonly use a word that is not referenced in the built-in dictionary you can add it in most applications. In the photo above we are highlighted on the word Brym. This particular application is giving us the option to learn the spelling. It will be added to the dictionary and will not show up as a misspelled word the next time I use it. By the way, to the best of my knowledge, Brym is not a real word.

# 200

# Templates

Templates come in handy for any file that you use with repetition. I'm going to show you a quick and easy way to turn almost any file on your Mac into a template. You can think about your daily workflow and think about files that you duplicate often, but for our example, we are going to make a basic return address template.

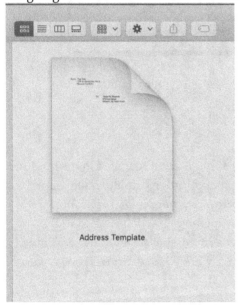

Address Template

In our example, we have created a word document with basic to and from information on it. In the past, you've probably made a file like this and duplicated it every time you want to make another address label. That's simply a step that is not needed.

The first thing we're going to do is create our original file. Save your file under a name that will be obvious to you in the future. In our example, we are saving it as Address Template.

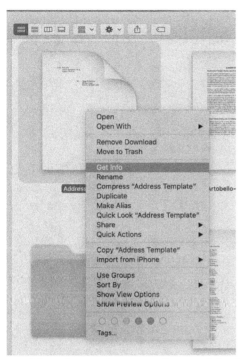

Now that we've created our original file we are going to turn it into a template. Right-click the file and go to *get info*. This will open up the info box.

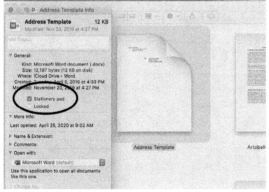

In the info box you will see a box to check for *Stationary pad*. Check the box and this file is now a template. Now in the future, all you have to do to make a label is to double-click the address template and it will automatically make a copy of itself labeled whatever the name of the file is followed by *copy*. You can go in and change that name to anything that you want it to be. The original template will remain unchanged as is. And it will be ready to go the next time you want to make another file.

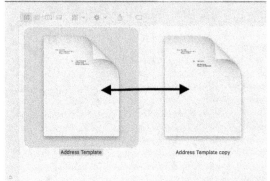

# 201

# Mapquest?

Maps is an underrated tool on the Mac, primarily because of the iPhone. We've become so accustomed to simply asking our phones to navigate to a destination that we don't think about the Maps app on the Mac, but paired with your phone, maps becomes a very powerful tool.

If you're accustomed to using online map websites like Mapquest, Maps has much of the same built-in functionality, but without the ads. When you launch Maps, click on the Directions tab in the upper left corner to get start and end directions. It will also show you a list of locations that you've been recently for easy navigation.

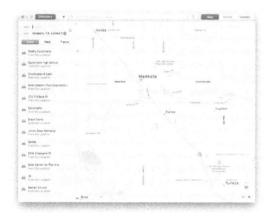

Maps will allow you to drop pins in locations to save them, change your look from a 2D to a 3D look, and give you information about the things around you by resting your tooltip on them. Explore the app, it can be incredibly useful especially when you're traveling.

# 202

# Inside Maps

When you leave your house, Maps is a great application for navigating the world outside. What you may not know is that Maps is also a great app for navigating your world *inside*. In this example, I have navigated to a local mall in the Maps application.

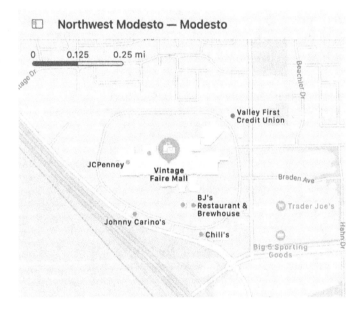

Pinching my trackpad I can zoom in to the mall all the way down to the actual room level.

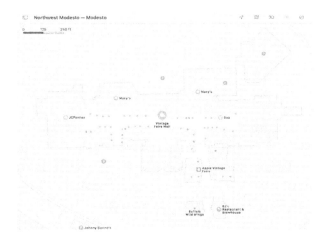

In the above picture I have it zoomed in to the point where I can see the layout of all of the stores. In the picture below I zoomed in even more to be able to see their names. I can now navigate the mall with maps just by moving around with my trackpad.

# 203
# Directions

A cool trick that Maps can do on a Mac is to send directions to your iPhone. Let's take the example of walking to work. Open Maps and if your starting at home, use your current location as the starting point in the directions tab. If you have your workplace listing in contacts, simply type work in the destination.

Click Walk and maps will calculate your best path. It will even show you the temperature and air quality on your walk if you have those options ticked in the show tab. Open maps on your iPhone. Now go to the share button and send the map to your phone.

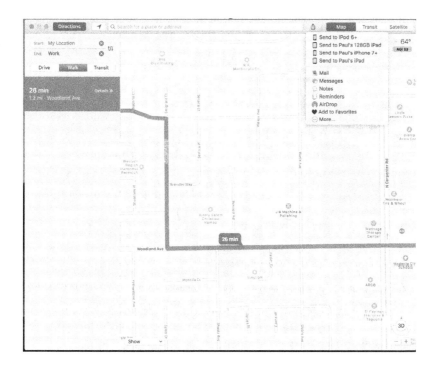

The current map with turn by turn instructions will be uploaded to your phone.

# 204

# The Music App

When Apple announced that they were doing away with iTunes as of the release of Catalina, you would have thought that they had set everyone's hair on fire by reading the backlash on various sites. Oh no! You can't get rid of my iTunes! What will happen to all of my music?

All of the worry and concern was, of course, was mostly unwarranted. The Music app is essentially iTunes lite. Your entire music library came over to Apple Music and is still available exactly the way it was, allowing you to sort by artist album or song. In many ways iTunes didn't go away, all of the clutter did.

The music app of course is geared largely towards Apple's music service. This is the moneymaking machine of the app. However, if you are a person who enjoys ripping their music from CDs or downloading your music from other sources on the web, the Music app will handle all of your music just like it did in iTunes.

If you find that the new Music app is sluggish or problematic with your old iTunes library you may want to rebuild it from scratch in Music. I had an extensive music library that came over from iTunes on two different machines. Both machines suffered from things getting mixed up and album art going away. On both machines, I rebuilt the music library in Music itself and have not experienced any problems from then on. If you use Apple Music service exclusively you will likely not encounter any such problems. If you are a person who installs their music from CD or MP3 file there may be issues that do not translate from one app to another and in this case, it's best to just create a music library native in the new app itself.

# 205
# Apple Music Media

If you're familiar with iTunes, you'll pick up with Apple Music without missing a beat.  If you've installed Catalina on a Mohave machine, you'll notice in preferences that your iTunes library is in fact, still your iTunes library.  If you go check out where your music files are stored, you'll find them in the same location, under the iTunes library name.  However, when you purchase a brand new Mac without a previous library, you'll notice that your music library file is now called *Media*.  The thought here is that eventually, the world will slowly move away from all things iTunes in regards to music, but it's going to take some time.  The term iTunes is not going to go away any time soon.  The music store is still called the iTunes Store for example.  In the future will we have the Music Store?  Time will tell how all of this will sort out, but for the time being, the transition will feel just a little bit clunky.

One of the big picture advantages of this change is that now every part of the old iTunes app will have a team designing and improving it specifically.  Over the next few years, we should see improvements and advancements in all of these apps without some being neglected over others.  The other big advantage will be in the simplicity of the new apps, leading to a better user experience with all of them.

For me, the most notable change in this new system is in how music is synced to your phone.  Apple has moved the syncing out of the individual apps and into Finder on the Mac.  This is so you can sync your phone once for all of your media, instead of having to sync it three or four times in all the different apps to get all of the different content.

# 206

# Remove Apple Music

Apple Music is a great service. You pay a subscription fee and you have access to an enormous music library as long as you continue to pay monthly for the service. But what if you could care less about Apple Music? There are many of us who only care about our own personal music library, and will likely never subscribe to the service. Wouldn't it be helpful if we didn't have to see the Apple Music section every time we fired up the Music app? If you find yourself in this camp, this is how to disable it, and never fear, if you change your mind down the road it's just as easy to put back.

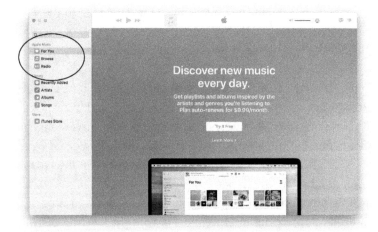

Launch the Music app. You should see the Apple Music section taking up a lot of sidebar real estate in the left pane. Now go up and click Music on the top menu bar and select Settings. Now uncheck show Apple Music.

# 207

# Music Equalizer

Here's a Music app feature that most users don't even know exists. Did you know that Music features a complete multi-frequency EQ tone control system? A system that's even programmable to your individual albums. Here's how to find it. While playing an album back, go up to *Window* on the menu bar. Click it and select Equalizer. You will be presented with a ten band graphic equalizer. Check to on box and move some sliders. Voilà! You're a sound engineer! Note that the EQ is in its own window, meaning that you can move it anywhere on the screen, or minimize it to move it out of the way.

You're not a sound engineer and you have no idea how to use a 10 band EQ? Not a problem. When you open up the preset dialog box you'll find a vast number of pre-made presets with common EQ curves to choose from. Find the one that makes your source sound best to your ears. You can still manually tweak these presets to get your tracks to sound just right.

Have a few favorite albums that you play all the time? You can save your custom made presets and give then each a custom name, like the name of the album for example. You can also rename the existing presets.

Another way to use this EQ is to attach it to the tracks of an album. You can do this by first going to an album. Then select all of its track by clicking on the first song, then shift-clicking on the last. Control-click on the highlighted list and click Get Info. Edit items and go to the options tab. Here you'll find the ability to attach an EQ curve to the songs so that it alters the tone every time you play them back.

# 208

# The Music Library

Your music on your Mac is stored in your Music library. This folder is on your Macs hard drive by default, but it can also be located on an external hard drive if you have purchased a computer with too small of a hard drive to accommodate a large library. Your Music library can also be reached over a network in case you wish to play media in another room, on another device. To find out where your current library is located, open Music and from the top menu bar click on *Music* and open *Preferences*. If you click on *Files* you will find the location of your Music Media folder. This is also where you would go on a new machine to set up a location rather than letting your computer pick a default one.

Knowing the location of your library is important for several reasons. First, if you're choosing to store your library on an external drive, make sure that that drive is configured for backup when time machine backs up your computer. It's also a good idea to manually copy your library to another drive simply as a hard manual backup if you should ever need it. I go one step further by keeping a copy of every album in my library on a separate thumb drive. This gives me the ability to share an album with someone or copy selected albums to another computer. I then take it even one step further by keeping a copy of the thumb drive on a second identical thumb drive. If all of this paranoia seems like it's coming from a person that has lost an old previous iTunes library on a PC, you'd be right. If PCs teach us anything, it's how to keep things backed up.

# 209
# Music Visualizer

This fun little feature has nothing to do with how your music sounds, but in how your music looks.  As the name implies, the visualizer creates a visual representation of the music you're listening too.  Think of it as an interactive screensaver on your computer.

While playing anything in Music, go up to *Window* on the menu bar and select *visualizer*.

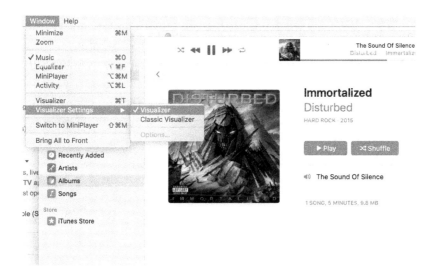

Here you will have two types of visualizes to choose from.  The classic version, and the latest version.  Experiment with both to see which one you like the best for whatever you're listening to at the time.  Once one is checked, select Visualizer to turn it on.  To exit the visualizer click escape.

# 210

# Music MiniPlayer

Now and then while working on your computer it's nice to have a little music running in the background. The Music app gives you a way to still have basic control over what's playing without taking a lot of your desk space away with the Music app. This feature is called the MiniPlayer.

The MiniPlayer interface is toggled on and off in Music by going up to the *Window* option on the menu bar. Click it and choose *Switch to MiniPlayer*. You can switch back to the full Music interface at any time by going back to *Window* and choosing *Switch from MiniPlayer*.

The MiniPlayer window can move anywhere on the screen. In its minimal state it will show you only the album art, but hoover your tooltip over the art and you'll get basic controls. Click on the list icon in the lower-right of the window and you'll expand the window to include information like the song list and upcoming tracks.

The MiniPlayer continues to work with the Apple keyboard just like when the full app is in use. You can still pause, play, skip songs, and adjust volume from the keys just as before.

# 211
# Quick Listen

This handy yet relatively unknown feature is great for people who are using their Macs for music production. Those that do this it's not uncommon to end up with folders on your computer that have a lot of generic tracks with labels like track one, track two, or track three. If you're just glancing at these tracks you'll have no idea what they are unless you actually listen to them. Quick listen allows you to preview any audio track on your Mac without launching the Music app.

Sometimes you may have several audio files on your desktop or in your downloads folder and you simply want to know what a track sounds like. This is especially true if you come across a track that has an obscure name. It's also helpful if you've downloaded a number of albums in your downloads folder and you want to go through and quickly give a listen to some tracks to find one in particular or discover whether or not you like a particular album.

To quick listen to any audio file click the file and then hold your finger on the space bar. As long as you hold your finger on the bar you will get a preview play of the track that's highlighted. When you take your finger off the bar, the track will no longer play.

# 212

# Music Artwork

If you purchase your music through the iTunes Store, you'll automatically get your album artwork with your ordered album. If you rip an album from a CD, Music will search its database and download the artwork for you. But what happens when you rip a CD or put an album into Music from another way and Music does not display the artwork? What if for instance, you have an album in MP3 format on a thumb drive that you're transferring to Music? Fortunately, with a little effort on your part, you can fill in those places in your Music library where a generic blank icon is being displayed instead of artwork.

First, go to Google and search for the artist followed by the name of the album. Next click on *images* to switch the search to an image search. Now, look through the album cover images. You're looking for a cover that is at least 500 pixels by 500 pixels. When you find your desired artwork, click on the image to get the full version of it. Control-click the artwork and select save as. You can now save it to your desktop.

In Music, click the album that you need the artwork for. You will now be able to single-click the first track and shift-click the last track. All tracks in the album will now be selected. You can now control-click any track and choose *Get Info*. It will ask you if you're sure that you want to edit items. Click *edit items*. You will now be able to go to the artwork tab and add artwork. Search for the artwork on your desktop and add the artwork. It will take iTunes a few seconds to populate every song in the album with the new artwork graphics.

A faster method, though it be a little more obscure, is to hover your tooltip on the blank generic album cover icon. A more icon will materialize in the lower-right-hand corner that's the round circle with the three dots in it. You can get to *more information* from that location as well. A third and I believe the fastest way to do it is to simply drag the artwork from your desktop onto the blank icon. This should populate all of the songs on that album.

# 213

# Wallpaper

Mac gives you a few options when it comes to wallpaper. First, you could choose one of Apple's stock static wallpapers. With each new incarnation of Mac OS, we get some added fresh stock photos to use, and they're usually themed to the operating systems name.

The second choice is to use Apple's dynamic wallpaper. This is a static image that changes with the time of day. If it's morning, your wallpaper will look like morning in the location you've chosen and as the day becomes night, so does the wallpaper.

The third choice is to use your own photos. This is my personal favorite as it allows you to customize the look of your machine. On my machines, I have a constant rotation of all of these photos set to change every half hour. Because I don't care for all of Apple's stock wallpapers, I've created a folder in documents folder to store my wallpapers.

# 214

# Custom Wallpaper

If you choose to use your own photos or ones found on the web, here are a few tips and tricks that will make the process easier and assure good results. Mac screens are very high resolution. If you have a new Mac with a 5K Retina display, you have one of the highest quality screens that you can buy for a computer. Not just a Mac, but any computer. These displays look awesome, but if you use a small resolution photo as a wallpaper, it's not going to look great. Fortunately, you don't have to pay exact attention to your screens exact pixel dimensions as Macs will size just about any photo to look great on your screen. What you do need to do is find the highest resolution wallpapers that you can find in order to take advantage of that great looking monitor!

An easy way to do this on the web is to search for HD wallpapers. There are numerous sites out there that cater specifically to free downloadable wallpapers. Every six months or so I will go out on the web to see what's new. New wallpapers are uploaded daily to the web, so it's an ever-changing landscape out there.

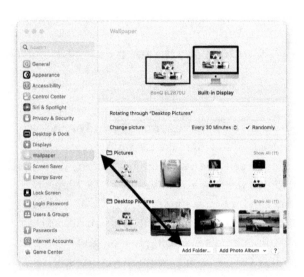

This next trick is simple, but it will make it much easier to get your own and your downloaded wallpapers onto your machine and keep them organized. I will create a folder in Documents called Wallpaper. Now anytime I see a photo I like on the web I will save it to this folder. In System Settings, I add this folder as a picture location by clicking the Add Folder button in Wallpaper. You only have to do this once. Now the Mac will use my own photo collection.

# Signatures

Mac makes it easy to place your actual signature on any electronic or scanned document. Just open anything in preview and click on the signature button.

The dropdown will show you any signatures that you currently have stored on your machine, and it will give you the option to create one. If you have multiple people using a home machine such as a husband and wife, you can create and store multiple signatures here.

When you choose to create a signature, you have the option of importing one from a picture or creating one by signing your trackpad with your finger.

Your signature is now stored on your machine and you can electronically sign any document simply by opening it up in preview and choosing the signature button. Signatures show up as a graphic that can be moved to any location on the document and can be resized by using the four round handles around the signature.

# 216
# Mail

There's a few options out there for sending and receiving email on a Mac, but the actual mail app that's built in to the operating system is still likely the best choice for most users. My wife is the CFO of our corporation and her mail app of choice is Thunderbird. I've learned enough about Thunderbird to know that it's a great alternative to Mail, but for my own use, I keep coming back to Mail on all of my machines for a number of reasons.

Mail gets updated in some way almost every time Apple publishes a major OS update, about twice a year. It's designed from the ground up to work hand in hand with the rest of the Mac's operating system with useful features that span across the rest of your daily workflow.

The Mail app actually pre-dates the iMac itself. Its roots can be traced all the way back to Steve Jobs and the NeXT computer. Its original name was, as you might guess, NeXTMail. It was developed as part of the NeXTSTEP operating system and it was acquired by apple in 1997.

Mail is relatively easy to configure and use and while Thunderbird users might point out that the rules function is not yet up to par in Mail, the integration with the rest of the Mac ecosystem is reason enough for me to keep using Mail as my main email app.

Mail allows the user to set up as many email accounts as you like and manage them all in one place. It allows you to set up multiple folders and subfolders which Mail calls *mailboxes*, so you can keep organized.

# 217
# Setup Email

Setting up email on your Mac is relatively easy however the process is slightly different for every type of email provider out there. Fortunately, your Mac will walk you through the process for your particular provider.

In Mail open up the Mail menu and you will see a tab for *accounts*. Clicking this will bring up the Internet accounts window. You will see a List of your accounts in the right pane and option to add an account. Click on your particular type of account and you will get a dialog box. Just start filling in the information. You'll need all of your account information before you start this. You get that information from your Internet or email provider. If you do not see your email provider in the drop-down list click *Other Account.*

Now fill in the initial information and click *sign in.* Once you do this it will open up a dialogue box for the remainder of the account's information. Once this process is complete, you will have your account added to the accounts in Mail. You can have multiple accounts set up in Mail so you can add a new account at any time.

# 218

# POP


When you set up your email on your first Mac, you will note that there are two major different types of email technologies that you must choose from when you set up an account. The first is pop, the second is IMAP. Pop is the more popular of the two and works a cross-platform whether you're on a PC or Mac. It has the advantage of being very stable and popular. It is also very easy to set up and maintain.

The easiest way to understand the differences between POP and IMAP is to note that IMAP gives you the ability to sync across all of your Apple devices, and pop treats each of your devices as an individual entity. When I got my first Mac I set it up as a POP email account because that's what I was used to. I understood how it worked and I understood what all the settings meant. In time I had a number of devices running email in the Apple ecosystem and they were all running under POP. Eventually, I understood the superiority of IMAP when it came to syncing my account crossed all of my devices and I switched all of my machines over to it.

My best advice with POP is to use it only if you have to. IMAP has so many advantages in the apple ecosystem that it is the clear choice for the Mac user.

# 219
# IMAP

As we said in the chapter prior IMAP is one of the two major technologies you can use when you set up an email account. IMAP up has an advantage over pop in the fact that it will sync across all of your Apple devices. This means if your iPhone is set up to IMAP and your MacBook is set up to IMAP you will see the same email file structure on both devices. If you delete an email on one, it will delete it on all. This may not be to your advantage if you in fact want to keep your laptop clean of one email account such as a work account for example, and you want to keep all of those emails on your work machine at another location.

So which Technology is the one to use? That answer depends on what you plan on doing with your email and how you use it. If you want multiple machines to function independently, you want to use a pop account. I will typically set up pop accounts when a person has many accounts that they are juggling. Work accounts, personal accounts, and perhaps other accounts associated with websites, etc. If the person is setting up a simple email account, and individual with a single email account, for example, I will usually set it up as IMAP.

# 220

# Switching From POP To IMAP

At the time that I made the switch to Mac, I had decades invested in the PC ecosystem. To say that I was entrenched would be an understatement. One of the areas that I was solidly invested in was PC email using the normal PC based POP system. It took eight years to fully make the change from POP over to IMAP on the Mac. Once I did, I wondered why I never took the time to make the switch.

We've previously gone over the differences between the two systems, so this chapter will simply be an instructional guide in how to make the switch. When I went from POP to IMAP I made the transition in one day. Now you may only have one computer to change over, but at the time I had to make the switch on three laptops, an iMac, an iPad, and an iPhone simultaneously.

All of my machines had different folders set up for sorting email and while 80% of the folders were basically the same, there were differences on all of the machines. The first thing I had to do was determine which machine was going to be the master template for all of them. I chose my oldest, an eight-year-old MacBook Pro. The next step was to go online to my webmail to look at the actual account. Because I had been using POP mail I found that the online account still had emails in it dating back six years! My first order of business was to delete anything from the account that wasn't current. I sorted by date and deleted everything that was prior to the current month. Next, I noticed that there were actually a few folders online that had been created years ago when I was setting up an old iPad. The emails contained in them dated back to 2014. Those had to go! After cleaning house, I was now ready to start switching over the machines.

I went to my oldest son, the eight-year-old MacBook Pro, and deleted my pop email account. To do this you click on Mail in the menu bar and select accounts. You can then click on the account that you want to delete and click Delete Account at the bottom to remove it.

After deleting all of your old POP accounts, you can put the new IMAP account(s) back in by clicking Add Account.

Now you can begin to create new folders in Mail in which to sort your mail, only now you'll only be creating those folders once, and all of your emails will be sorted, moved, or deleted only once on whatever machine you're on and it will be mirrored over all of your devices.

# 221

# Mailboxes

In order to stay organized in Mail, you're going to want to set up mailboxes. Think of mailboxes as a folder organizational structure for your email. In other words just like you would use folders to store files on your hard drive, you will use mailboxes to store emails in your Mail program. By grouping your emails that you are keeping in this fashion you will be able to go back and find a particular email that you're looking for.

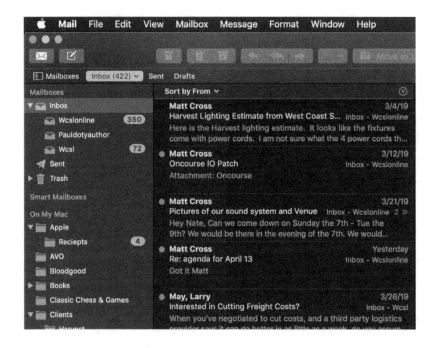

If you look at the example above you will notice that on my laptop I have three different email addresses coming in. Every time you create a new email address they will show up here automatically under your inbox. That's as automatic as mail gets. But if you notice below you will see a section called On My Mac and you will notice a list of folders and subfolders. You can now create as many folders and subfolders as you want to organize the emails that you want to keep.

Right-click on inbox and create a new mailbox for emails that you know that you will be keeping. You can then right-click on that mailbox and create subfolders. For example, you may have a mailbox called bills. In that mailbox, you may have other subfolders with the various utilities that you pay on a monthly basis. There is no limit to how many you can create. To save an email, drag the e-mail into the mailbox that you want it in.

# Unwanted Email Accounts

One of the distinctive that makes an Apple an Apple is your computer's ability to predict your needs. If you set up an IMAP email account on one machine, it will ask to populate the account on your other machines for example. Often Apple will take it upon itself to make some changes automatically. This is a great feature when Mac gets it right, you begin to feel like you have a servant who anticipates your every wish, but what happens when Mac gets it wrong? Unfortunately, this will occur from time to time, and it can be frustrating, but with a little attention, it can be set straight when it occurs.

Apple is famous for changing settings on your phone or computer after updates. From time to time you might find strange changes on your system like features switched off or on that where not previously. I recently did an update on my MacBook and noticed that when I went to Mail for the first time following an update, I now had a new email account amongst my numerous others. It was an unused Google account and Mail was showing a syncing error with it in the form of a little lightning bolt icon.

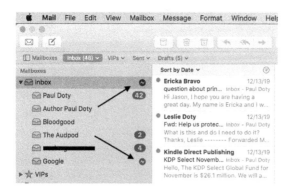

This was an unused Gmail account. It exists because I have a

Google account that I use for a shared calendar for my business. After the Apple update, Apple found the Calendar account and then anticipated that I would want the associated Gmail account added to my Mail app. Apple got it wrong. Fortunately, it's a Mac, and it's an easy fix.

The first step is to close the Mail app. Then go to System Settings and open Internet Accounts. There you will find your various accounts including the offending one. My first clue that something was amiss with the settings is that my Google Account said Mail, Calendars instead of just Calendars.

Click on the account and you'll see all other the options that are turned on for it, whether you turned them on, or Apple. In this case, the Mail checkbox became checked during the last update. Unchecking the Mail box restored normal operation to the Mail app.

Go through all of the switches and make sure only the features that you are using are switched on. In my case, Calendar should have been the only feature.

A great way to keep your inbox clean is to use rules. A rule will automatically deal with any email that you set up a rule for ahead of time. In my example below I will set up a rule in order to deal with a daily onslaught of failure notice emails from GoDaddy.

A few years ago I set up a new email domain for myself. I then had all of the emails sent to the old domain forwarded to the new one and an email was automatically sent to the sender to inform them of the new email change. The problem with that is that every time an email was automatically sent to a sender who was a *Do Not Reply* sender, a failure notice was generated by GoDaddy and sent to me. This meant that I was getting a few dozen failure notice emails a day. Here's how I unclogged my box with a rule.

With the first offending email highlighted, I navigate to Mail/ Settings/Rules. I then click *Add Rule*. Now I'm going to name my rule Failure Notice and tell the rule that if that term shows up in the subject, move it to the trash.

Once a rule is created it will ask you if you wish to run the rule on your entire inbox.  Click apply.  Not only has it rid your inbox of the offending emails, but it has set a rule for all future emails!  The rules list will only apply to the computer that you're on, so all of your computers can have different rules.  There are many more ways to configure rules.  Look through the various drop-downs and configure each rule to specifically meet your needs.

# 224

# Sharing Rules

IMAP is awesome for sharing your email across devices. You can share your email rules across devices as well!

Just go to System Settings on all of your shared machines and click on iCloud. Click on iCloud Drive/Options. Check the Mail box and your sharing!

# 225

# Scam Emails

Phishing and email scams are nothing new. At this point, most of us are not going to fall for the email from the Nigerian king who wants your bank routing number so he can share his wealth with you. Unfortunately, there's a new wave of very clever email scams out there that have been extremely lucrative. Both prey on their victim's fears of being caught viewing pornography.

The first wave of these emails came after the security breaches of 2016-2017. Because of two major breaches in major corporations, millions of email addresses and passwords were compromised and sold on the dark web. Hackers then bought the information and sent emails to the victims demanding ransom in bitcoin, claiming that they had hacked their victim's computers, and recorded them watching porn. They offered the victims password as proof that they had control of their system.

Of course, they had the passwords because they were purchased in the breach, and if you think about it logically, if the hacker actually had compromised a machine, would it have not been a more effective incentive to send the victim a 5-second snippet of the supposed video?

Your account was hacked! Renew the pswd immediately!

You do not know me me and you may be definitely surprised why you're receiving this letter, proper?
I'm ahacker who burstyour emailand OSnot so long ago.

Don't attempt to talk to me or alternatively try to find me, it is definitely not possible, because I directed you this message from YOUR own account that I've hacked.

I've installed malware soft on the adult vids (porn) website and suppose you have spent time on this site to have some fun (you know what I really mean).

While you were paying attention to vids, your browser began operating as a RDP (Remote Control) that have a keylogger that gave me access to your monitor and camera.

Then, my software programgatheredall information.

You have entered passcodes on the sites you visited, and I caught them.

Surely, you are able change each of them, or perhaps already modified them.

But it doesn't matter, my malware updates it every time.

And what did I do?

I generated a backup of every your device. Of all files and personal contacts.

I created a dual-screen movie. The 1st screen shows the clip that you were watching (you've the perfect taste, wow...), the second part shows the recording from your own webcam.

What should you do?

So, I believe, 1000 USD will be a inexpensive price for our small riddle. You will do the deposit by bitcoins (in case you don't understand this, try to find "how to purchase bitcoin" in Google).

My bitcoin wallet address:

In the second wave of these scams, the technology has become ever more sophisticated and convincing. In this version, the hackers are using a special piece of software that will create an email that mimics the victim's own email account. The victim receives an email sent from their own address. This supposedly proves that the hacker has control over the victim's digital world. The reality is that this type of email is easy to fake, and again, if the hacker actually had a video of the victim, they would be offering it as proof.

What does one do if you are receiving scam emails? First off, you're not alone. Almost all email accounts are going to be targets of these scams. If it's a generic one like the photo above, simply delete them. If it is a scam from a known business or corporation, most will have a special email address listed on their legitimate websites where you can send scam emails to in order to report them to the company.

# 226

# Email Signatures

Mail allows you to set up multiple signatures for use over multiple email accounts. A signature can be as simple as your name and email address, or as complicated as a paragraph long copyright disclaimer. It can be anything that you might want to routinely add to multiple emails in order to save time retyping the same information over and over again.

To add signatures, click on Mail on the menu bar and go to Preferences. Now click on signatures. Go to the account that you wish to add a signature too and click the + symbol. Give your signature a name in the left column and add the signature text in the right. If you have multiple accounts, you can add the same signatures to multiple accounts by copy and paste. Note: You'll have to restart Mail after putting in new signatures to get them to automatically show up. When you go to compose an email, you'll see a dropdown list of the available signatures for that account.

# 227

# Sign An Email Document

As a business owner, I am asked to sign documents that are sent to me in emails all the time. Sooner or later you will have something sent to you and an email and you will need to sign it and send it back. How do you do that when it is a PDF attachment?

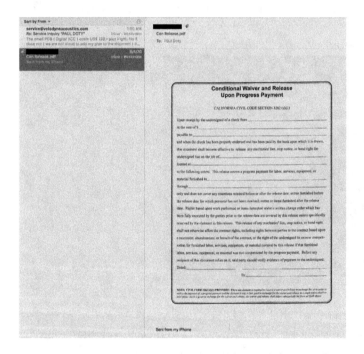

I will click the attachment in the email and it will open up in Preview. Once it is open export the file as a PDF to your desktop or location of your choice.

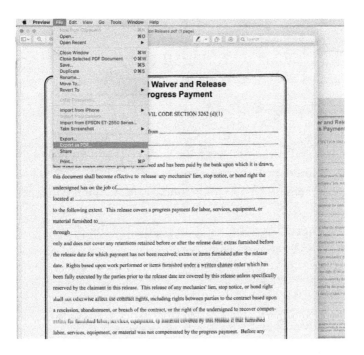

Once the document is opened in Preview you can then use the markup tools to add text to the document. There are icons for adding text and signatures to the PDF. After you have filled out your PDF it will be saved when you exit. You can now send the form back as a PDF and keep the original for your records.

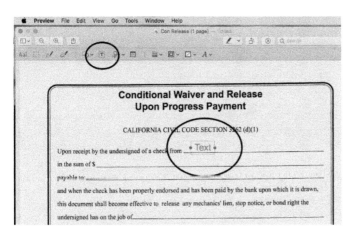

# Email Flags

Most people probably know how to create folders in the mail application and sort emails into them. But what if you have a folder that has different projects contained within it? What if you wanted to mark certain emails in that folder and associate them with specific projects? Apple Mail allows you to do simple email flagging. Let's say you have a specific project and you want all of the emails pertaining to that project to have a red flag.

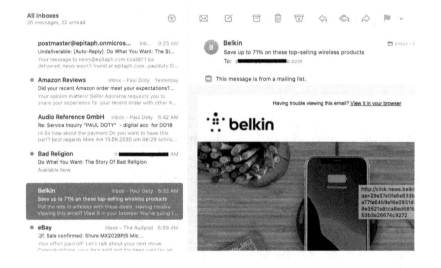

While the email is highlighted just go up to the flag icon and open the dropdown menu. You'll see seven different colors that you can use to differentiate your emails. Assign one color to a specific project. You can get rid of a flag simply by clicking it again while the email is highlighted.

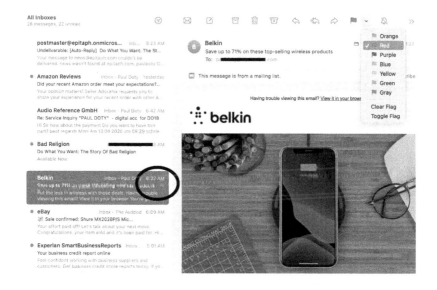

# 229

# Large Attachments

Depending on what email service you have 5 MB is really the largest file you're ever going to send over email. Until the release of Catalina, there was really only one good way of sending a larger attachment in an email and that was to put it in a Dropbox folder and create a link that could be sent to the recipient. Now, Apple will let you upload the large attachment to iCloud.

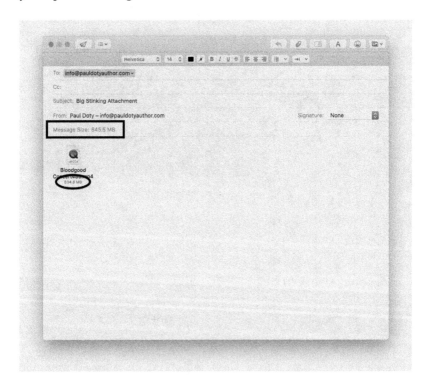

Here we can see a very large file trying to be sent by email. 845MB is far too large for any service to forward. Apple Mail will ask you if you would like to send the attachment using Mail Drop. Mail Drop will put this attachment in your iCloud Drive for 30 days. All the recipient has to do is retrieve the file on their end. The file will delete after 30 days.

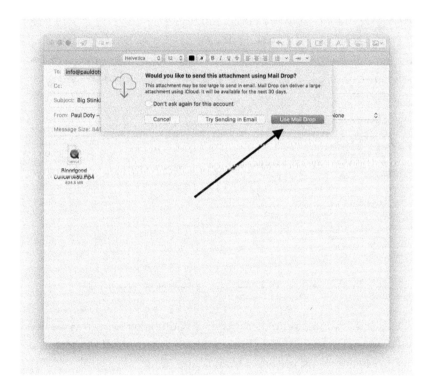

# 230

# Phishing

Phishing is the art of trolling for low hanging fruit.  It preys upon the computer semi-illiterate and the elderly, which makes it particularly diabolical in my book, literally.

This type of scammer will craft an email by stealing the identity of a known and trusted entity.  In our example below we see a scam email posting as JP Morgan and Chase Bank.  Two known and trusted financial entities.

The email is informing us that our account is on hold and we need to take action to reinstate it.  The email is clearly from JP Morgan and the reinstatement link is clearly from Chase Bank....or is it?

I'm about to show you a way to check the credentials of any email that you might get in order to see if it is fake.  If the forger is good, they can get around the way that I'm going to show you, so if a suspected email passes this test, but it still doesn't feel right, contact the company directly by known secure means.

The first thing we're going to examine is the true sender.  A forger with little HTML skill can craft an email with anyone's name as the sender.  Place your tooltip on the little down arrow to the right of the name and it will reveal the true source of the email.

In this example, we can see that the forger is using a German domain (.de) and it is clearly NOT JP Morgan. Next, we can rest our tooltip on the Chase Bank link to see where it is actually directing its victim too.

Again, we can clearly see that this is not a link to **chase.com** as the link impersonates. It's likely a virus loader or a fake webpage designed to gather the victim's credit and banking information.

# 231

# Split Screen

You have two ways to work in your environment in the Mail app. The first is the classic window method. In this method, Mail shows you your mailboxes down the left side, what's in your inboxes in the next column, and a preview pane on the right.

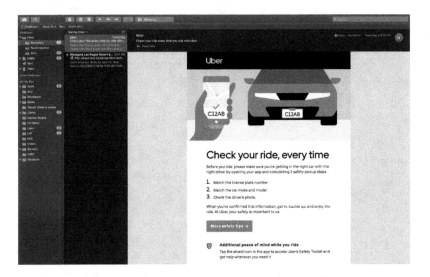

If you go to compose an email, you'll get the email in a floatable window. This classic view works well if you're working in a number of open windows that you want visible.

There is however another method of working in Mail called Split Window. This mode allows emails to be composed in a fourth pane to the right of the standard three. The advantage of this mode is that it will allow you to bounce information between multiple emails.

You might be previewing an email from one individual in the third
pane while composing an email in the fourth pane. You can then drag
attachments or text from one to the other. The panes are also
adjustable by dragging their edges. To enable this feature, open
Settings under Mail and select the General tab. Check the Prefer
opening all mailboxes in split view when in full-screen box. Close and
make sure you are in full-screen mode in Mail. Now when you
double-click an email, it will open in a fourth pane.

# 232

# Font Fix

If you're like me, you can't stand Mails default font size. It's way too small. If this is you, follow me to font salvation.

Go to mail and open Preferences. Under the Fonts & Colors tab click Select on Message font. Next select 18. There, fixed. You're welcome!

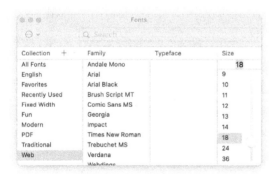

# 233

# Mailbox Fix

Every now and then a mailbox may become corrupt on a Mac. Mac computers are usually rock solid, but they are still computers, and as such problems may still arise. Recently, I was moving a large amount of folders from one email account into another in Mail. After a while, I began to have syncing issues between the various computers that were accessing those mailboxes. On my main computer, I could no longer delete certain emails and on the other computers those emails were not showing up at all. The mailbox had become corrupt.

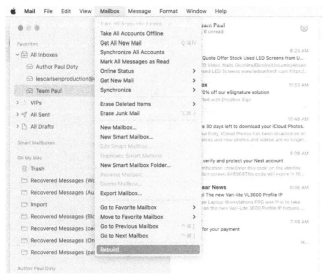

If you're a QuickBooks user you are already familiar with the concept of rebuilding a company file. Mac gives you the ability to rebuild a mailbox in Mail if one becomes corrupt. Highlight the mailbox that you're having issue with and go to Mailbox on the main menu. There you will find a button to Rebuild the mailbox. Give it some time and Mac will likely find the problem and fix it. After rebuilding, test the mailbox to see if functionality has been restored.

# 234

# Address Dropdown

In Mail, if you open up an email from someone, there is a very powerful yet simple thing that you can do with the sender's address. If you look at it in the upper left-hand corner of the email you will notice a dropdown menu. Click that dropdown menu and you will be presented with a number of options and some very important information.

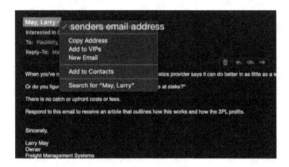

The first thing we will look at is the sender's email address itself. This is very important, especially if you receive an email that you think maybe a scam email. In this area at you will see the actual email address that the email originated from. If you get an email supposedly from your Internet provider wanting you to verify your login information for example, and you go to this address and find out that it's a stolen email address from a lawyer in New York, you can immediately recognize the email as a scam.

*Copy address* allows you to do exactly as it says. This is a fast way to copy an address and paste it into an email or another document.

A very useful tool here is *Add To Contacts*. Clicking this will immediately put a new contact into your contacts list with all of the information that your Mac currently has on it.

If you are being harassed by an email or you can also choose to block a contact from this dropdown as well.

# 235

# Unsubscribe

There's nothing that will make you feel more popular and more loved than hitting the fetch email button in Mail and receiving over one hundred unsolicited emails, right? Spam email, it's the bane of your computer. Who has time to sift through it all? Spam can be really annoying, and like death and taxes, it's a fact of life, but there are steps that you can take to help reduce the amount of it that you must deal with.

Simply deleting spam email is not the most effective way of dealing with it. If your messages are coming from a legitimate source such as a recognized food chain, or hardware store, or other business, then they will, by law, offer a method to unsubscribe in the email itself. This will usually show up as a small unassuming link at the bottom of the email. Remember, they have to provide this by law, not by choice, so they usually don't make it stand out as an option, but if you look closely, you'll find it.

After clicking on the link, you will usually be taken to a website to unsubscribe. Carefully read all of the instructions there to properly unsubscribe as some are tricky by design. Just pay attention.

Legitimate companies will have the unsubscribe option, but what if you're being spammed by companies or individuals who are not following the law? They can actually be reported to the government. If the appropriate government agency receives enough complaints, they will take action against the offender. When you receive this type of spam, forward the entire email to **spam@uce.gov**. If the offender spams you once a day, report it once a day. As the saying goes, the squeaky wheel gets the grease.

# 236

# iMessage

Built into every Mac is the ability to use iMessage. In a way, iMessage is like belonging to an exclusive club. It allows Apple device users to send information back and forth that would not be possible on a standard SMS (Short Message Service) device. Think of iMessage as texting on steroids. Of course, iMessage can receive a standard SMS text from an Android device, but its capabilities multiply when you're communicating with another Apple user.

iMessage shines bright when it comes to security. iMessage messages are encrypted with end to end encryption which virtually eliminates the possibility of an outside hacker intercepting your communication. Apple itself touts the fact that they cannot decipher your iMessage communications, so iMessage becomes the perfect method for getting a sensitive message to another individual, as long as that individual is another Apple user. Let's say that your spouse needs to know the password to your Netflix account. If you're in separate locations, there's a number of ways that you could communicate that information to each other. One would be in an email. If you're in a hotel and sent the information in an email, you'd be trusting that that information would not be visible on the hotel's network, or intercepted anywhere on the web, and you'd be trusting not only your own email provider but the hotel's unknown internet provider as well. That's a lot of trust.

iMessage on the other hand sends your message point to point with end to end encryption. Apple then stakes its reputation on the fact that even they cannot intercept or decode it. How do you know that they're telling you the truth? Well, if you think about it realistically, Apple's reputation is worth far more than your Netflix passcode, so you can be pretty confident that you're safe. Just remember that anyone with access to your unlocked iPhone physically, could still pick up your phone and simply read a text.

# 237

# Configuring iMessage

Set up your iMessage account by launching iMessage and go to Settings by clicking on iMessage from the menu bar. You'll need to have your iCloud account set up before this.

The first option to configure is the ability to share your name and photo with others. The next is how long messages and data are stored in iMessages. This option can be set to delete information in a month, a year, or can be set to keep them forever. From this page, you can adjust the text size of your messages.

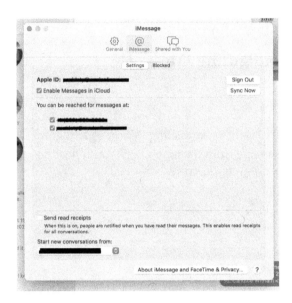

In the second window, you can configure the phone numbers and email addresses associated with your account. Using both email and cell numbers will greatly improve the usability of iMessage. Enabling iMessage in iCloud here will also allow you to share iMessage across multiple devices. This may not be desired if you only own one Apple product, but it adds so much more functionality to iMessage if you have multiple devices.

# 238

# Managing Messages

How long do you think Messages has been around?  You might say well we've had Messages for a long time on the Mac and you'd be wrong.  What you've had for a long time on the Mac is an application called iMessage.  Messages is actually an application that was developed for the iPhone and the iPad and it came over to the Mac during the Big Sur era replacing the old iMessages app.

With Messages came a lot of functionality that you previously did not have on the Mac.  For example, if you control-click on an individual in your Messages list you'll see a number of things that you can do with that message.

Have you ever had a conversation with someone in Messages only to go back a few days later to retrieve some important information and have a hard time finding the original thread?  I don't know about you but it happens to me all the time.  Messages gives you the ability to actually pin a thread to the top of your page whenever you open up messages.  Now your important contacts and message threads will be at the very top and you'll be able to go back to them instantly instead of having to scroll through to find an old one.

You can also open up different threads in different windows.  This comes in real handy if you're talking to two different people about the same topic.  You can have both of them open at the same time and communicate with both of them simultaneously without having to switch back-and-forth.  Windows on a Mac, what a concept.

Other fun features are available here.  You can hide alerts altogether from someone who is possibly annoying you or delete a conversation  This is particularly handy when dealing with those pesky spam messages.

# 239

# Searching In Messages

Have you ever needed to locate some information that somebody sent you months ago in Messages? It's always a fairly important piece of information and you have to dig back by scrolling back and back and back and back and if you're lucky, you might find it. This problem was all too common in the old iMessages app but it has been addressed in a big way in the new Messages app in Big Sur.

By default, Messages will open up in a very compact view. Just the icons down the left and messages on the right. If you rest your tooltip on the line between your contacts and the message body a new tooltip will appear allowing you to drag the pane to the right to expand it.

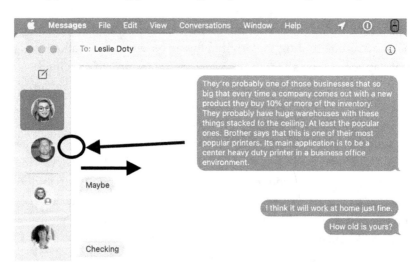

Once this area expands you will now have a search feature that you can use to find a previous message, even if it's months old.

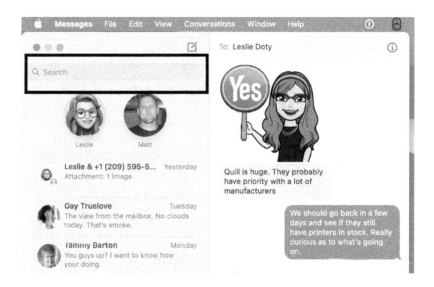

In this example, I am using a photograph that my wife sent me while she was waiting in line at Winco during the great pandemic of 2020. I chose this photograph as the demo because it was months old. Two months to be specific. All I needed to do to locate it was to go into the search bar and type the word Winco.

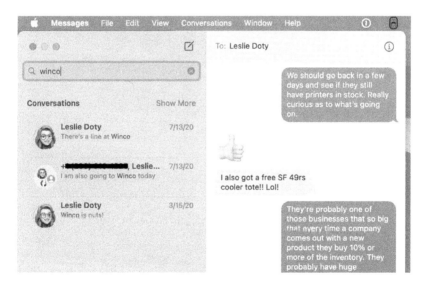

Winco was found three times in various threads on my machine. One instance went all the way back to March, seven months earlier. Highlighting each of these would show me the thread that I was looking for. And there's the picture! If this had been a critical piece of information, I would've just saved a lot of time and frustration.

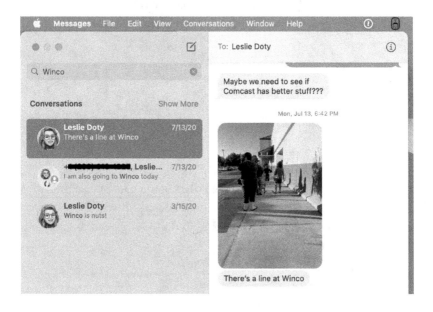

# 240

# Text Inserts

I remember when the new animated Memoji came to the new iPhones for the first time. Apple created a lot of jealousy because you couldn't use one of these new features unless you went out and bought a brand new iPhone. Even though it was a telephone it was light-years beyond your Mac computer as far as what it could do when texting. What's wrong with that picture?

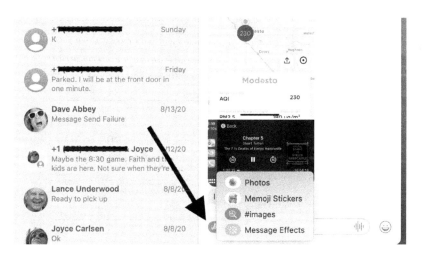

The iPhone was a much bigger revenue stream at the time then the iMac. It was the star product that got the shiny new chips first that allow them to do all of these fun things. In time these applications have trickled down to the Mac.

For the most part, you have Catalyst to thank for that. Catalyst is an application that allows developers to bring iOS applications to the Mac. This means that an application that is developed specifically for the iPhone or iPad will be able to be adapted for use on the Mac. Messages is a prime example of this new technology.

Now in Messages you can insert all of the cool effects that you can do on your phone when it comes to sending a message. Just open up the little icon in the left of the text space and you will be able to insert photos, emojis, animated GIFs, or use special effects in your texts.

If you've already set up memojis on your phone everything will transfer over to your Mac via iCloud. You will not have to program things twice. You can also go in and alter your Memoji on your Mac which is a much bigger screen than on your phone.

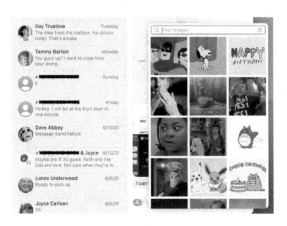

Animated gifs are now easy to use in Messages on the Mac. No more installing third-party applications, although you still can.

# 241

# Data Over iMessage

iMessage works great on your Mac for sending text messages to other computers and phones, but if you're sending to another Apple computer or iPhone, iMessage really begins to come alive. If you text a non-Apple device from your Mac, you'll be limited to standard SMS text, but if your recipient is another Mac, a wealth of options becomes available to you.

iMessage users can send just about any type of data between devices, not simply text characters. If you're texting an Android device that uses MMS, you'll be able to send basic photos to the device, but that's about the end of the road. If you're Apple to Apple, the world of data now opens up to you, limited mostly by the size of your data plan itself. iMessage users can send texts, photos, links to websites, location and map information, and even files across the system.

iMessage also has the ability to share this data between all of your own devices if iCloud is enabled on your Mac. I'll point out where to do this in the next lesson, but when iCloud is enabled, you will be able to send data to an individual on one device such as your Mac and be able to go home, pick up your iPad, and see the same data that you sent from your work Mac. You can then continue the same conversation on the second device and it will appear like you've been on the same device all along on your recipient's end. Just make sure that iCloud is enabled on iMessage on all of your devices.

Remember that you're limited to data transfers with other Apple device users. If you try to send data to a non-user, your data will not be sent, or you'll be limited to text.

As of Ventura, Apple also now gives you the ability to edit a text after sending it. You can even delete a text if the recipient hasn't seen it. This ability goes away after a short amount of time so you have to catch it pretty quick, but it can be a lifesaver.

# 242

# Apple TV

When I was growing up if you wanted to watch TV you would turn on a box in the living room that had three channels on it. The display was black and white and everyone pretty much memorized everything that was on every channel. Today you watch TV by turning on your TV on your Apple TV on which you watch your Apple TV app which will allow you to watch Apple TV+. Did you get that? That wasn't very confusing, was it?

This could easily be a chapter on exploring all of the various reasons why apple would name so many products *Apple TV*, but instead, we will be focusing on the Apple TV app on your Mac. If you are a cord-cutter you already know the joys of having to log in and out of multiple services in order to watch Hulu, Netflix, Amazon Prime, and a host of others. The TV app is Apple's attempt to group all of your services into one application.

I have to admit, for me, I'm not yet a fan. At this time this application is in its infancy. Its attempt to declutter the streaming world has only managed to make it worse by cluttering all of the services into a single pile on your living room floor. The app is clunky and you never know what programs are free, which ones you already subscribe to, or which ones you have to purchase to watch until you've clicked through a few screens, wasting a good amount of your time in the process.

I applaud Apple's attempt to list out available channels like an old-style TV, but there needs to be a way in future versions of the app to customize these icons, otherwise you're just back to surfing channels that you may not get in the first place.

In the Settings window, several adjustments can be made to the quality of the available stream. Older Macs may not be able to play a stream at as high of quality as a newer Mac, so Apple gives you the ability to adjust quality here.

The application also has some good controls for families and parents who might want to set limits on ratings, etc.

The bottom line for Apple TV is that it is a new product. Future versions should not be judged on initial rollouts. For the time being, this app is not the end-all to TV clutter, but an addition to it. What it is, is a first attempt to build a product that has the potential for a bright future. Time will tell.

# 243

# Share With Apple TV

Over the years I've had four Apple TVs. I used the first incarnation of the device as a small media server in my living room to hold music for playback through my stereo, a sort of iPod for my home theater. As years went by, I eventually ended up with a 4$^{th}$ generation Apple TV in my bedroom as a streaming box, and a full-blown media server computer hooked up to my home theater in the living room. With this setup, I have the best of both worlds, because I can share my media server's Music library over my home network to my bedroom via sharing on the Apple TV. In other words, if you have an iMac on your network, you can share its Music library throughout your house, as long as you have Apple TVs hooked up to whatever system you wish to have content playback on.

To do this, make sure all of your devices are first on the same network and all are running the latest update of their respective OS. Then make sure you're signed in to both devices with the same Apple ID. Now open Music on your Mac and turn on Home Sharing by going to File/Home Sharing/Turn on Home Sharing. On your Apple TV, you will need to turn on Home Sharing as well by going to Settings/Accounts/Home Sharing.

Here's where some people get hung up. If your music is on your Apple TV, then you would go to the Music app on the Apple TV to find it, but in this scenario, your music or content is NOT on the Apple TV, but on a remote computer, so go to Computers instead and choose the library located on the remote machine. Once set up, you'll be able to enjoy your library throughout your house!

# 244
# Apple TV+

In 2019 Apple continued its effort to become a major player in the TV broadcasting game by taking a giant leap forward with the introduction of its own streaming service Apple TV+. Apple has a history of other products that have come in late to the game and have either become great hits like the Apple Watch or the iPhone or misses like the Newton PDA or the HomePod speaker. In the future, the failure or success of Apple TV+ will be judged on its content, not on it as an original idea.

At launch, Apple had very few programs compared to other services like Netflix. It takes a good amount of time and money to build that kind of original catalog especially if it's going to be one of quality. Because of this, knowing that their debut would be thin, Apple has basically given away the service for free to most customers in the first year in order to get people hooked on the available releases, and to get the app running on as many Macs as possible.

I suspect that Apple TV+ will eventually fall into the hit category for Apple. What will be required for that to happen is time. Time to develop the content and work all of the bugs out of the hardware and software.

**Update 2022.** As expected, Apple TV+ has become a player with many new noteworthy shows. Content like ted Lasso and For All man Kind have become quality staples, helping to establish the service as a contender. Apple shows no signs of slowing down and at just $7 a month, the service is priced right.

# 245
# Photos

Photos is Apple's application for managing your photo collection on your Mac. This application can be used in two ways, and we will look at both of those ways in this lesson.

The first way is to allow photos to completely manage all of your photo collection. The application works wonderfully if you are a person who does not take many photographs in a given year. The reason I say this is because in order for the photos ecosystem to work, you need to be using iCloud Drive to store your photos so they are available on all of your devices all of the time. If you are a photographer who takes only a few photographs this is great because you're not using a ton of space for storing photographs.

However if you are a heavy photographer you will find that this proposition will get very expensive, very fast. Photos are not small files and they take up a lot of room on whatever storage medium you decide to store them on. So if you are using photos to manage your collection, you are going to be storing all of your photos locally on your Mac and maintaining a photostream in the cloud. This is going to come at a premium. You will be spending money every month on a lot of iCloud storage space and you will have to own a Mac with a very large hard drive. Apple is well aware of this and they are happy to sell you that space, both on your new Mac and monthly in iCloud. Apple also knows that most people are generally unknowledgeable and lazy when it comes to managing their photo collection. Photos is an answer to this dilemma for the user and a great revenue stream for Apple.

The second way to use the application (and it's the way that I use the application) is to use it solely for projects and manage all of your photographs separately on a separate hard drive manually. The photos app will give you opportunities to make slideshows and do other things like creating books, calendars, and cards. For me, the best of both worlds is to manage my photo collection manually and use the best features of the photos application for working with my pictures.

# 246

# Retouch

I love photo editors like Photoshop and Pixelmator Pro. They give you the ability to retouch photos and make good photos great. But what if you're trying to get the job done on the cheap? The Photos app that comes standard on a Mac actually gives you much of the functionality of these higher-priced apps, and it's built into the system. Take retouching and scratch removal for example.

Here I have a photograph from the 1800s with a fair amount of scratches and imperfections.

To clean it up, simply open the photo in Photos, choose to edit it, and open the retouch tool. The tool will allow you to set a size for the edited area. Next pick a large area in the photo with a good background. Option-click this area to set it as the source for your photo retouch. Now click and drag over the areas that you wish to retouch.

Your retouched photo can now be exported back into your picture storage location, or you can continue to edit and enhance.

# 247

# Vignette

Built into your Mac is an easy way to add a vignette to any photo. To accomplish this, launch Photos and drop the photo, or a copy of it, into the app. Go to edit and choose Vignette.

You'll get a wide range of variables that will produce vignettes from subtle to pronounced. Play with the three elements until you've achieved the effect you're looking for.

Your vignette photo can now be exported.

# 248

# Slide Shows

There's a couple of ways to do slideshows on a Mac. Within the operating system itself, you can do a quick down and dirty slideshow by highlighting several photos within a folder and then hit the option key at the same time you hit the spacebar. This will start a basic slideshow of the selected photos. I call it down and dirty because you will have no options for speed or transitions. It will simply do a slideshow that will run automatically or you can hit the pause and advance one slide at a time.

If you need something more produced and more permanent, then try using the slideshow producer in the Photos app. With this option, you can make quality professional looking slideshow presentations for special events, weddings, memorials, or graduations.

Put all the photos that you wish to include in the Photos app and choose Slideshow from the My Projects menu. You'll be able to arrange the photos, pick a suitable theme, and set it to music if you wish.

# Fast Crop

One of the most popular alterations that you will want to do with your photographs is the simple crop. You could open a fancy program like Photoshop, or Pixelmator Pro, and get the job done but there is a simple and fast way to do quick crops on the Mac without opening anything.

In this first picture, we have a photograph of a laptop with a race car as its wallpaper. What if I simply wanted a picture of the car? The answer is quick crop. With the image on my desktop or anywhere on my computer for that matter, I simply double-click the image and it will open in Preview automatically. Now without opening anything else I can take a mouse and left-click the upper left-hand corner of a box that I want to quit crop and drag it to the bottom right. As it drags you can see that the computer is giving me pixel information about how large my image is going to be when I crop. This may be useful if you are cropping for the web. When I am happy with my crop I simply let go of the mouse. Now I'll go up and open *tools* where I will find the command *crop*. Click *crop*.

What I am left with is a new cropped version of the image.

You can also fine-tune your crop before pulling the trigger by putting your tooltip on the little boxes in the corners or sides of the crop lines, then drag them to where you want the crop to be.

# 250

# Adjust Size

Sooner or later you'll run into a situation where you have to make an image bigger or smaller. I ran into this very situation the other day when I was posting an auction on eBay. I had an image from the web that was about 400 pixels wide. I had it saved to my desktop and when it came time to upload the image into the auction I got a warning message that the image had to be at least 500 pixels wide. At this point, I had two choices. One, I could go searching for another image, or two I could simply resize the image to make eBay happy.

Fortunately resizing images on a Mac is a very easy process. Go to the image and double-click it. The image will open in preview. From Preview you can go to tools and select Adjust Size.

Adjust Size is going to give you a lot of options. You could use the top box to squeeze the image into a specific window size but most people will probably want to leave it on custom and set the exact size that they want for themselves. In this case, I have changed how I am viewing the image from inches to pixels. I have an image with a width of 500 and in this case, I am going to expand it to 600. If you leave the scale proportional box checked all you have to do is change one of the dimensions and when you hit enter or tab the other dimension will be adjusted proportionally.

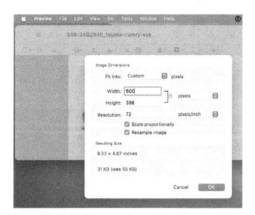

Once your image is the size that you want it to be click OK. The image in the original location will be converted to the new size.

# 251
# Black & White

There may be times when you need to quickly convert an image from color to black and white. Yes you can open the photo in an application like photos, or Pixelmator, or any other third-party application, but Mac gives you a super quick way to almost instantly convert a photo.

First, make a duplication of your color photo, if you want to save the original color version. That way the original is not affected and can be altered in another way if need be in the future. Now double-click the duplicate photo and it will open up in preview. Select Tools from the top menu and click on adjust color.

Next move the saturation slider to the left. You now have a monochrome image. You can make further adjustments if needed, but often this is all that is needed for a great black and white image. Close the window and you'll be left with the altered image.

# 252

# Crop a Photo

If you scan a photo into your Mac, you'll often time need to crop it to be straight. You also may want to crop to simply remove an element from a picture. The Mac offers a simple way to accomplish this, once again, without opening the photo in another editing app.

First double-click the image to open it in Preview. Your tooltip will now change from an arrow into crosshairs. Place the crosshairs in the upper left corner of the photo, left-click and hold the mouse button as you drag the box to the lower-right-hand corner of the photo and release. Don't worry if it's not perfect, you can use the blue dots to reposition the sides or corners to make it perfect and if you still make a mistake, simply use command Z to go back in time for another go at it.

Once you get it right, select *Save* from the file menu. Your cropped photo will replace your original.

# 253

# Rotate a Photo

While the Mac OS has an included photo editing app (Photos), there's actually a lot that you can do to fix many basic types of problems with photos while the picture is simply stored on your machine. Let's look at a few common problems.

First, the rotated photo. Now while I absolutely love the camera on the iPhone, it's not without its problems. One issue is that it's not incredibly foolproof when it comes to choosing between a landscape photograph, and a portrait. Sooner or later, you'll import a series of photos off your phone only to find a few laying on their side. Yes, you can rotate them in the phone itself, but if you've already moved them to your computer, never fear. Just follow these easy steps.

Control-click the photo or tap it with two fingers if you're using a laptop or trackpad. Click quick actions. You'll now be able to rotate your photo. Keep rotating the photo until the orientation is correct. There's nothing more that you have to do to save it, the photo will now forevermore be correct.

While you're in the Quick Action menu, hold the option key and you will get an option to rotate to the right.

# 254

# Remove Background

If you use your Mac for graphics, you'll eventually need to make a background of an image transparent. This would allow you to overlay the image onto another with the bottom image showing through the removed portion. Now normally on a computer, you would need an expensive graphics program to accomplish this, but Mac allows you to do it within the operating system itself.

First, you'll need an image that has a solid background. Grab the image and save it to your desktop.

Next double-click the image to open it in Preview. Choose to show the markup tools by clicking the markup tool icon. Then choose the Instant Alpha tool to get a crosshair. Place the crosshair in the center of the area that you want to remove.

Left-click and drag the area to fill the portion that you want to remove. Your image will now have ant trails in the chosen area.

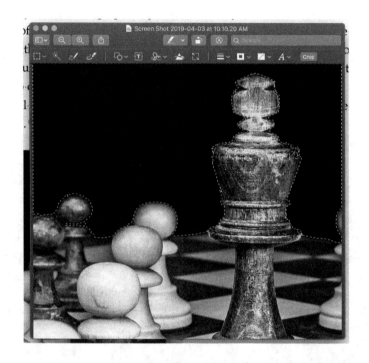

All you have to do now is to hit the delete key and the background will be removed.

# 255
# Light Adjustment


I do not use the Photos app on the Mac for storing and sorting my photos. I take care of those tasks manually, so I have more control over the process. Photos does have a few other features however, that are useable as standalone. The photo editor within the app, for example, can do more than the basic editor in preview. You may already have an editor like Pixelmator Pro with more professional features, but for the more casual photographer, many of the same basic edits can be done right within Photos.

The first thing you will need to do to edit a photo is to import it into the app. If you have your photo collection on a separate hard drive you can simply copy the photo you wish to edit. Open Photos and while on the photos tab on the left, go up to edit on the menu bar and select paste. You'll now have a copy of your original photo imported into Photos, and your original will remain safe and untouched.

In this example, I've imported a picture of a cat. Double-clicking the photo will open it for editing. Clicking on the edit button will open up a handful of editing choices including Light.

Clicking on the Light arrow will open a dropdown menu with many editing options. Clicking Auto will use the computer's intelligence to analyze the photo and make all the appropriate changes needed to fix the photo according to its programmer's liking. The reverse arrow will return it to its unedited state.

You have a second and third method at this point to further edit the light levels. You can further take advantage of the computer's artificial intelligence by dragging the center bar in the filmstrip area in the dropdown. As you do, the computer will slide all seven parameters to different locations in order to accomplish the different looks. You can also take manual charge and slide any of the individual parameters yourself.

Once you're satisfied, click done. You may now export the edited photo by going up to File on the menu bar and choosing Export. As you save it, it will allow you to change the file type, save location, and change the name, among other things.

# Adding Shapes

Mac OS gives you two quick ways to add shapes when applying mark up to an image. There are numerous examples in this book for instance where you've seen me circle something on a photo to draw attention to a specific detail, like what button to press, or what icon to select. You may need to ask a computer savvy friend a question about something, and you might want to text them a screenshot for instance with an option circled or underlined. Mac makes it easy to do just that with its markup tools in preview.

The first method is to open a photo or screenshot in preview and click on the notation tool icon.

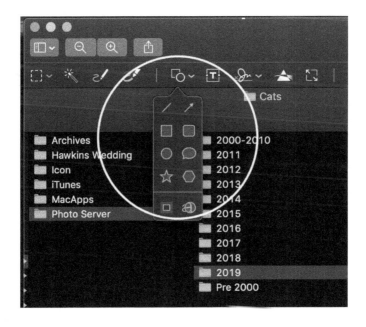

This will give you the ability to create custom predetermined shapes like arrows, squares, and circles. Once you've created one you can move its location or resize it to meet your needs.

In the next method, you can use the sketch tool to hand draw basic shapes like circles, squares, or triangles. When you complete the squiggly hand-drawn object, your Mac will interpret the correct shape and turn your drawing into an editable perfect shape.

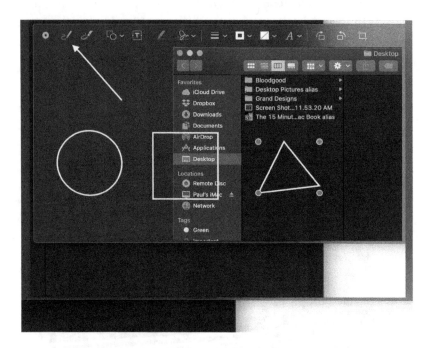

# 257

# Adding Text

You can also add text to any image that you might have on your Mac. Bring up the image in preview and select the text tool. The text tool is the square box with the letter T in it. You will immediately be able to start typing text onto your image. Don't be concerned with where the text is showing up on the image, the placement is editable as well as all of the other elements of the font.

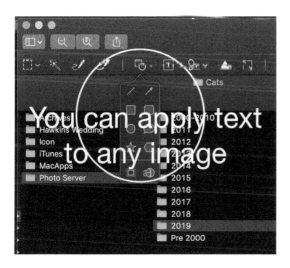

After you've entered your text you can adjust everything about it to make it perfect on the image. While your text is selected, open the text editing tool. It's an A with a dropdown menu arrow. Here you can choose a font, change the color, and alter the text in other ways much like the way you would expect to in a word processor. Drag the individual corner and side boxes to alter the text box itself, or move your tooltip to an area on a side to get a hand instead of an arrow. Now you can move the entire text box around the image.

# 258
# Printing Photos

Unless you know a few secrets, printing photographs on a Mac can at first seem like a chore. Let's say you have a photograph on your desktop and you want to send it to your printer. If you double-click that photograph it opens up in Preview and while Preview gives you a way to print it, it gives you no control over the size of the photograph. If you want a specific size photo like a 5 x 7 there is no easy way to do this from Preview.

In order to have control over a photograph's specific printed size, we must first open that photo in a separate application. There are numerous applications available that will do this including the Photos app that is built into every Mac.

To print a photograph open the Photos app and drag the photograph into it. Your photo will show up on the *Imports* page. When you click on your photo it will become highlighted with a blue line around it. After it is highlighted go up to file and choose *Print*. You'll now have the option to print your photograph in various popular photo sizes like 8 x 10 or 4 x 6. What if you want to print it in an odd size? That's not a problem there is a box where you can choose *Custom*.

# 259

# Image Capture

Image capture is a utility that lives on every Mac. It is used for bringing images into your computer from outside sources like a phone, an iPad, or a scanner. You can find this utility by going to your applications folder. Although I use this utility all the time, I do not put it in my quick launch area. The reason being, I can program this utility to open every time I plug in my phone by default. You can trigger this from within the utility. The first time that you open it however you will need to go find it in your Applications folder and double-click it.

Once it is open go ahead and plug in your phone. At this point it, should populate in the pane to the left of the window and you should be able to double-click your phone to get a look at all of your photos contained on it. If your phone automatically launched another program like finder or iTunes, close those applications. Notice the lock to the right. You will have to physically unlock your phone with your passcode in order for the utility to access all of the photos on your phone.

Once you're connected you can go down to the lower-left-hand corner and you can set the utility to open your phone automatically every time your phone is plugged into your computer over USB. Now instead of defaulting to something like iTunes or folder, your phone will launch Image Capture automatically every time it's plugged in thus no need for a shortcut on your desktop.

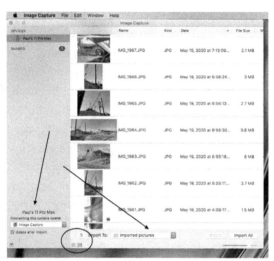

An important item to set up initially is where you will import your photos too by default. For my workflow, I prefer to have an empty folder on my desktop continually, called *imported pictures*. Every time I import pictures from my phone they end up automatically in this folder and they can sit there until I'm ready to sort them into albums on my external photo server drive.

Another important control by the *Import To* dropdown is the view button. As you can see there are two different views. The first view in the top photo is the information view. This will show every photograph on your phone with all of the metadata information associated with that photo. If you want to simply see the photos alone, click the multiple box icon and it will look like the photo below.

Another important box to check or uncheck is the delete after import box. This will tell the computer what to do on your phone with the photographs after the import happens. Do you want to leave your photos on your phone? Or do you want them deleted automatically for you so you are clean and ready to take more pictures.

Working in tandem with the view buttons is the view slider. This can be found in the lower-right-hand corner under import all. Sliding this bar back-and-forth will change the size of the photos that you're looking at in the window.

Now you can choose what photos you wish to import off of your phone whether it be one photo or all of them. If you simply need to import three or four photos go through and click those photos so they have a checkmark on them. These will be the only ones that import. You can choose all of them by clicking the *Import All* button.

After hitting the *Import* or *Import All* buttons the computer will complete the task automatically. Sit back and watch the import process happen. Note that some photographs will take longer to import than others, especially videos. If you have a long video expect to watch a slow progress bar. This is normal. When the process is done all of the photos will disappear from the window and they will all be in the folder that you have told the computer you want them in.

# 260

# Photo Booth

Remember the old photo booths at carnivals when you were growing up? You could pile into the booth with your friends and pay a price to snap silly Polaroid photos with your friends. Photo Booth does the same thing essentially, all from within your Mac OS.

Launch Photo Booth and you'll be given the choice between taking a photo or making a video. You can select between the two by clicking the icons on the lower-left of the window. The icon in the center will tell you if you're taking a picture or making a video. Click this button to snap a picture or start and stop the video.

Using the effects button allows you to have some fun.

Photos taken with Photo Booth can be opened in Preview and can be saved to your Mac for use in other applications.

# 261

# Screenshots

My wife and I are avid poker players. Over the years both of us have gotten a few Royal flushes. Anyone that plays poker knows how hard it is to get a royal flush, and once you get one how proud you are of it. The vast majority of our poker takes place online. Because of this, we're always ready to take a screenshot if we manage to get that elusive royal flush.

There are many reasons why you would want to take a screenshot. Sometimes it can be as easy as wanting to save a photograph from the web that you otherwise couldn't download. You may want to text something to a friend who is helping you out with your computer. The reasons go on and on.

Fortunately, with Mac OS, Apple has made it incredibly easy to take a screenshot. All you have to do is hold the command key, the shift key and hit five on your keyboard. You will then be faced with a menu of options. In this menu you can capture the entire screen, capture a selected window, or captured a selected portion of a window. You can also record your screen if you want to make a movie, but know that it will not capture sound, only video. On the right, you will have an option dropdown menu that will be where you tell the computer what you want to do with the document you captured. You can save an item to your desktop, your documents folder, or to the clipboard. You also have other options available to you here. Once you've made your selection left-click on your mouse key to take a picture. It will save the image as a PNG by default, Apple's standard graphic.

PNG's can be used just about anywhere, on the web, Facebook, or in most graphics programs. You can also send a PNG to any other Apple user.

# 262
# JPG Screenshots

When you take a screenshot with your Mac it is saved to your computer as an Apple standard PNG file. The application gives you no option to change this to any other format. This is fine if you're taking screenshots for yourself or taking screenshots to share with another Apple user. The problem comes in however if you are sharing that photo with a non-Apple user as PNG is an Apple standard. Wouldn't it be nice if the screenshot app allowed you to save to a universal format like JPEG? Well with a little programming skill, you can do just that. Now, don't be afraid of the phrase *programming skill*. Anyone with even basic computer knowledge can perform the hack I am about to teach you.

First off go ahead and take a screenshot of anything and save it to your desktop to confirm that your machine is saving as a PNG file. Once you've saved a screenshot to your desktop, right-click the screenshot and click on *get info*. *Kind* should be a PNG image.

Now let's do some programming on our Mac to change that file format for the future. Open up your terminal app and type in the following command: *defaults write com.apple.screencapture type JPG* and hit return. You've just programmed your Mac to save as a JPG instead of a PNG. Go ahead and take another screenshot and check to see what format it's saving in. If it is not saving as a JPG, reboot your machine and try another screenshot. Your machine should now be saving in a universal standard capable of being used on any PC or Mac.

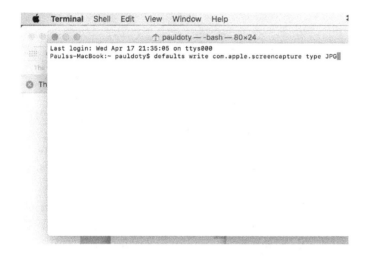

By the way, if that's the first time that you've done any programming on your Mac, congratulations! The Terminal app is a good place to get your feet wet!

# 263

# Encryption

Apple prides itself with its wonderful security on the Mac. Modern Macs have great features like finger print recognition, and facial recognition is just around the corner. All Macs have the ability to require a log on code for an individual to access it. But what if you want to encrypt a sensitive file to share with someone or take extra steps to make sure a folder on your machine is hidden from prying eyes? All Macs give you the ability to encrypt individual files and folders so they cannot be opened without a unique password.

To learn how to do this, let's create a text file on our desktop in either Word or Pages. It can be anything, but let's just type a document that says Test and save it to our desktop with the name Test. Next create a folder on your desktop and move the file into it. Call the folder Test as well. Now go to Launchpad and open Disk Utility. Select *file* and choose *New Image/Image from Folder*. Select the test folder on your desktop and click choose. Next set encryption to 128-bit. You will now be prompted for a password. Think of this as a key to your locked file. Choose something unique to any other password you're currently using on your machine. In other words, don't use the same password as your log on as that will defeat your second level of security. Plus, if you're going to share this file with another person, you can do so without revealing your log on code to your computer. Next save it as a compressed image.

Depending on the size of the disc image you are creating and the speed of your machine, it will take anywhere from a few seconds to several minutes to render an encrypted DMG file to your desktop. When it has completed, you'll have a fully encrypted file that cannot be opened unless the person opening it has the key. Lastly, do not check the save to keychain box when you enter your password to unlock it. This will defeat the purpose of using a lock to begin with.

When finished you will need to move the original file to the trash and then empty your trash.

# Keychain

Keychain, or rather Keychain Access, is an application built into your Mac's OS that will automatically run in the background any time you come to a website or use an application that needs security access. If you visit your bank online for instance, you will need to enter an account name and password to get into your account. This application remembers all your passwords and account logons for you and will log you in automatically if you choose to remember a password when you're prompted too by the application.

That's easy enough to understand, but what you may not know is that you can access Keychain anytime and make alterations to it if necessary. Let's say for instance that you've entered an incorrect password on an account, and Keychain keeps trying to put in the incorrect key whenever you visit a site. That can be annoying. Fortunately, you can launch Keychain Access from Launchpad and delete any erroneous entry that you might have made.

Once you've launched the application you can go to an entry, secondary-click it, and have access to either see the actual password information by choosing *Get Info*, or delete the entry altogether.

Once you've clicked *Get Info*, you then have the option to click Show password in order to see what password is listed.

There are two things we should touch on with Keychain. First, remember that anyone who has access to your computer's logon code has access to *all* of your logon codes. Secondly, there are password vaults out there that are far easier to use and edit than Keychain. 1Password is my application of choice, but there are many. These third-party applications will also run at the same time as Keychain, so in a sense, you're always getting the best of both worlds when using a third-party application.

# 265

# Keys to the Castle

Have you noticed that everything in your modern digital life revolves around keys? It seems like every account, every website you visit or log onto, and every device you use has passcodes. Passcodes are the modern equivalent of keys. When I was a kid in grammar school I would always see the janitor walking around later in the day. He would have a huge ring on his belt with a massive amount of keys on it. Later as technology changed, the janitors would carry fewer keys because many locks could be keyed the same.

Today we are the custodians of our digital world. That world also has a lot of keys. Some of us are really good custodians, some of us are horrible. What type of custodian are you? Are you continually losing your passwords and log on codes? Are your locks easy to pick?

Like it or not, passwords and log on codes are a necessity for living in our modern digital world. Yes, better methods of security are here like facial recognition and fingerprint authentication, but there will always be a need to give a trusted person away to open your house. Because of this, keys or passwords are not going away anytime in the near future.

The Mac operating system deals with keys and passcodes by means of an application that runs in the background called Keychain. Any time you save a password anywhere in your digital world, you will be asked if you would like to save it to Keychain.

While keychain works great, there are third-party applications that work even better. An application that many trust and use is an application called 1password. This application, as the name implies will allow you to keep track of all of your log in passcodes in one place using one universal password. It will also generate strong passwords for you if you tend to come up with passwords that are easily hacked.

# 266
# Manage Safari Passwords

As you browse the net, Safari will remember your various passwords for the websites that you visit. You can also access a list of those passwords for the sake of management right from Safari. Every now and then it's a good idea to take an audit of your password inventory. If you haven't done this in a while you will likely find that you have duplicates or passwords for sites that are no longer in use. It's a good idea to keep this list tidy on your machine. You can access this list by going to your Safari menu and choosing Settings. Once the pop-up box comes up choose passwords. From this screen, you can manage your password list in any way you see fit. Look for duplications or passwords that are no longer in use. Safari will also tell you if there are problems with passwords such as duplicates or passwords that are easily guessed.

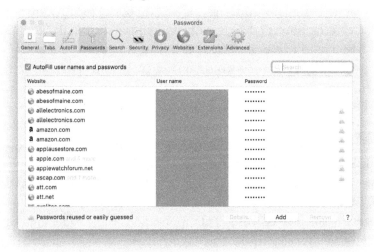

# PDF Encryption

On the Mac, any PDF file can be encrypted. This comes in handy if you want to hide the contents of a PDF from prying eyes or if you want to send a private PDF file to another individual. Take the PDF that you wish to encrypt and open it in Preview.

Now from the File menu go down to export as PDF. Yes, I know it's already a PDF, but we are going to use the encryption tools this time when we save it.

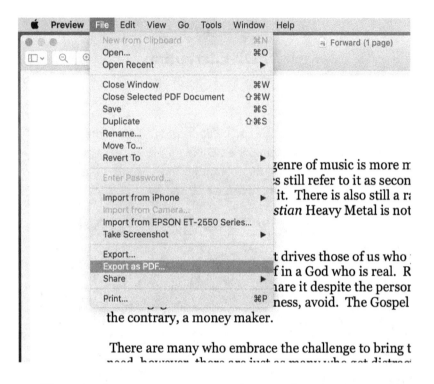

Here you can give it a new name if you wish under Save As. Now before clicking Save, look at the area that allows you to encrypt. Check the Encrypt box and give your encryption a password. You will have to enter this twice for verification.

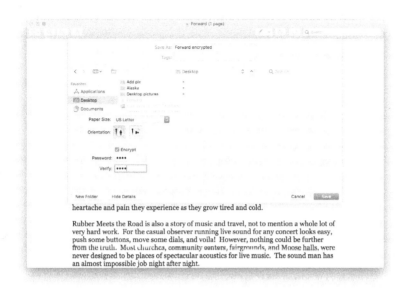

heartache and pain they experience as they grow tired and cold.

Rubber Meets the Road is also a story of music and travel, not to mention a whole lot of very hard work. For the casual observer running live sound for any concert looks easy, push some buttons, move some dials, and voila! However, nothing could be further from the truth. Most churches, community centers, fairgrounds, and Moose halls, were never designed to be places of spectacular acoustics for live music. The sound man has an almost impossible job night after night.

Clicking Save will now give you an encrypted version of the file.

Anytime this file is opened from now on, you will be prompted to supply a password. If the password does not match its encryption, the file will not be able to be opened.

This document is password protected.

Please enter the password below.

Password

# 268
# Screen Sharing

Built into every Mac is the ability to control another Mac remotely. This feature is built into the OS by way of iMessage. This feature can come in handy if you ever need to troubleshoot an issue on another Mac in a remote location. All that's needed is for both computers to be online and both Macs logged into messages with your Apple ID's.

To use the feature, open Messages and go to a stream of a previous conversation with the person who's Mac you need to control. With their thread highlighted, go up to Conversations on the Messages menu bar. Select Invite to share my screen or Ask to share screen depending on if your the one doing the sharing, or the controlling. The person on the other end can give you permission to either view your screen or take control of it. If you take control, you'll be able to run that Mac like you're sitting in the room with it and because you're connected via messages, you'll be able to talk with each other during the session, just like you can do with a FaceTime audio call.

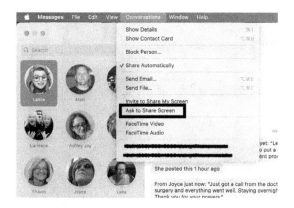

When you're finished with your session, all you have to do is end it by clicking End Screen sharing which is found in the screen sharing icon in the menu bar at the top of your screen.

# 269

# Multiple Screens

Nothing says power user like running multiple screens on your Mac. Almost any Mac can have multiple screens whether you're on a laptop, a Mac mini, or a full-blown powerhouse iMac. The number and resolution of your external monitors will vary with the type of Mac you own, so you'll have to do some internet research on your particular model to find out how many monitors you can run. A MacBook for instance will be able to run an additional monitor. A thirteen-inch MacBook Pro will be able to run two additional. A sixteen-inch MacBook Pro will be able to run four additional, giving you a whopping five monitors! That's awesome if you have a desk big enough for all of them! Desktop models can even run more if they are powerful enough. You'll have to do the research to find out what you'll need to run additional monitors on your particular setup.

My home workspace consists of a full-size 5K iMac screen with a secondary 27" 4K monitor. This setup fills my available desk space and provides a large amount of digital real estate for multitrack audio recording, and it's the ultimate workspace for a writer. My wife is a power user CFO running three monitors in her workspace in her office with Quickbooks on one screen, email on the second, and the internet on the third.

Multiple monitors are all about real-estate. The more screen, the more digital desk space for multiple windows and applications to be open at the same time.

# 270

# Sidecar

Sidecar is a new feature as of Catalina which allows you to use an iPad as a second monitor. The iPad must have an A8 processor and generally be one that is around 2015 or later. If you're wondering if your iPad can be used as a second monitor, check its product details. There are websites set up specifically for that and we'll cover those later in greater length.

Sidecar is turned on by going to the sidecar section in System Settings on your Mac. The best experience will be with an iPad Pro with an apple pencil. In fact, there are many things that you will need an Apple Pencil for an order to access them on the iPad once you're using it as a second monitor. I guess we can get to tip the hat to Apple at this point for creating yet another use for an iPad for those that don't own one previously or never knew that they needed a new one to begin with, and of course, while you're at it, you're going to need that apple pencil as well.

When you do have this set up however you will be able to essentially take a fully functional desktop system with you on the road. If you are a person that works on photography or audio files or video, this could be a game-changer. Imagine having a full-on two-monitor desktop set up with you in a hotel room that you simply pop into a backpack and head off to the next location.

At this time there are not as many applications that support sidecar as you may like, but in the coming year or two expect most of your apps to add sidecar support.

Once you are using sidecar your iPad can either be an extended display or a duplicate display. The duplicate display comes in handy when you are editing something on your main display with an Apple Pencil. An extended display comes in handy when you need extra real estate to spread windows across.

# Contrast

Ever wish that a cheaper, lower-resolution monitor could look as good as a Retina display? Here's a trick that will help a lessor then Retina display have better definition and contrast. You may even find that you prefer it on your high-end Retina display.

Apple gives you the ability to run your laptop or desktop in what they call Contrast Mode. This mode will extend the contrast of any display by making bright things brighter, dark things darker, and by adding bolder frames around anything in a box. It will not alter or interfere with anything you're doing on your computer, and you can quickly switch back and forth between the modes once you learn how.

To access this feature, open your System Settings. Your natural inclination at this point may be to go to the displays section, but you'd be wrong. Instead, open up the accessibility section.

You'll now have many switches to play with to adjust your contrast and other monitor settings.

# 272

# Screensaver History

The screensaver is one of those relics from the past that no longer has the same function as it did when it was first introduced, but we still refer to it by the same name, even though the name has nothing to do with its actual modern-day function. I work in the theatrical lighting industry, and almost everything I work with falls into this category. The controls on my lighting console are called handles because if you go back sixty years in history, large handles attached to rheostats were used to dim lights down. We call the filters that we put into conventional theatrical lights gels because at the time of their invention, gelatin was used as their material, and today we use plastics. The same is true for the screensaver.

Back in the early days of cathode ray tube monochrome monitors (black and white, black and green, or black and amber TV screen looking monitors), we used to have a problem with screen burn-in. When an image was left on the screen for an amount of time, the image would begin to permanently paint itself onto the screen, and you'd begin to see a shadow of the image, even when the screen was showing something else. Early programmers came up with a workaround program that would randomly change the screen image on those early computers that kept different images on the screen when the screen was not in use, thus saving the CRT screen. It didn't take long for these early programs to evolve into artistic expressions for the individual computer users. They could soon be personalized with photos and different artistic patterns that reflected the user's personality or likes and interests. The screensaver experience morphed in time into a way of customization and personalization rather than the needful screen saving tool of its original intent.

# 273

# Mac Screen Saver

Screen savers today are used more for keeping prying eyes from seeing what you're working on when you walk away from your machine, rather than protecting the screen itself. You can access the standard Mac screen savers by going to *System Settings* and selecting *Screen Saver*. When you click on the Screen Saver button you'll be presented with an array of built-in Mac screen savers. This set is universal to all Macs. You can preview the various types by clicking on them one by one. A preview will play in the box on the right.

The first set of screen savers revolve around photographs. By default, they are set to stock Mac photos but each can be customized with photos of your own by setting up a specific folder on your Mac with pictures of your choosing.

The next set are geometric patterns and random graphics. The message screen saver is the classic Mac screen saver. It will default to your computer's name, but you can change the message to whatever you like.

Many of the built-in screen savers have options to customize the particular screen saver in some manner. If options are available you will be presented with an option tab under the screen savers preview window. One popular option is the ability to add a floating clock to your screen saver.

For those who like surprises, you can tick a box to randomize your screen saver. When checked, this option will pick one at random from the entire list.

Remember to set your screen savers start time. If this dropdown is set to never, your screen saver will never start. Set it short enough to kick in if you walk away from your machine for an amount of time, but not too quickly as to annoy you while you're trying to use your machine.

# 274

# Displays

The *Displays* tab in *System Settings* is where you want to come to adjust your various monitor settings. You may have one monitor attached to your computer or many, all will be controlled from this window.

In the past we've been able to right click on an individual monitors background attached to our computer system to get details on that specific monitor. All has been condensed now into this one window, and you can get individual information by simply clicking on the individual monitors displayed.

# 275

# RAM

One of the decisions that you will make when you purchase a Mac is how much RAM to get. RAM or Random Access Memory is the playground on your computer where your applications play. Your RAM size will determine how many applications you can have open at once and because when your machine runs out of this space it will begin to write and read to the hard drive to make up for it, it will determine how fast your machine will operate as well. PCs have an advantage over Macs in the fact that they are usually user-upgradable whereas Macs have their RAM permanently residing on the processor chip. Because of this, it's important to max out the RAM of your machine with as much RAM as you will likely need for the computer for whatever you plan on using it for because it's going to have to last you for the life of that machine.

Macs today will start with 8GB of RAM. This amount of RAM will allow you to do many things. These machines make great netbooks and will run almost anything you throw at it with the limitation of one or two large programs at a time. They do not make great machines for power-hungry tasks like multi-channel sound recording or video editing. Book writing software like Scrivener will also be frustrating at the 8GB level as there will be times that you are waiting for the computer to catch up to your typing instead of enjoying a fluid experience on the device. An 8GB machine is great for email, basic word processing, non-memory hungry games, and small spreadsheet projects. They are not your first choice for hardcore graphics and various types of editing applications.

Your next bump is 16GB of RAM. Unless you're purchasing a computer specifically to use as an email reader and web surfer with minor app usage, I recommend 16GB as your minimum amount of RAM. This amount will allow you to do just about anything on a Mac, and do it fast. Why then would anyone need more than 16GB? One simple word, multitasking.

Now we enter the world of the power user. 32GB and up is the realm of the heavy-duty user who's working with huge files or editing movies. While 16GB of RAM will let you edit a half-hour movie fairly painlessly, 32 and up is the land that you want to be in if you have an hour and a half movie to render., and if you're this kind of user, the more RAM the better.

# 276

# Hard Drive

Very few Macs are available today with old-style mechanical optical hard drives. Although this type of drive is cheap, it is also fragile and undependable. Mechanical drives fail. It's not a matter of *if*, but of *when*, and because Mac computers typically have all their guts integrated onto their circuit boards to save space, a failed drive means a computer serviceable only by Apple in most cases.

The modern hard drive uses a solid-state memory chip instead of a moving mechanism inside the machine. As a result, they are quieter, faster, cooler, and more reliable. They are also more expensive, but prices are falling on them every year. These solid-state drives are known as SSD drives.

Some iMacs offer a hybrid solution with a device called a fusion drive. This is a drive essentially made up as a hybrid of both solid-state and mechanical. While faster than an old school mechanical hard drive, I still don't recommend them because of the potential for failure. If you're buying a new computer today, this is one of the key areas that you're going to want to spend your money on. Get an SSD drive, and get as large of one as you can realistically afford.

128GB is the smallest SSD's available for a Mac and I do not recommend them. Their size is too small for any computer that is going to have a normal amount of apps on it. The only place this small of a drive might work is in a machine that is used only for web surfing and email.

256GB is the absolute smallest SSD that you would want. It has enough room for an entry-level computer user who doesn't run many apps.

500GB is the goldilocks area of SSD. It's large enough to accommodate almost any user, yet priced well below a 1TB drive.

1TB and up are awesome drives if you can afford them. A 1TB drive is a great size for someone working with a MacBook Pro on the road who needs much more storage on it than just enough room for its apps.

# Hard Drive Size

Apple gives you a fast way to check the hard drive size on your machine. There's a number of reasons why you would want to do this over the course of your Mac's life. Perhaps you want to see how much space is left on your hard drive. If your Mac begins to slow down it maybe slowing down because there is less than 20% of your hard drive space left. Or you simply may wish to see how big your hard drive is to begin with.

In your System Settings you can click on General/Storage to see your drive.

Clicking on Storage Settings will give you a breakdown of what's taking up room on your machine.

# 278

# Hard Drive Space

Buy a computer with a small hard drive (256-500GB) and you'll save a lot of cash, but spend a lot of time cleaning files from the hard drive. Buy one with 1TB or more and you'll put out a lot of dough, but you'll be bothered with cleaning files far less. The choice is yours, but even with a large internal drive, you're still going to need to do occasional house cleaning.

To manage your computer's hard drive space go to System settings/General/Storage. You'll have options here to optimize your drive. You can even delete clutter in the lower section by clicking on the information icons

# 279

# Upgrade SSD

Upgrading your SSD drive inside your machine is one of the fastest ways to increase performance and storage for your Mac. The first thing you're going to need to know is what kind of Mac you have. You will need to go up to the Apple logo in the upper left-hand corner and click on About This Mac. Write down the information for your machine.

There are many places on the web to get an SSD drive and many manufacturers out there. Crucial is one of the best and they have a great website for determining whether or not your SSD drive is upgradable. Even if you buy another product from another manufacturer you can still use this website to determine if your drive is updatable. The crucial product is a great product at a great price so they do have my recommendation.

On their website, you will either scan your computer using their software or you will click *select  computer* and enter the information manually. Entering manually has the advantage of not having to put any additional software onto your machine. *Scan computer* has the advantage of doing the task automatically.

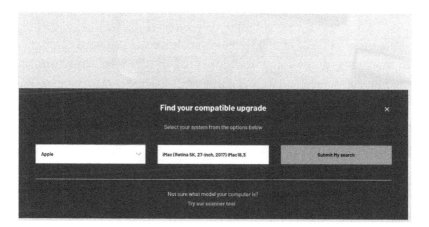

Basically, you're going to want to buy the largest drive that you can afford. The larger your drive the better the performance of your machine. Also, the larger the drive the more storage space you'll have on your machine. I mentioned the other first because people tend to overlook the fact that a larger drive would give you more room for your machine to work. A computer will continually write files to the blank portion of its internal drive. The more space that you have available here will mean the fewer slowdowns that you encounter in computer performance especially when doing a large task like upgrading the operating system.

The installation of an SSD drive is fairly straightforward. Once your machine is apart you will simply plug the drive in. There are many helpful tutorial videos out there on YouTube and a little research will allow you to do this fairly simple task yourself without paying a lot of money to have a shop upgrade it for you.

# 280

# Upgrade RAM

Like updating your SSD drive a good way to find out if your ram is updatable is to go to crucial.com. Again you will need to go to your *About This Mac* screen and find your computer type. Once you're armed with this information, go to the website and either select *Scan computer* or *Select computer*. Personally, I have always had better luck with manually putting in the information under *Select computer* but by all means, give *Scan computer* a shot.

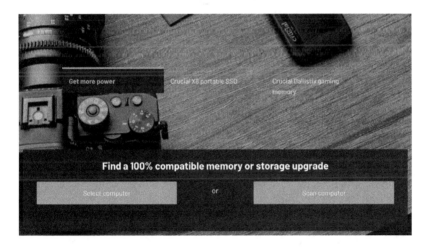

Once you've put the information in you'll be able to use their website to determine if your computer is upgradable and if so what ram modules will be needed for the upgrade.

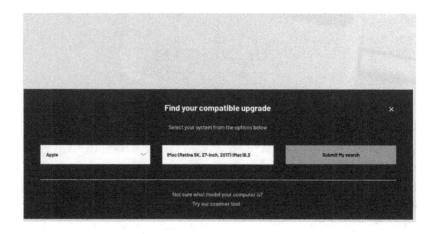

The rule of thumb with RAM is the more the merrier. RAM is one of those areas that will almost always increase the performance of your machine by giving it more room to stretch out and work.

Installing RAM is fairly straightforward. Usually requires taking the bottom off of a laptop or a back panel off of an iMac. The ram modules themselves snap into place. This is a fairly easy upgrade for the DYI individual. However, if you are shy about working with electronics, you may want to call upon a friend who is more tech-savvy.

# 281

# Drive Repair

It's been said that a mechanical hard drive has two functions. Number one, to store and retrieve data. Number two, to fail. In recent years hard drive quality has greatly increased due to SSD technology. However, we still use a good amount of old-style optical drives in our computer systems, especially for external storage.

When drives fail they will fail in one of two ways. They will either have a software level failure such as a corrupt table of contents or they will have a mechanical failure. If your hard drive suffers a mechanical failure, unfortunately, there's not a lot you can do for it except to replace it. However, if it suffers a software level failure, you can oftentimes fix the drive on your own by using a utility on your Mac called Disk Utility.

If you suspect a problem with your drive launch Disk Utility and highlight the drive that is having an issue. You will notice that there is a mother directory, and there will be child directories under it. Start with the mother directory by highlighting it and click *First Aid*.

First Aid will warn you that what you're about to do may take up to a few hours. Make sure you have the time to do it! Click run and everything else is pretty much automatic at this point. The computer will go through and check all of the necessary things to find out if there are any errors on the disk. If there are it will attempt to fix it. If it can't fix one it will give you a report at the end. If it does repair it, it will tell you what it did to fix it.

Now go back and run the same test on the child directories. All of these tasks could take between a few minutes and a few hours depending on how much data is on the drive and how much damage has been done to them.

Built into every Mac is the ability to repair a disk that may be having issues. If you suspect that you have an issue with a hard drive of any type, launch Disk Utility and select the drive that you wish to check.

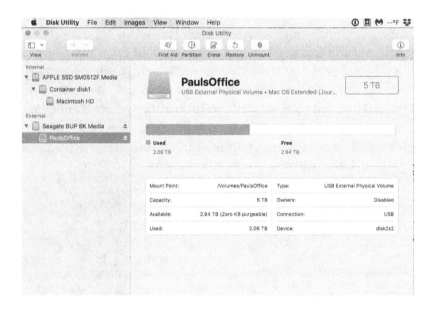

Select First Aid from the options to launch a fully automated scan and repair of the disc volume. The utility will scan the drive, giving you a progress report for every step. If it encounters common issues that are repairable, it will carry out those repairs.

If the drive passes, it will let you know. If it needed repair and those repairs were successful, again, it will let you know. If the drive failed and the situation is unrepairable, it will tell you that as well. Unfortunately, these issues may not be software in nature. A hardware failure usually means the replacement of the defective drive.

# Full Disk Access

One of the best features about your Mac is its security. There is not a personal computer on the planet more secure than a Mac. However you will find out that at times you will want to grant full access to a app on your machine. Because this is giving an application access to secure and sensitive files, you will have to do this manually.

Two programs that I have given full access to on my machines for example our Malwarebytes and App Cleaner. Malwarebytes has full access because I want it to be able to scan every part of my machine for malicious software. App cleaner has full access because anytime I delete an application from my system I want to find every single trace of it everywhere on the computer. These are just two examples, you may have others.

To grant full disk access to an app you must first open System Settings and go to Full Disk Access.

Here you can toggle full access on or off.

# 284
# Formatting a Hard Drive

With Mac, you format drives with an app called Disk Utility. When you launch it, you will see all of the media connected to your computer whether they be internal hard drives, external hard drives, or portable thumb drives.  To format a drive, choose the last partition on that drive and click Erase.  You will be prompted to name the new drive and choose what format you'd like to use for it.

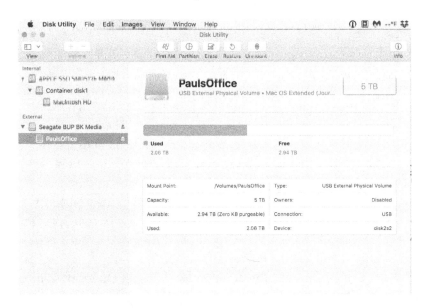

Formatting on the Mac is lightyears faster than formatting on a PC. You will come to appreciate this if you've ever spent any time formatting drives on a Windows machine.  The biggest decision that you'll have to make is what format to use.  If your drive is going to be used by a Mac exclusively, then absolutely format it as a mac drive using Mac OS Extended.  If it's going to bounce between a mac and a PC then it must be formatted in one of the slower PC FAT32 versions.

# 285

# Thumb Drives

Like hard drives, thumb drives, or flash drives share many of the same uses and characteristics. They are now becoming so large, that they can be seen as legitimate portable storage. Some are even larger than the hard drives that come in entry-level Macs.

A word to the wise with thumb drives. Stick with known brand names. There are a lot of cheap knock off thumb drives out there on the internet, and with these little guys, you get what you pay for. I'm going to assume that you care about the information that you're taking the time to store on one of these drives, so it makes sense to buy a product that you can rely on to load after it's been in a drawer for a year.

These little wonders can be used to transfer information between machines or as storage for libraries of information. They're cheap enough now that you can own several and dedicate them to specific tasks. I have sticks that do nothing other than house music libraries. Others for things I routinely do at my work like house updates for pieces of equipment. I utilize a label machine to put sticky labels on them all to keep them organized. If a stick is going to be mac specific, I re-format it initially to be a Mac-only stick. If it's going to need to be read by a PC, I will leave it formatted for PC.

My wife uses a number of sticks for back-ups for Quickbooks in our business. She might have one stick labeled weekly with weekly backups and one labeled monthly for a backup of the backups. The bottom line is that these little guys are good cheap mass storage now and they provide an easy way to transfer data between machines.

The drawback to consider? Because of their size, they're also easy to misplace or lose.

# 286
# USB Drives

Adding more hard drive space on your Mac is as easy as plugging in an external USB hard drive. These drives are readily available everywhere and prices have dropped tremendously over the past few years. External USB hard drives are available in inexpensive traditional mechanical optical style drives or the new and expensive solid-state variety known as an SSD drive. The major differences between the two are speed and dependability. SSD's are much faster and more reliable than a mechanical drive and they are more expensive for it.

USB drives have many uses including, but not limited to being an excellent choice location to back up your computer to. They can also serve as external storage for large libraries like music or photos.

In my home system, I use an internal 500GB SSD drive to store my OS and apps on for the operation of my computer. I have a 5TB drive as storage for my photos, music, and file archive. I have another 5TB drive attached as a backup drive for the entire system.

When you buy an external drive, you'll need to make a decision on how you want to format it. Most drives, while Mac compatible, come formatted for PC and there's a very good reason for this. As such they are compatible with both systems. Mac, however, uses a superior file system called Mac OS Extended (Journaled) that is much faster than the PC system. The drawback is that you will only be able to use it on a Mac. When you buy a drive, you'll need to decide what it will be used for and format it accordingly. If it will live on your Apple system and never see a PC, by all means, re-format it for Apple so you can take advantage of that speed, reliability, and compatibility. If you're formatting a drive for the purpose of moving files back and forth between a Mac and a PC, you'll want to stick with a PC format.

# 287

# USB C

I bought my first PC around 1990. At that time most computers had four different connectors on them. They had a VGA port for connecting a monitor, a printer port for connecting a dot matrix printer, a din connector for connecting a keyboard, and a serial port for connecting a mouse. All four of these connectors were large multi-pin ports.

The problem with the serial port is you could only connect one thing at a time. Compared to today's computers you can see where this configuration was greatly limited. In time the printer port, the keyboard port, and serial port gave way to a universal serial bus or USB. The USB allowed us to connect a series of serial devices to a computer on a universal bus. Versions over the years continued to get faster but basically operated in the same way. Once again time came where computers became so fast that they needed a faster way to handle serial connections. Enter the universal serial bus version C.

Without going into pages of specifications that will mean nothing to most people reading this chapter, the bottom line with USB-C is that it gave us a new bus system that can do far more than the old USB-3 standard can do, and it can do it much faster. Video and power transfer can now happen within the universal serial bus greatly enhancing the features of all computers.

When this redesign took place the engineers also looked at the fact that the old antiquated USB-3 system had a flaw in its basic nature and design. It was continually being inserted upside down by users. For years we would flip that little sucker back-and-forth until we figured out the way it went in the hole. This is a problem that has been dealt with ingeniously with USB-C as the connector can be inserted either way into its socket.

We are so entrenched in USB-3 however it's going to take years for computers to completely go over to USB-C. Apple is doing its part by no longer selling its high-end computers with USB-3 ports. Yes, you can still plug in an adapter in and use all of your USB-3 devices, but Apple has chosen to take a step into the future to force the issue. Love it or hate it, in the end, I think it's the right thing to do.

# 288

# USB-C Cable Speed

In the early '80s, I was working at a Hi-Fi store called The Federated Group. We sold high-fidelity home entertainment systems, components, and accessories. You could make good money selling the big systems if you knew how to read people and cherry-pick your clients who came in the door. It took a lot of time to sell a big system, but the reward was worth the time invested.

Another strategy for making good money was to hang out at the register and wright up all of the little accessories that would walk up. One of the more lucrative accessories were high-end speaker cables. In those days there were famous name brands that made high-end specialty cables that were supposedly engineered to actually sound better than normal speaker cables. Of course, the joke among all of the employees was that the cables sounded no better than a normal wire of the same gage, and the customer was paying a lot of extra money for a fancy looking product. A $60 12-gauge specialty cable did sound better than a $3 18-gauge brown zipcord speaker wire, but it sounded no better than a $6 12-gauge zipcord.

The same take away applies to USB-C cables when it comes to charging speed for your MacBook. The look of a cable has little to nothing to do with its performance, but size does matter.

I bought some great looking USB-C cables on Amazon. They were quite inexpensive and they did do the job of transferring data and charging my laptops, but, because the manufacturer saved money by cutting cost on the internal cable gauge, they do not transfer current to the computer as fast as an Apple cable of larger gauge. The result is that while they work, they do not charge a device as fast. So, buyer beware, and buyer be educated to the physics involved.

# 289
# Apple Cores

Every apple has a core, except for your computer. It likely has more than one. Computer cores are for the most part semi-irrelevant for the basic user as most modern computers come with plenty of cores to get basic computing jobs done. It's usually only the power users that are rendering video or working with multi-track recordings that take notice of the number of cores that a machine has, but if you're going to master the Mac, it's a good idea to have a basic understanding of what a core is and why the number of them is important.

Your computer has what's called a multi-core processor. That means it has a single electronic chip brain that is in fact, the thinking part of the computer. Inside this chip is a number of cores. Think of each core as a standalone computer capable of running applications separate from the others. If your computer has four cores, it's like having four individual computers all handling different tasks and apps simultaneously. Speed, efficiency, and capability all rise as the number of cores goes up.

In an i3 processor chip, you will find 2 cores. In an i5 chip you'll likely find 4 cores, and in an i7 chip might find 4 or more.

To find out how many cores your computer has go to the Apple logo in the upper left-hand corner of your screen and click it.

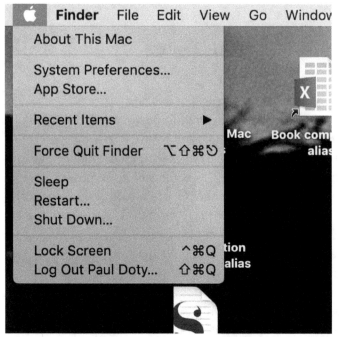

Now we're going to access a hidden menu. If you press and hold the option key you'll notice that *About This Mac* becomes *System Information*. While holding that option key, click *System Information*. You'll be presented with this window that will have your core information on it.

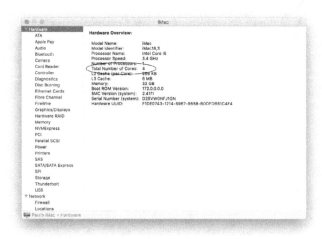

# 290
# Battery Levels

Checking battery levels on a Mac is easy. When I say battery, your mind might automatically go to picturing a laptop battery but remember, more and more Apple accessories are running on rechargeable batteries. The trackpad, Magic Mouse, keyboards, Bluetooth headphones, and other accessories all now run on rechargeable batteries, and all can be monitored on your Mac.

For example, if you're using a Magic Mouse and keyboard on an iMac, put your tooltip on the Bluetooth icon in your menu bar and click.

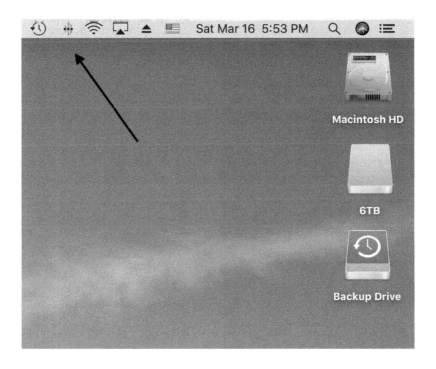

If you have any peripherals running with internal batteries, you will be able to click on them individually and see their current charge levels.

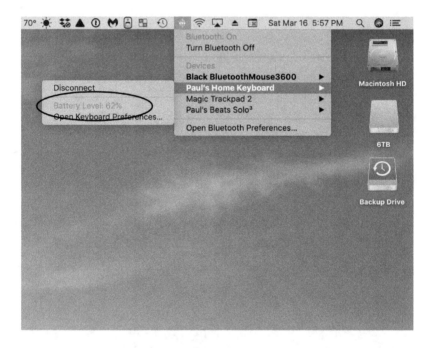

If you don't have a Bluetooth icon in your menu bar, go to system preferences and click on Bluetooth. There will be a checkbox for adding it.

# Energy Saver

The *Energy Saver* page in *System Settings* is where you will go to set up the various energy related settings on your iMac. The information that you see here will vary from laptop to desktop.

In our kitchen we have an elevated television above doorway that hides a Mac Mini that serves as the kitchens computer. My wife uses this computer to view recipes or television, while she's in the kitchen. One of the important settings for that computer in Energy Saver is the ability to *Start up at automatically after power failure*. Because the Mac Mini is elevated behind the TV, it is somewhat difficult to get to without a stepstool. If there is a power failure, this computer will automatically re-fire and go back about its business when power is restored.

# 292
# iMac

The iMac is Apple's version of the desktop computer workstation. Many people today choose to buy MacBook Pros instead of iMacs because they have become powerful enough to do the job of both in most cases, but there are some real advantages to having an iMac in your home or office. First off, there's that screen. Today's iMac computers look amazing, and if you're a power user with multiple apps open over a solitary screen, then the iMac is your best choice for a stationary computer.

When purchasing an iMac, storage is not as important as RAM. It's very easy and economical to add storage to an iMac by way of external hard drives. A 500GB SSD drive in your iMac will be plenty of storage space for most users apps, but again, if you can afford more, the more the merrier.

RAM is where it's at with an iMac. If you're planning on using that awesome Retina display for movie editing or similar adventures, then 32GB and up is your playground. A professional setup will typically have 64GB or better and will be found in recording, movie, and photo studios.

The iMacs offer more ports on them than a traditional laptop and those ports can be expanded by adding dongles or hubs. They will also have the power and drivers needed to run multiple monitors at high resolutions, not just a second monitor.

An iMac in your home or office will give you a stable static place to be able to expand, work, and play in an environment with a permanent feel. For years I used a MacBook Pro as my road laptop, and as my home workstation. While it had many great advantages which we'll look at in a few chapters, it had the occasional frustrating disadvantage of *oh, I can't use my computer because I left it at work.*

# 293

## Mac Studio

The Mac Studio as the name implies is the choice for hard core production users wether you're in a recording studio or video editing suite. When you need pure horse power, and money is a secondary concern, choose the Mac Studio. So what makes these little boxes so desirable to working professionals? Simply put, the numbers are staggering. And big numbers = big performance. These beasts come with M series max and Ultra chips that are simply the most powerful processors out there. Do you want 64 cores of GPU, 128GB of RAM and an 8TB SSD drive? If your answer was I don"t know what that means.....then the Studio was not built for you. But if your projects demand the best that the computing world has to offer.....this is it.

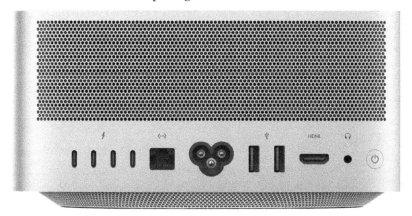

# 294

# MacBook Air

The MacBook Air is designed to be everyone's everyday laptop. This mid-level computer will sometimes confuse people during the buying process because its price point overlaps the other computers in the lineup. My advice to people is while the cost is certainly a consideration, what you plan on using a laptop for should be your reason for deciding between each of the Mac laptop lines.

If travel size is your reason for purchasing a laptop, go with the MacBook. Now as of the writing of this book, the MacBook is no longer available, but I'm leaving it in this update of the book as I anticipate its return.

If you're interested in a cost-effective day to day laptop computer for school or home, go with the MacBook Air as you will get more performance for the money at the sacrifice of weight and size. If you want a full-featured portable desktop on the go, get a MacBook Pro. If you need the size and speed of the best, then it's the Studio.

Once you've clarified the why of what you need, you'll then be free to look within the specific lineup of those machines to decide which one will suit your current needs.

One thing to consider with any laptop needs is your future with the product. Whichever computer you decide on, always consider your future growth with it. A hard drive that's just big enough to meet your needs today, may become bothersome three years down the road. One of the wonderful drawbacks of owning a Mac is its life expectancy. The laptop you purchase today will likely still be with you in eight or more years so look to the future as well, especially when it comes to RAM and hard drive size.

MacBook Air adds a few features over the MacBook. With this notebook, you'll double your USBC ports to two and you obviously get a larger screen. While it would be a gross comparison to think of the MacBook, Mackbook Air, and MacBook Pro as a netbook, notebook, and laptop, those are the traditional category roles that they fill. All three however do it in a vastly superior way to most of their PC counterparts which in the end is one of the major justifications for their price.

# 295

# MacBook Pro

Today's MacBook Pro is the professional workhorse of the industry. It truly is the portable full-featured mobile desktop. In fact, so much so, it is not uncommon to see people choosing the MacBook Pro over an iMac as their home or office machine, capable of docking to a monitor, only to head out the door when its user leaves.

MacBook Pro doubles your USB-C ports again over the Air bringing the total to four. At four pounds the MacBook Pro is the heaviest in the line and can seem heavy if you're used to a MacBook, but let's not forget that you could expect double that weight just a few years ago in a full-size premium laptop. After all, the MacBook Pro is not really about weight, it's about the ability to take a fully capable desktop machine with you on the go. It's a serious machine for serious users.

The ability to run up to 64GB of RAM will allow you to use the Pro for serious video editing and other extreme rendering projects. Even the 16GB version is quite capable and at home working with multi-track audio and professional photo rendering. If you're an audio engineer, musician, writer, number cruncher, or multitasker, the 16GB version has everything you need. If you're a filmmaker, or routinely run multiple memory-hungry apps simultaneously, go with the 32GB.

As far as hard drive size, you'll want at least a 500GB SSD to store all your apps and you'll likely add a portable hard drive for your large files if you're working with audio or video. Choose a 1TB drive if you need room on your machine for a large project or two on the road. If you're a video editor, you may want to go with a super-sized SSD, but you'll find out that it comes with a super-sized price tag as well.

# 296

# The Mac Mini

2018 saw the long-neglected return of the Mac Mini. The original intent of this micro wonder was to give people a relatively cheap introduction into the world of Mac. It was stripped down to the bare bones, allowing the user to bring their own monitor, keyboard, and mouse, but its compact size thrust this little guy into the professional world of media servers and hidden presentation machines in board rooms. I can't recall how many of these little wonders I installed back in the day in corporate Zoom rooms, neatly tucked behind TVs on walls. Apple took notice and finally responded to the cry's of professionals and home users alike to update and bring this little wonder back.

The Mac Mini returns as a powerful network server and professional media box. It's still at home as a standalone computer, but Apple has supercharged this little box into a monster. With the edition of the M1 Mac Mini's, you can still get a great little Mac for around $600, however, spend more and you'll find out that the computer has grown up into a powerful tool that has found its way into all areas of professional computing.

Now, for the consumer, who's going to want a new Mac Mini? This Apple reboot is going to come in handy anywhere space is at a premium. It can hide just about anywhere. There will be those that embrace it as a customizable desktop. There will be those who push it into service in home theater systems as a media server, and it will once again thrive in the corporate IT world of media installations in restaurants, bars, and boardrooms.

For consumers, one of the great things about the Mini is its adaptability. It's not uncommon to see these little guys passed down to serve in other applications when replaced by a more powerful computer.

# Fan Control

From time to time you might want to take control of your fan speed, or see what the temperature of your CPU is. While there is no easy way to do this on a Mac natively, there is a trick little downloadable app called Macs Fan Control. You can download the free or paid version at **www.crystalidea.com**.

Once installed the app will allow you to take control over your Macs internal fan(s). On the right of its window you'll be able to see your internal heat sensors on various components on Fahrenheit or Celsius.

One useful feature will allow you to periodically run your fans full blast for a time to blow out any dust bunny build up in your computer.

# 298

# Battery

The Macs energy settings have been located under Energy Saver in System Preferences up until the release of Big Sur. Now they can be found inside the Battery App. The energy setting is a way that you can manage the energy use of your machine. The settings in Battery will likely look different depending on whether you are using a laptop or desktop computer.

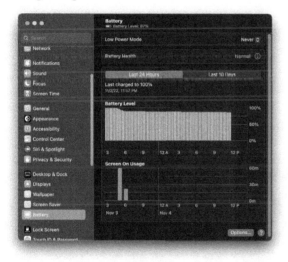

This app will tell you everything you need to know about your battery including when to replace it.

# 299

# Key Lights

Apple laptops feature backlit keys on their keyboards. If you've ever tried to use a laptop in the dark with unlit keys you will understand just how great this feature is. What you may be unaware of is there are ways to control the intensity of your key lights and turn them off completely if you want to save your battery.

If you open your System Settings and go to the Keyboard icon you will see two key boxes for controlling your backlight on your keyboard. The first checkbox will allow the computer to automatically adjust to ambient light. Once this box is unchecked you will be in control of the intensity of your keyboard light instead of your computer.

The second checkbox will allow the computer to automatically kill the keyboard lights after a certain amount of inactivity.

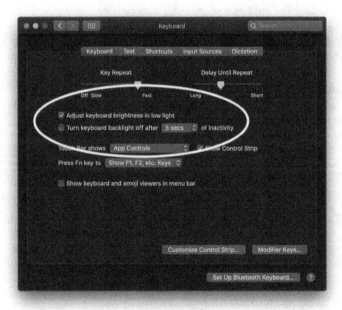

Once you uncheck the *Adjust keyboard brightness in low light* box, you will then have manual control over the intensity of your key lights. These controls can be found on your function keys at the top of your keyboard or if you have a MacBook Pro you can access them on the Touch Bar by simply pressing the over arrow to open up more hidden buttons.

Once this area is open you will have a keyboard brighter and a keyboard darker button. You can tap the down button until the on-screen display gives you a circle slash. At this point, the keyboard LEDs will be off completely. Going to Control Center will also give you a button for keyboard brightness. When you push this it will open up a box with a slider to adjust your key brightness up or down.

# 300

# Using Your Mac As A Phone

If you own an iPhone you can use your Mac computer as a telephone. Your Mac will use your phone to make the actual call but your computer will be the interface that you use to control it.

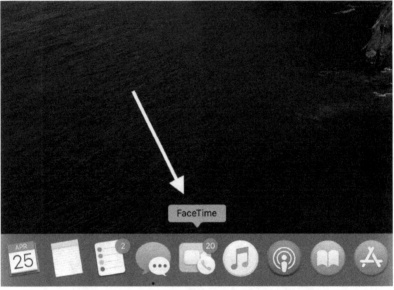

You can originate a call in a couple of different ways. The first is from opening the FaceTime app and simply searching for a number to call. Your FaceTime app will give you a list of the last calls that you have made in the pane on the left. Click on the number you wish to call and the computer will dial it for you. Otherwise, you can use the search function to search for a number in your contacts.

Another easy way to make a call is from the Internet. Often times you will be searching for a business or organization and you will come across the telephone number for them on the Internet. Your Mac will Display that telephone number as a clickable link.

# West Coast Sound & Light

| Website | Directions | Save |
|---------|-----------|------|

5.0 ★★★★★ 4 Google reviews

Theater production in Stanislaus County, California

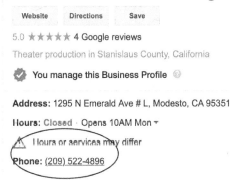

✔ You manage this Business Profile ⓘ

**Address:** 1295 N Emerald Ave # L, Modesto, CA 95351

**Hours:** Closed · Opens 10AM Mon ▾

⚠ Hours or services may differ

**Phone:** (209) 522-4896

If you click the link in your browser your Mac will automatically call the telephone number. A dialog box will show up in the upper right-hand portion of your screen with a button to click that says *call*. Once you've made your call simply talk at your computer screen. The microphone in your Mac will pick up your voice and the speakers on your monitor will allow you to hear the person on the other end. If you are using your Mac and your phone rings, you will also have the option to pick up that phone call on your computer instead of your phone by clicking the answer button in the upper right-hand corner dialog box.

# 301

# Keyboard

The keyboard setup can be found in System Settings. It controls a number of basic functions for the keyboard that you have hooked up to your Mac. If you are using an Apple keyboard the default settings will probably work just fine but you can still tweak them here to get the keyboard to feel exactly the way you want it to.

If you're using a wireless Apple keyboard you will be able to monitor its battery level from this screen.

# 302

# KeyGate

In 2016 I set out to get myself a travel laptop. My previous machine for this purpose was an Acer netbook that was amazingly fast for a cheap Windows laptop. It had an eleven-inch screen and it was so cheap ($250 at Costco) I had bought two, one for myself and one for my wife. It was made of plastic and was incredibly light. To be honest, over the years that little Acer was one of my favorite machines, fulfilling a specific task.

By 2016 I was fully entrenched in Mac with my 15″ MacBook Pro and I was looking for something lightweight in the Mac world for travel. At that time Apple's smallest offering was the relatively new 12 inch MacBook. Because this machine was going to be a full-power road dog, I specced the machine with nearly maxed-out specifications. At the time 8GB RAM was the most that you could do in a MacBook and I really needed 16GB for hardcore writing and music production. Rumor had it that the 16GB version was a year away, so I hatched a plan to purchase and temporarily use my wife's future travel laptop with the plan to purchase a 16GB version for myself the following year. My wife's needs were much more comfortable with 8GB's of RAM. She uses her travel MacBook primarily for web surfing and email.

So I ended up purchasing a shiny new MacBook in Rose Gold, as that was her color of choice. Granted, a lot of men would have been a bit uncomfortable with a pink laptop, but being quite comfortable in my masculinity, I rocked that rose gold on the road for over a year until I purchased my current 16GB space gray MacBook. To this day I miss the rose gold finish as that really is a good looking laptop. My wife loves it by the way.

All of this introduction brings me to the point of this chapter. From that laptop forward, all of my computers have had the butterfly keyboards that everyone seems to love or hate. In fact, being a 2016 model, the rose gold laptop has one of the first generation butterfly keyboards. Now if you believe all of the press out there concerning Apple's supposed woes concerning sticking keys with these keyboards, you might be apprehensive about buying an Apple laptop. All I can tell you is that out of my three machines that have the first two generations of butterfly keyboards, I have enjoyed a 99% success rate with them with almost no issues. Alright, perhaps you were alarmed with 99% instead of 100% and perhaps you caught my use of the word *almost*.

My first machine (the pink one) did have a small issue once. With what I do for a living, my computers are subject to harsh environments. They will often sit outside in hot temperatures at festivals and fairs. It's not uncommon for them to be in dusty and windy environments. Once I had a key stick on my first butterfly generation MacBook. One key simply stopped working. I thought to myself, *oh no, here we go*. As it turned out, I simply got a can of compressed air, gave the sticking key a shot of air, and the offending little spec of dust likely blew out and the keyboard returned to normal. I've had no issues with any of my machines sense. I suspect that many of these so-called *KeyGate* issues are nothing more than a speck of dirt that is able to be dealt with in the same fashion. I would not hesitate to buy or recommend an Apple product with these new keyboards and if you do ever have an issue, Apple has sense put repair and upgrades in place for those who have had problems.

# 303

# Magic Mouse

If I'm being honest, I have a love/hate relationship with the Magic Mouse. The biggest advantage of Apple's mouse is compatibility. I've used a number of bluetooth mice with different Macs. Some are pretty solid, others, not so much. Even the most solid third-party mice have their moments of frustration when it comes to solid connectivity.

Apple's Magic Mouse on the other hand, is by far, the most stable mouse made for the Mac. The older generation used batteries, and the new incarnation uses a rechargeable battery that uses a standard Apple lightning charging cable.

So what's magic about the Magic Mouse? The mouse is basically a combination of a standard mouse and a trackpad. The glass top of the mouse is capable of reading gestures similarly to using a trackpad. Although the mouse has no physical buttons, it is capable of discerning between left and right clicks. You can also use your finger to scroll.

What do I hate about the Magic Mouse? It tends to be harder to use for a hardcore long time Microsoft mouse user. Often times you'll find yourself making erroneous moves because of the top of the mouse being active. It comes down to what you're accustomed to. You can actually turn off all of these special functions in System Settings so it responds like a normal mouse, but why would you want to pay the premium price for all that "magic" only to disable it?

You can zoom a document or webpage by holding the control key on your keyboard while running your finger up and down on the surface.

The last vent I have for the mouse? When the power runs out, you have to charge it with the cable. What do I hate about that? It's on the bottom of the mouse. That means you cannot charge the mouse and use it at the same time. Who thought that was a good design? If your power runs out....you're done.

# 304

# Trackpad

Every Apple laptop comes with a built-in trackpad. Apple also makes a trackpad for the iMac called the Magic Trackpad. For years people have clamored for a Mac with a touchscreen, but Apple feels like they have all of the functionality of a touchscreen available to Apple users and then some by way of the trackpad. The new Mac user will instantly be familiar with the basics of a trackpad if they've ever used a Windows PC in the past. The basic function of point and click is second nature.

The Magic Trackpad however is a gesture-driven input device giving Mac users far more control over their computers than just a simple pointer pad. The device is highly configurable and like the mouse, you'll find a configuration section for it in System Settings.

Who needs a trackpad on a desktop machine? There are many answers to that question, but in my opinion, the must-haves are any user who's doing any type of serious photo, audio, or video editing.

With any new trackpad or laptop, the first thing you're going to want to do is to go in and configure your trackpad to your working style. The first thing I turn on on all of my machines is the tap to click option. Why this function does not come on as the default is a mystery to me. This function will allow you to simply tap the pad to click instead of having to press it all the way down.

Next, you'll want to go through and turn on any gestures that you think will be useful in your particular workflow. The various gestures are easily toggled on and off and if you hover over each section with your tooltip, the computer will even show you an example of the gesture in use.

# 305
# MagicBridge

Twelve South is a company with specialty products for the Mac. Right up front, let me mention that I am not paid to endorse this product, nor am I affiliated with them in any way, other than that I buy and use their product.

One of their most essential products in my opinion is the MagicBridge keyboard and trackpad holder.

This gem can be picked up on Amazon for around $27 and if you're a photography, video, or audio enthusiast, it's a must item and well worth the price.

This handy device clicks a standard Bluetooth Apple keyboard and trackpad together to fuse them into one integrated device.

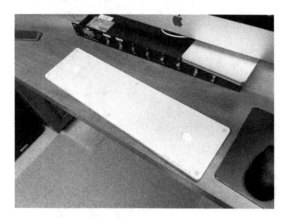

This fusion is not permanent, and the trackpad can be moved to either the left or right side of the keyboard. Holes are provided on the bottom to pop the components back out, and slots are provided on the back so both can be charged by cable without removing them from the bridge.

I use one bridge in my studio for audio recording and video production. It speeds your workflow because you never have to think about where your trackpad is or chase it around the desk. I use another as a remote control for my media server in my living room.

# 306

# Microsoft Mouse

The Microsoft mouse can be your saving grace if you are coming from the world of PC over to the Mac. It allows you to control your new environment with an old familiar friend. Right-click, left-click, point, and scroll. All of your old favorites are here, and they all work as they did on the PC.

When it comes to computers, my motto has always been the right tool for the right job. If you're going to run Windows on your Mac for any reason either through Boot Camp or Parallels, I highly recommend using a Microsoft Mouse, or a mouse designed for PC when you do as it will give you the greatest compatibility and old school PC feel.

Having said that, if you're sticking to the Mac environment, I'd recommend weaning yourself off of a PC mouse in time, for a few reasons. The first reason is the functionality. Your Mac is capable of much more functionality than a PC mouse can offer. The second is the connectivity. The best wireless PC mice use a plugin USB dongle. That means always having a hub or dongle plugged into your machine. Microsoft does make a Bluetooth mouse without a dongle, but the radio inside of it is not as stable as a Magic Mouse, which is why a Bluetooth Microsoft Mouse costs twenty dollars and a Magic Mouse costs between eighty and one hundred. Apple's catchphrase of *It just works* comes into play here with reliability, but it does so at a price.

In my digital world, I use a combination of all three input devices. Microsoft Mouse, Magic Mouse, and trackpad. All three offer a unique set of advantages and disadvantages. I bounce between them all, using the best input device for whatever my needs might be at the time.

# Network

You can access your network settings by clicking in System Settings and going to *Network*.

For the most part, you'll probably never have to go into network settings and change anything. The only time you should change something here is if you know exactly what you're doing. Changing any of the settings here can knock you off the Internet or your home or office network. The settings should be adjusted by someone who understands and is very familiar with not only network settings in general, but the settings of your particular network.

# 308
# Wi-Fi

Most people log onto a computer network and that's it. They will log into the router in their home and surf the web with little need to switch routers or networks. There are those out there however that use their laptop for professional uses. Many of these uses will require them to switch from network to network. I am a sound engineer and my profession requires me to jump from Wi-Fi network to Wi-Fi network all the time. An example of this might be when I am logged into a router that is attached to a sound system so I can operate it with my laptop. I may have to jump out of that router into another to get on the Internet. In the days before Catalina, the only way to accomplish this was to go up to the Wi-Fi icon in the menubar and turn off Wi-Fi and then turn it back on and log into a different router. This was the long way around the block. Mac now gives you the ability to bounce between networks without logging off, and the Big Sur era perfected the look and feel.

Clicking on the Wi-Fi symbol will bring up an uncluttered view of your current networks. Other networks around you will be hidden behind the other networks dropdown. You can still turn Wi-Fi on and off from this box, but you don't have to do it to switch networks. Simply select the network you want to join or bounce too.

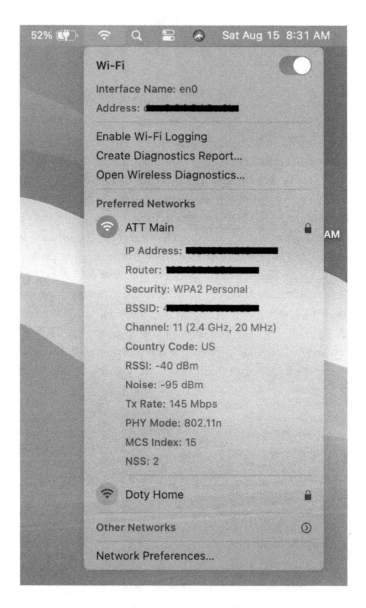

If you option-click on the Wi-Fi symbol the box will open up with all of the information surrounding the network you're currently on. You will also be able to perform various diagnostics from this box.

# 309
# Networking

Apple Macintosh. It just works!

That's the promise from Apple marketing and Apple fans, but it comes to networking, it's not always the case. Networking is a tricky business with any computer system whether Apple or PC. Even more so if you plan on combining both systems on a single network. The hardest thing about networking is making sure that you have all of the places ticked on your computer where you need to provide permission. Apple security is tight and part of that security are layers of permissions. If you're having difficulty networking two Apple computers together, try looking in these areas to see where the permissions are set. A Google search will also provide a myriad of other places that may not be listed here.

The first place you're going to want to go to is sharing. Get to Sharing by going to System Settings/General/Sharing. In this area you'll assign the various permissions for this machine over the network.

# 310

# Games

As stated previously, the Mac is not famous for being a gaming platform but rather a creative platform. If you were to look on any of my machines, you wouldn't see a large selection of games.

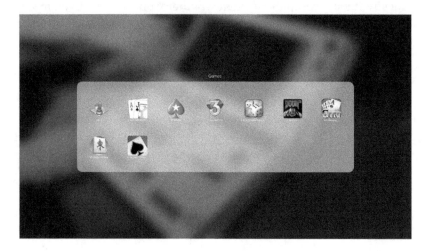

Serious gamers are likely to still be using a PC to run their favorite games, but there are a wide variety of games available on the Mac platform with more coming all the time. There's plenty of standards available in the App Store like Sims and the like.

If your a casual gamer like I, you'll find a good amount of free or near-free titles in the store that will entertain you while you're trying to pass some time while waiting for your plane or relaxing at home. Moonlight Mahjong and card games like Gin have been long time favorites of mine, so check the App Store out, you're sure to find a few favorites, even if you're not a serious gamer.

# 311
# Chess

To be honest, the Mac is not famous for being a gamers machine. It's just not where they shine. PC is still king in that arena, but that's not to say that there are some good games available on the system. Every Mac comes with a semi-simple chess app preinstalled called *Chess*.

Now growing up, chess was my main game of choice. I started learning the game in grade school and honed my game on the road, playing chess with great players and a grandmaster while riding in tour vehicles on long rock and roll tours during the eighties. The problem with chess was that I seldom had a worthy opponent once I came off of the road, so I soon switched my game of choice to poker. Back in the eighties, if you wanted to play a game of chess, you had two ways to do it. First, find an opponent to play, or second, buy an expensive chess computer game to play against an artificial intelligence. Years later, chess would become a standard offering as a computer game on both the PC and the Mac platform.

But is it any good? In the first paragraph, I stated that the Mac chess version was semi-simple. Here's what I mean by that. Chess on the Mac is a very powerful opponent. In fact, most players will not be able to beat it from level three on. In fact, being the geek that I am, I've played the Mac chess app against a vintage chess board computer from the eighties just to see how it stacks up and the Mac will beat the standalone computer game on its level four setting, while the standalone computer has ninety-nine variations of levels. This is why I refer to it as simple. The problem with the Mac chess app is that it does not have enough variation ability to be a good app that you can enjoy and grow with over time. Most players will eventually learn to beat it on level two, and then lose interest in it as the jump to level three is so steep, they'll simply never be able to beat it, and if they manage to, it will be one out of fifty or so attempts. What the game needs to make it a viable app for a chess player is the ability to place more parameters on the computer brain like limiting it's think time or disabling it all together on your move time. Until that happens, the built-in app will, unfortunately, be semi-simple, and real players will lose interest in it after a few plays.

If you are a chess player, my recommendation is to explore third-party apps and enjoy using the Mac for online chess play with real players.

# 312

# Apple Arcade

If you're a serious gamer, you're on Windows 10 and that's just the way that it has been. A few years ago Apple set out to remedy that situation, or at least develop a platform that could compete in some slice of the marketplace.

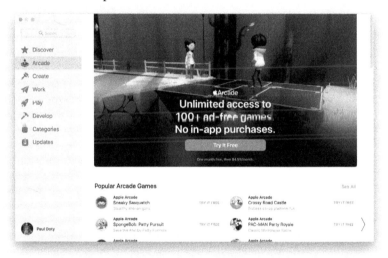

Apple Arcade was born! A platform for Apple to call all its own. At any time, first-time users can try Apple Arcade for free for 30 days. Apple hopes that you'll get hooked on at least one of their many games and want to subscribe. The service is relatively cheap after the trial period. Will Apple become a world-class gaming platform like Windows? That remains to be seen, but they may be happy enough with a little lucrative niche in this vast marketplace.

# Fonts

Every Mac comes with a generic set of preinstalled fonts. These are popular fonts that you're going to encounter on the Internet, or on documents that people might send you. You can access all of the fonts on your machine by clicking on the Font Book app.

Font Book will show you all of the fonts installed on your system and it will give you ways to arrange how you view them. There is also a plus box in the lower-left-hand corner where you can click and install other fonts that you may have downloaded from the Internet. Another easy way to install a font is to simply double-click the downloaded font itself and it will begin the installation process as well. Once a font is installed it will show up here in Font Book.

# 314

# Other Apple Fonts

Every Mac computer comes with a large set of preinstalled fonts. From time to time Apple will add new fonts to your system through the Font Book app. These fonts however will not automatically download to your Mac. You must go into the Font Book and choose which ones you would like to download.

While in Font Book select all fonts in the left pane. You will now see a list of all fonts available for your Mac from Apple. You will notice that some fonts are grayed out. These are fonts that are available but are not automatically downloaded onto your machine.

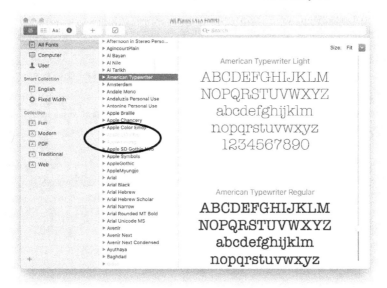

As you select these fonts with your tooltip you will be able to see a preview of the font in the right pane. If you find a font that you want to download simply click the download button in the upper right-hand corner of the window.

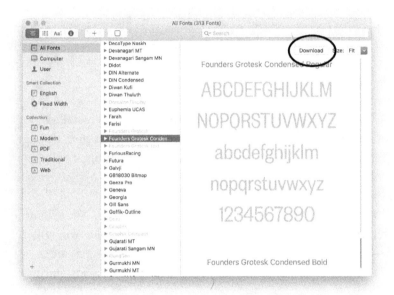

Most fonts come as a font set. This means there are a number of types and variations of the same font within the package. This is normal for fonts. You will get a window warning you of this when you first click *Download*. If you understand this and never want to see this window again click the *do not ask me again* tab and it will never bother you again.

In seconds your new font will be on your machine and it will show up in black instead of gray. It will also be available in all of your other apps that use various fonts.

# 315

# The Perfect Font

Have you ever been working with a graphic or word document and needed a specific looking font? Your Mac comes with many generic fonts that will work for many documents, but there will be times when you need a specific specialty font. Fortunately, there are tons of free specialty fonts that you can add to your Mac, simply by going out on the internet and downloading them.

I was putting together a quick Facebook header the other day and needed a racing font. I jumped on one of the many free font sites out there **1001freefonts.com**. On that site, you can find almost anything in the way of a custom font. The fastest way is to use the search bar at the top of the site. In this case, I simply typed in *Racing*.

I was given a filtered list of many fonts from the site and I ended up picking the very first one, a font called Furious Racing. After clicking on the font you'll see a chart of what all the characters look like in the font. To download the font to your Mac just click DOWNLOAD. A dialog box will appear allowing you to accept downloads from the site. You'll find the download in the form of a zip file in your downloads folder. Double-click the zip file and you'll get the actual font. Double-click the font to install it. If all goes well you'll see the font now listed alongside all of your other custom installed fonts. There will also be a box with a sample of the font.

After installation open your program of choice and your new font should be listed with your other fonts ready to use!

# 316

# Font Share

Once you start downloading new fonts onto your machine you'll soon run into an annoying problem. You'll save a document on your iMac in iCloud and then head off to a coffee shop with your laptop only to find that you don't have the same font on that machine when you try to open the document for editing. My solution is to create a folder in iCloud called Fonts. Whenever I download a new font I place it in this folder before installing it. Then I install that font from that folder on every machine I own. Now I have a fixed library of all of my favorite downloaded fonts at the ready. This comes in handy whenever you buy a brand new machine. Now you can go to the folder and install all of your third party fonts in one quick session. It also gives you a quick collection of fonts to share with someone else by sharing that particular folder with them.

# 317

# Convert to MP3

Eventually you'll come across an online video that you'd like to have as an MP3 file. As you may already know, many video files online contain copy-written material, so I'll spare you the in depth lecture, and simply point out that it's a bad idea to use someone else's work for monetary gain, but there may be times when you simply need a track for personal use. Wouldn't it be grand if you could simply download the audio portion of an online video as an MP3?

Many free online sites will allow you to do just that. Some work very well, and others are hit and miss. I use the word *free* in the sense that you do not have to pay money for this service, but be aware that many of these sites exist to make money from their advertisers, and oftentimes the advertisers are of the unscrupulous variety, attempting to get you to download maintenance type applications for your Mac that are fronts for delivering adware. So the bottom line there is be discerning, but don't be afraid to take advantage of the service.

The site that I currently use for this is **www.2conv.com**. The reason that I use this service over others is that for one, it works consistently, and secondly it is easy to use. Many sites work reasonably well but will not allow you to use their service in the United States or other locations. This site seems to work in just about any location. Making a conversion is relatively simple. First go to the site that has the video that you want to convert. Next highlight the URL of the video and press *command C* to copy it. Open up another tab in Safari and go to **www.2conv.com**. Use *command V* to paste the URL into its window. Then click convert. After conversion takes place there will be a button that will allow you to download the converted video. It will take a few minutes for it to fully download to your downloads folder. When it's done you will have a MP3 version ready to use.

# 318

# ClipGrab

If you don't want to use an online solution there is a free downloadable app out there that works great for downloading and/or converting videos called Clipgrab. Download the app from clipgab.org.

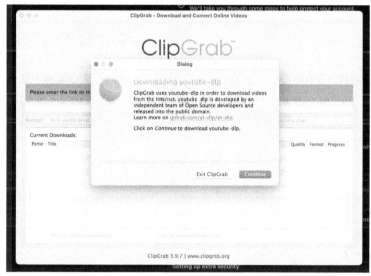

It uses an open source engine called YouTube-dip. You'll download this app once and then you'll be good to go. This app is free, but if you find yourself using it after you may want to make a donation.

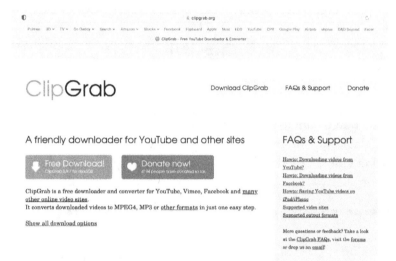

You can search videos from within the app but I find myself manually entering in the information I want to convert on its second page. Here you can convert the video into other formats and save them wherever you want.

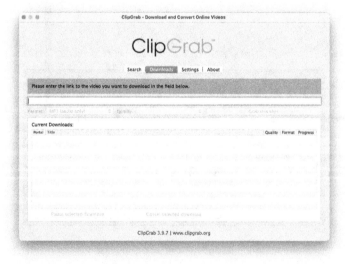

# 319
# Activity Monitor

Activity Monitor is a diagnostic app that you can run to watch your system's resources in real-time. The app can monitor your CPU usage (your actual computer chip) & your memory (Your RAM). These two activities determine the speed of your machine. The processes that are using the most power or RAM will be displayed from the top down showing you the percentage of use and amount of RAM that it's consuming. If you have 16MB of RAM and you constantly exceed that number, slowing down your machine, then it might be time to buy a larger computer to meet your needs.

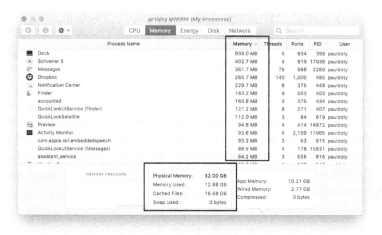

If need be, you can stop a process by double-clicking it. You will get an option to quit the process. Another area that you can monitor with the app is energy consumption, disk usage, and network activity.

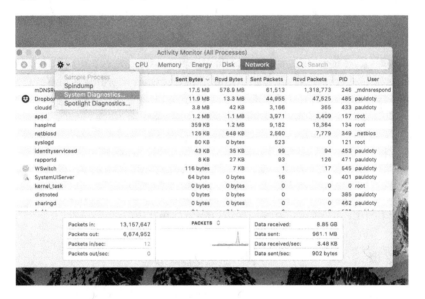

A computer technician can run a system-wide diagnostic from the app as well by using the dropdown by the little gear on the screen. A report will be generated with a massive amount of computer process information. It may be gibberish to you, but it just might help a tech pinpoint a problem with your system.

# 320

# Spotlight

When you're new to Mac, finding files can be frustrating, especially if you've let your Mac save a file to a default location instead of picking a specific location for the file yourself. This is where Spotlight comes in handy. Spotlight is the little magnifying glass in the upper right-hand corner of your screen.

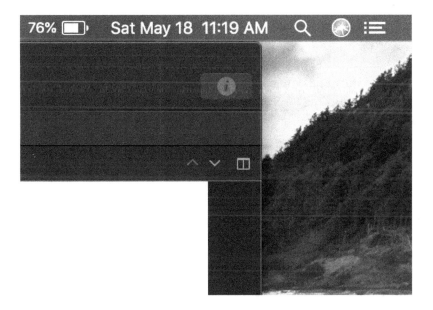

Clicking it will bring up a spotlight text entry window that will allow you to type the name of the file you're looking for. Your Mac will locate the file for you. What could be easier than that? I'm glad you asked. Like most tasks on a Mac, there's an even easier shortcut for power users. Just Command-click the space bar at any time and a Spotlight window will appear!

# 321

# To Do

To Do is one of the best list applications I have found for the Mac. This application was known as Wunderlist until it was purchased by Microsoft. Because it is an MS application you will have to have a Microsoft account to log into it initially in order to use it. I know some people may have an aversion to having a Microsoft account, but it's not a big deal even if that's the only thing you use your account for. Set up is really nothing more than giving Microsoft an email address and password.

When Microsoft bought this application they bought a good working mature one with a built-in base of users. They took a year or so out to develop To Do as a standalone application based on Wunderlist. Both applications existed for a year or so simultaneously until Wunderlist was eventually phased out in 2020. They have done an excellent job of retaining the original application and enhancing it by adding new features and new ways to customize it. An example of this is the ability to alphabetize items that have already been checked off of a checklist.

This application runs on both the Mac and the iPhone and integration between the two is seamless. What you update on your phone will be updated on your Mac as they both use a shared account.

Other notable features are the ability to share specific lists with other people. You simply click share and the application will automatically send an invitation over to the person you wish to share with. After they accept this you will now have a shared list. This is outstanding when using the application for grocery lists. Grocery lists can also be accessed via an Amazon Echo device with Alexa if you have one.

Even though Wunderlist was around for many years, to do is still in its infancy and it is getting daily attention by its developer. Couple that with the fact that the application is free makes To Do a winner.

# 322

# Reminders

The Reminders app is one of those areas that works across your entire Apple ecosystem. It shines the brightest for those of us that are fully entrenched with Mac computers, Apple Watch, and iPhones. Reminders allow you to ask for a reminder, and then your digital world will remind you of that reminder at the appropriate time. Set a reminder on your iPhone to turn the water off in an hour and your iMac will remind you an hour later while you're answering your emails, or whatever you're doing at the time. Reminders work great even if you only own one Apple product. Of course, if you ask for a reminder on your laptop and then turn it off before the reminder happens, your experience is going to fall short. What can you do besides go out and buy more Apple products?

You can set a reminder on your computer in a few different ways depending on the model you have. If you have a MacBook Pro with Touch Bar it's as easy as touching Siri and saying *set a reminder for three PM*. On the Siri enabled machines, just click Siri and do the same. You can even click the Reminders app and add a reminder manually, or manage your current reminders. If you use family sharing, you can share reminders across multiple family members as well.

# 323

# The Unarchiver

If you've used computers for any length of time you will become familiar with the concept of compressing or archiving files. In a nutshell, what this process does is compress the size of a file by eliminating bits of information that are not necessarily needed. Then it is able to be reassembled at a later time thus savings on space on your hard drive.

If you've used a Windows machine you're probably already familiar with programs like WinZip. But what if you're on a Mac? Can you compress files on a Mac? The Answer of course is yes and there are a number of applications out there for archiving and un-archiving files. One of the best ones in the App Store is a little app called the Unarchiver.

This is one of those applications that gets installed on every one of my machines on day one. Sooner or later you will have to unzip a file and this application is a great one for doing just that. First off it's free. I like free. Secondly, it has many options for various types of compression. You'll probably put this application on your machine and forget it's even there, but it will go about its work anytime you need to unzip a file.

# 324

# Amphetamine

No, this chapter is not going to be a lesson on how to stay awake and play video games on your Mac all night. Amphetamine is a free utility in the App Store that will allow you to keep your Mac awake for what they call a *session*. It's a great application to install on any machine on which you wish to have total control over when the machine sleeps or more importantly preventing it from doing so.

For me, this application is machine specific. There are certain ones that I install it on and others that I do not. For example, I have no need for it on my iMac in my home office however I will use it on my laptops which double as production machines.

My MacBook Pro will often time be used as a mobile multi-channel recorder at concerts. The last thing I need on that machine is for the computer to go to sleep halfway through a recording session. Even if it is on battery, I want it to remain on, even if I haven't touched it in over two hours.

I have other machines that I use professionally for corporate Zoom sessions. It's not uncommon at one of our corporate events to see a table lined with MacBooks and MacBook Pros. All of these machines have to remain on during the entire event.

It's also helpful on my travel laptops to have it installed in case I want to do some major downloading in a hotel room. It will allow me to go to sleep and leave the computer running all night. The computer will stay awake and never shut down allowing it to complete its job.

The operation of amphetamine is quite simple. A toggle switch on your menu bar turns it on and off. When it is on it is considered a *session*. It is also quite configurable to be able to turn itself on and off automatically by use of its menu.

# 325

# Find My App

The Find My application on your Mac is used to locate and track all of your devices. If you were to lose a computer or phone or an iPad you would be able to come to this device to find out where it is and what its current battery level is.

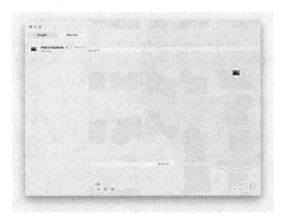

In the left-hand column, you'll see a list of your devices on a given account. On the right, a map will open up to show the approximate location of that device at any given time.

If you've lost your phone or MacBook there is a handy feature that is found by right-clicking on the device. From this screen, you are able to play a sound on it to locate it in your house or wherever it might be. You can also mark the device as lost or completely erase the device if you have sensitive information on it.

Another fun feature is to find a person. Not only can you find your iPhone, but you can find your wife. And to be clear, you'll have to have a wife with an iPhone to begin with, your Mac won't actually find you a wife.

# 326

# How Find My App Works

The Find My app was introduced in Catalina. It allows you to meet up with friends and find missing devices. It could even help you find your MacBook if it is lost or stolen. The Find My feature used to be simply buried in iCloud. It was something you could turn on or off on your iPhone. Now it is a full-blown app available on your computer.

To turn on Find My Mac for your computer go to System Preferences and click your Apple ID, then click iCloud. There you will find a box to tick called *Find My Mac*.

When you open up the **Find My** app you will be able to track either people or devices. Through this app, you can even find a device that has been turned off. Apple has taken advantage of the fact that there are now so many Apple devices in the world that at any given time there is almost always one or more Apple devices near your lost or stolen device. Apple takes advantage of the Bluetooth and Wi-Fi capabilities of these devices to ping and pinpoint lost devices in the background. Essentially, we are all in this together and if any one of us loses a device, the entire Apple community will help find it, whether they know they're doing it or not.

When you first activate this program, you may notice devices included on the left that you no longer own. You may have sold the device or have gotten rid of it in some other fashion. If you click on a device you will have the ability to remove the device from your list. If it is a stolen unit, you can even erase this device from this list so the thief is unable to retrieve any sensitive information from it.

# 327

# FOLX

FOLX is a torrent application for downloading torrents on the web. It comes in two different versions, a free version and a paid one. The paid version has many professional features including the search engine built into it. If you're using the free version you will still have to search for torrents on a torrent search engine site.

After installing FOLX, find a file that you want to download you will click the torrent or magnet link and it will automatically launch FOLX. Once it launches you will get a window that shows the torrent and will need to click OK to begin downloading it.

The reason FOLX shines is that it is very straightforward and very simple to use. Once you start downloading a file it will show up in a window. You can pause the download by hitting the pause button. It will show you the progress of how fast you're finding the torrent bits and assembling them on your computer. At any time before a file has fully downloaded, or after it has downloaded, you can right-click the box to delete the task or delete the task with its files and its entirety. There's also a number of other controls that you can use that those will tend to be your main ones. FOLX is a product of Eltima software and they can be found at **mac.eltima.com**.

# 328

# App Cleaner

Another place that your Mac shines is when it comes to uninstalling an app. The PC uninstall process is a little on the time-consuming side and with a registry, you'll often not get the entire program uninstalled, even after running the uninstaller. On a Mac, you simply remove the app from the applications folder and throw it away.

There are some apps however that may leave a small part of themselves behind even on a Mac. An application might create a secondary file or folder with configuration information, etc. The thought here is that if you ever reinstall the app, your previous information is retained. To be sure that you are removing every single part of an app on your Mac, you can use a handy free downloadable app called App Cleaner.

App Cleaner can be downloaded from the site **freemacsoft.net/appcleaner**. Once installed, you can use it to uninstall an app in one of two ways, and both are quite simple. In the first method, launch the app and simply drag the unwanted app's icon into the center area of App Cleaner.

The second way to uninstall an app is to click the box in the upper right of the app and start typing the app's name. When App cleaner finds the app you're looking for, it will allow you to remove any part of the app that you wish. To completely remove it, simply check all the boxes.

# 329

# Currency Conversion

There's a lot of great apps out there for the Mac. Every time you may need to perform a new task on your computer, you'll likely find yourself running over to the App Store to see what apps are available for a specific needed task. On occasion, you will be pleasantly surprised to discover that the Mac has many hidden talents and may be capable of a function or task without the download of a new app.

Take currency conversion for instance. The Mac has the built in ability to do this for you, whatever country you may be in, as long as you have an internet connection. No additional apps are necessary! To invoke this ability, simply type a monetary value into Spotlight (the magnifying glass icon in the upper right of your computer). You'll be immediately shown common conversions and you'll be given options for other common related tasks as well.

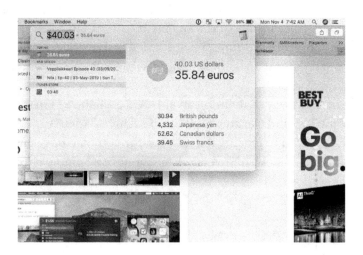

You can also get to Spotlight by holding down the command key and pressing the .space bar.

# 330

# Background Sounds

Here's a fun feature that many Mac users have no idea exists. You may work in a noisy environment and wish you had a way to drowned out noise so you can focus more on your work. You can do so with a handy little background noise machine that is built into your iMac. To access this go to *Accessibility/Audio* and turn on Background sounds. Most people will likely choose a soft rain.

# 331
# Spotlight Results

Spotlight search can be an amazing tool. It searches an amazing amount of things and places to bring you the information that you need. But sometimes that information is just an overload. If you find that you are using spotlight search for just specific things, you can go in and fine-tune Spotlight to search for exactly what you want and ignore all of the other things out there in the world. By default, every category of spotlight search is turned on. But you may only want to use Spotlight to find apps on your computer. You could literally uncheck everything except applications if you wanted to and spotlight would become your personal application launcher assistant.

You will find Siri & Spotlight in System Settings.

# Quick Menus

There are two places by default on the dock where you can quick launch items through quick menus. One is Launchpad in the other is System Settings.

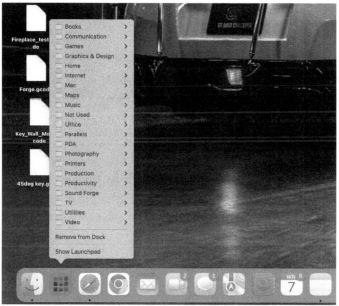

If you place your tooltip on Launchpad and left-click and hold the button, it will open up a shortcut menu to all of the folders that are in Launchpad. After a moment you can take your finger off of the button and the menu will stay allowing you to navigate it. You can then scroll through them and pick an app just like you would if you were in Finder or in Launchpad while it is open. This can be a very quick way to launch programs.

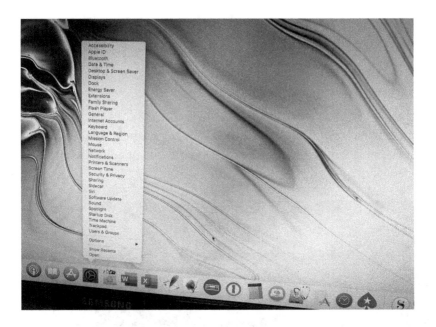

If you rest your tooltip on System Settings and left-click, you will see all of the System Settings that are available when you open the window. You can click on any of the System Settings now from the quick menu just like you would if you had actually opened the window.

# 333

# The Books App

Looking at things from the perspective of a writer I have to admit that the Apple Books app is one application that I'm just not sure of where it's going. When you publish a book you have a several places that you can publish it today. The largest platform reaching the widest audience is Amazon.

Because this book is a Mac specific one it was really the first time that I seriously considered putting a book in Apple's bookstore. The books in the Apple bookstore are essentially specific to Mac in format. Just to say that they are read on Apple devices. Kindle books on the other hand can be read on a Mac or a PC or on a Kindle book reader for that matter. Therefore most authors will tend to go with this other platform over Apple.

So what is Apple's vision for Books both now and moving forward? To be honest I don't have an answer to that question. Up until recently Apple had a specific application for writing books for the Apple bookstore called iBooks Author. That application has been abandoned and the functionality has been written into pages. One wonders if this is simply a streamlining of applications or a sign of what's to come in the future to Apple Books.

For now, as an author I just sit and watch to see where Apple is going to go with Books in the future. In the meantime the app is available to everyone on a Mac, and there are many free and paid titles in the store though they be specific to the Apple platform.

# 334

# Screen Record

Mac allows you to make a screen capture movie of anything you're doing on your Mac. You could make a how to video of how to use a particular app for example, or send a short movie to a friend showing them how to do something.

This feature works the same way that the screen capture works. Press Command Shit 5 to get into the screen capture menu. Now instead of using the three screen capture options on the left, you'll be choosing from the two screen record buttons in the middle. One will capture only a window, the other will capture your entire screen. To start recording, press the record button on the right. By default, screen record will do just that. It will record only what you're doing on the screen. To add your voice to the recording, open up the options menu before you start and click Built In Microphone. Now your voice will be added to the movie.

To stop a recording, press command shift 5 again to get the menu back and hit the stop button. The Mac will automatically save your video as a Quick Time movie to your desktop. You're now free to do anything you want with it. Upload it to YouTub, text or email it if it's not too big, or edit it in iMovie.

# 335

# The Mac Computer Users Group

If you are on Facebook and you own a Mac, then becoming a member of The Mac Computer Users Group is a no-brainer. Membership is free and so is the instruction and advice that you're going to get from the professional admins and other Mac users like yourself.

Everyone is an expert is something, and no one is a expert on everything. The Mac Computer Users Group takes the strength in numbers approach to problem solving on the Mac as it is Facebooks largest Mac user forum. On the site you can ask any Mac related question and because of the sheer number of users, you will immediately start getting answers to help you with your issue or offer advice.

As a professional sound engineer and Mac writer, I am always quick to jump in and offer advice in my area of expertise if someone is having issues with audio recording on the Mac or the like. When I encounter an issue that I've never seen before I have a place where I can go and get advice as well. Again, we all need help from time to time and there is no better place on the internet to get it.

The site also has live streaming guests on from time to time and I have had the pleasure of speaking on a handful of these events. Everything is free and open to all Mac users. The admins who run the group are professional computer repair people who care about the end users of the Apple product and have a lifetime of experience in the Apple ecosystem. You can find the group on Facebook by simply searching *The Mac Computer Users Group*.

# 336

# Tech Talk America

I have a friend who is an online teacher by the name of David A. Cox. David runs a website for Mac users called Tech Talk America. He first came into the public eye on the network television show Shark Tank in which he introduced his unique brand of teaching via the Internet. He has produced more how-to videos on the Mac operating system than anyone else I know of. Once more, David is a charismatic individual and a phenomenal teacher. His videos are interesting and easy to follow for any level of Mac user. Once more his online classes are free.

David makes a living by providing services to individuals and companies as well as taking donations for his free online classes, so if you are so inclined please support him. You can find his website at **www.techtalkamerica.com**. There you will be able to watch his classes on virtually any subject you might be interested in when it comes to Mac. You can subscribe so you don't miss future episodes and you can support him financially from this location as well. Another way to find his classes is to do a YouTube search for Tech Talk America. There you can subscribe to his channel and see the vast library of videos that he has produced on all of the various subjects in the Mac universe.

# 337
# Apple Insider Podcast

The Apple Insider podcast is the place to go to hear all of the latest rumors and news surrounding all things Apple. It is an independent podcast by knowledgeable Apple enthusiasts. The Apple Insider is a serious podcast for anyone who wants to keep up with all things Apple. The show covers everything imaginable including guesses as to what's coming down the pike.

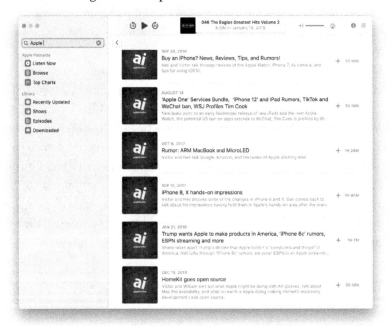

The podcast is free and readily downloaded in the podcast store. AI has been around for a number of years so it's the perfect place to binge listen if you are a new subscriber. The episodes are long and it's the perfect go-to podcast for those who commute.

# 338
# Apple Live Events

Apple has always been a company that has marched to its own beat. One of the ways that this is evident is in the companies policy to handle its own product reveals on its own terms. While the entire tech world gathers every January in Las Vegas for the Consumer Electronics Show, Apple chooses to handle its own events at a completely different time of the year. While walking the endless floors of CES, Apple is eerily missing from the event. This has worked well for Apple by keeping the companies new products from being lost in the clutter and madness that is the CES show.

The Apple event in September is where Apple typically releases their new operating systems while the spring events are where we are teased with what's coming in September. Apple will also have smaller events in June and October. These events are theatrical, a tip of the hat to Apple's founder, the late Steve Jobs. Apple will likely keep this tradition as Apple fans have come to expect it and look forward to these events every year with the passion that people have with their favorite sporting events.

Every year Apple attempts to up its production game on these events and they've become quite impressive. Apple has even built a semi-dedicated theater at their new complex to showcase these events. Watching an Apple event is exciting and entertaining. They can also be amusing at times. It doesn't take long at each event for you to discover the *catch word* of the show. This might be a word like *exciting*, or *incredible*, whatever it is, you'll be tired of it by the end and someone somewhere has surely made a drinking game of it.

The best way to keep up with Apple events is on the Apple website. It's also the best place to watch those Apple events live. If you miss an event live, they are archived on the site for a time and are usually available a short time later in the same day for viewing.

# 339

# The Genius Bar

The dictionary on your Mac describes a genius as a person of exceptional intellectual or creative power or other natural ability either generally or in some particular respect.

**180** ¶

**The Genius Bar** ¶

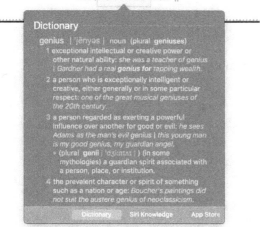

I used to find Apple's use of the word genius a little on the comical side until I actually read the definition of it. The word can simply refer to any person who has a natural ability in a particular respect. In this case, individuals who have knowledge of the Apple product.

The Genius Bar can be a useful resource for you if you're having an issue with your Mac. You do not have to be under warranty to make use of the Genius Bar, but you will need to call in ahead or go online to schedule an appointment if you don't want to spend the day waiting in line.

# 340

# News

News is Apple's curated news service. It's the modern-day equivalent of the morning newspaper with some major differences. First off it is updated throughout the day, not just when it hits your porch. It's not your father's newspaper. Secondly, it can be customized to your taste. Once it is set up Apple will go about the business of finding articles that they think you would like to read.

When you first fire up the app it will give you an opportunity to subscribe to Apple News Plus. This is the modern-day equivalent of a magazine stand. Almost all of the major magazines that you used to enjoy are now living in the digital world. This subscription service allows you to view any magazine you want for a single subscription price. Are the magazines that you like available? You can find out by taking a free one-month trial before shelling out any cash. If you are a person that used to subscribe to a lot of paper magazines, this is probably a really good deal.

Once you're into the app the first section you will notice is all the default generic news feeds. Learn about the hottest topics of the day and get the latest headlines. The next section is customized topics that you wish to follow. Apple will suggest other topics for you and they will appear below. You can move those topics into your followed list if there's something you like and you can ask Siri to never recommend them again if you don't.

You can use the search feature in the upper right-hand corner to look for topics that you might specifically be interested in. Once you find a new topic you can click on it and it will take you to what is currently being curated for it. If it looks like something that you want to subscribe to, click the plus arrow and it will be added to your following list. Come back every day for a brand new newspaper.

# 341

# Flipboard

While Apple has its own native built-in newsreader, there are other services out there that have been around much longer. My newsreader preference is Flipboard.

Flipboard allows you to set up your account with all the topics that interest you and then group your articles into magazines for reading at a later date. In the settings window, they also give you a way to control who your information gets sold to. There is a master switch that you can use to opt-out of their marketing. You can even go in and see who's buying your information.

As for the quality of the articles, every time Apple does a major Mac OS update I'll go back in and try Apple News, just to see if it's gotten better. So far I've always gone back to Flipboard.

# 342

# Weather

As of Ventura, the Weather app comes to Mac. Why it's taken this long is anyones guess, but you can now do on a Mac what you've been able to do on an iPhone for years. Use is simple. The only extra thing I would point out is if you double click on a module you will get expanded information concerning that module. The weather map for example is zoomable.

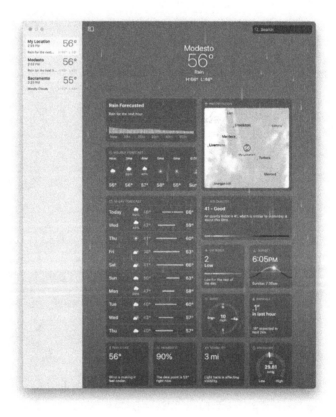

# 343

# Weather Bug

If you have an Apple Watch or an iPhone you already know the convenience of having updated weather reports with you at all times. But what about when you're sitting in front of your Mac? Other than the Weather app, the Mac has no built-in functionality for seeing a weather forecast on the menu bar. Fortunately, there are several third-party apps for monitoring and viewing the weather in detail.

I currently use an app by Weather Bug. It seems to be pretty accurate for most areas and I like the fact that it will sit on my computer's top bar with the current conditions and temperature.

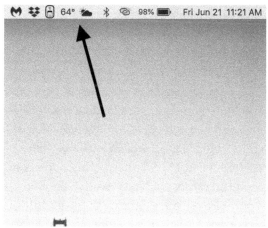

You can click the Weather Bug icon at any time to see additional information or change your location manually, just click the little gear for additional adjustments. If you want a less obtrusive weather experience without running an additional app try using a widget. You can set up a weather widget but of course, you will have to actually go to it to see it.

# 344

# Knocked Out of the Sky

In 2016 my company was contracted to provide sound reinforcement for the Bernie Sanders campaign. I was the main sound engineer for the San Francisco event. We were providing a sound system that reached a huge area in the foreground of the Golden Gate Bridge and at the same time we provided audio distribution for forty or so local and national news trucks.

I've worked over the years with most of the major candidates, on both sides, and these events all have one thing in common. The Secret Service. While we love them and literally trust them for our safety and protection at these events, they also create logistical frustrations for you as a sound engineer.

One area where this comes into play is with your wireless mic frequencies. We have to report all of our frequencies to the Secret Service that we use before an event so they know and can track/ monitor all of the frequencies that are in use. We will do a scan of all the frequencies in play at an event site and choose frequencies that are not in use for our wireless mics. Here's the problem with the Secret service, once soundcheck is over, twenty to fifty news trucks descend onto your event, all with powerful radios that may overlap on your frequencies. The result is your wireless mics quitting in the middle of your event, literally knocked out of the sky by a more powerful radio.

By now you're asking what this story has to do with your Mac? The same issues with radio frequency are present with your computer system. Today we have all manor of devices around our computers that emit radio frequency. Our phones, our mice, our keyboards, our microwaves, our florescent lights, our routers, our hard drives, and dozens of other devices are all emitting radio frequencies that can interfere with your computer. If you suddenly have interference with mice or keyboards behaving radically, or if your router starts dropping devices, you may want to look around your computer to see what is in proximity. You may think that you need a new mouse when in reality you simply may need to move an offending device further away.

# 345
# Removing An Unremovable App

Now and then you'll run into a situation where your computer might be loading an app at startup that you no longer need, or you don't know what it is. It might tell you that you have an issue with an app, but when you go to your app folder, you can't find an app by that name.

This happened to me recently on my Mac Mini that I use as a media server in our home theater. The mini had been booting sluggishly for some time and began giving me a message that it had an issue loading an app called NETserver. When I looked into my app folder, no app by that name was to be found. So what do you do in these circumstances to rectify the problem? In times like these, you have to be willing to become a bit of a detective.

Fortunately for us, Mac is a simple streamline product compared to a PC. Tracking down these rogue problems is a lot easier if you know how. The first thing I did after failing at removing the app by conventional methods was to simply do a Google search for information. As soon as I typed in *NETserver* Google began to populate other searches with terms like *How do I remove NETserver from Mac*. It's always a good sign when you find that other people have experienced the same or similar issue as you.

As it turns out NETserver is part of the printer driver for Brother printers. This mini two years earlier had been an office machine and in that office was hooked up to a Brother printer. When the computer moved locations the old printer was removed from it in the normal way that you'd pull a printer driver off of a Mac, but part of the driver remained behind. In this case, the answer was to go to the old printer drivers folder on the hard drive and drag the entire folder into the trash. By using Google, I learned that this folder could be found on the hard drive at *Computer/Macintosh HD/Library/Printers/Brother*.

There is a world of information out there at your fingertips and if you're willing to simply look for an answer, a Mac is just usually not that hard to fix.

# 346

# Slow Boot?

For PC users, the concept that your computer will gradually slow down and run more sluggish as days go by is an unfortunate fact of life. Not so for the Mac user. There are a few situations however that can cause your beloved Mac to feel long in the tooth. The good news is that there are a few easy fixes for when and if this happens.

The first common problem we'll look at is not the Mac's fault at all. A few weeks ago I had begun to notice that my work computer was starting to boot slower than all of my other machines. To be fair, I have to point out that this machine was my original Mac, a seven-year-old MacBook Pro. Now it was a screaming fast machine for its day with 16GB of RAM and a 500GB SSD drive, but my boot time on the machine had gone from well under a minute to almost two. I Googled a few fixes to try to bring it back to the start-up time of its youth, but to no avail.

Then I started wondering, what if it wasn't its fault at all? The machine had a number of peripherals plugged into it on power-up, what if something else was causing the issue? Well, it was easy enough to check, I powered down the machine and unplugged everything attached to it. I unplugged its external monitor, its external hard drive, and an external USB hub. I powered the machine back on and lo and behold, it powered up in under a minute, just like when it was new! I then proceeded to plug back in the peripherals one at a time until I found the offender. The problem was a sluggish external hard drive. The drive worked fine, but its age was showing. For the cost of a new external hard drive, I got back all of the speed of my computer's youth!

# 347

# NVRAM

Another issue that may cause a slow boot and other problems is a corrupt NVRAM. NVRAM, pronounced N.V. ram stands for Non-Volatile Random Access Memory, and it is the area of memory that contains the information for your Macs boot up. It stores things like screen resolution, your volume, and many other system settings on your Mac. Like any computer file, this information can become corrupt, and a corrupt NVRAM will slow down your boot time.

The NVRAM can be reset on any Mac by any user with a little knowledge, and some contortionist skills. To reset the NVRAM, do the following. First power down your computer. Now, take your left finger and hold down the option and command keys. With your right finger press the power button and immediately press and hold the P and R keys. You'll see and hear your computer begin to boot up normally, but then the screen will go black and you'll see and hear the process start over again. This is when the reset occurs. After the second startup boot begins you can remove your fingers from the keyboard and your computer will begin to boot normally with the newly written NVRAM file. After startup is complete, reboot your machine normally to make sure that the new NVRAM is doing its job.

This procedure is necessary any time an internal hard drive is replaced or a new battery is put into your machine. Perform this procedure as a last resort if you're experiencing boot issues, and you've eliminated the possibility of any external devices interfering with boot up. It's not harmful to your machine to do it, but as the saying goes, if it's not broken, don't fix it. Apple makes it hard to do this procedure for a reason, but having said that, if you're having issues, it's worth a try.

# 348

# Relocated Items

When you upgrading from some operating systems, you may notice a funny little quirk about the upgrade. Sometimes an OS upgrade will drop a folder on your desktop called *Relocated Items*.

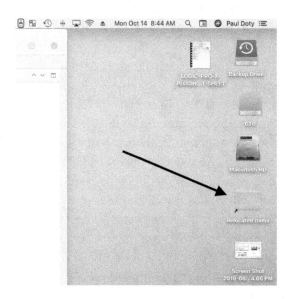

This little icon is an alias (or shortcut) to a folder on your hard drive with files that the new OS had to move due to updates in the new OS security protocols and methods. In most cases, this information is likely irrelevant, but to be sure, go ahead and open this folder and step through all of the subfolders to look at the information contained within. Look for anything relevant to you and if you find something, go ahead and move it to a location of your choosing. Chances are, you'll find nothing but computer-generated gibberish here. On all of my machines, I found that almost all of the sub-folders were actually empty, and one at the very end was actually locked, so I couldn't see its contents.

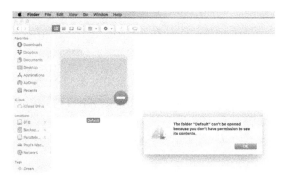

The Mac OS no longer allows apps to leave files in the root directory, so any of these files that have been left behind from really old apps and operating systems have been moved here. For the most part, these are usually orphaned files from apps that are likely long gone and this is the Macs way of cleaning house, however, and this is a big however, you should go through these folders and see if there is anything you recognize and keep. I have heard stories of people who had things like photos stored in their root directories and would have lost them if they didn't look before deleting this folder!

Once you've looked through the folders and like 99% of us determined that there's nothing here that you care about, you have two choices. One, you can get rid of the alias and keep the VERY small amount of files stored in this folder entombed on your hard drive just in case you find that you actually did need something there down the road. Or, you can delete the actual folder.

To keep the files but remove the alias, simply drag the alias into the trash. To delete the actual folder and its contents open finder and click Go/Home and search for *Relocated Items*. The folder should pop up so you can delete it by dragging it to the trash. After doing so you will still need to drag the alias into the trash as well.

# 349

# Frozen Boot

Occasionally a Mac will freeze on boot up. Typically the progress bar will simply freeze at some point and it will just sit there. The first thing to do when this happens is to attempt a power down and reboot. Holding the power button will usually allow you to shut down the computer and attempt a re-boot.

If this doesn't work, try removing all peripherals plugged into the machine, and try again. If it boots, the issue is not your Mac.

Still no luck? Then it's time to boot up in safe mode. Before you begin to start up your Mac in safe mode, you need to know what type of Mac you have. On your Mac, choose Apple menu and go to About This Mac. If you see an item labeled *Chip*, followed by the name of the chip, you have a Mac with Apple silicon. If you see an item labeled *Processor*, followed by the name of an Intel processor, you have an Intel-based Mac. Next Google the restart instructions for your particular Mac.

The first thing you'll want to do in safe mode is empty your recycle bin. Then go to finder and verify that your hard drive has at least 10GB open on it. If it doesn't, that's likely the problem. Move or delete enough files to get more than 10GB open. Remember to empty the recycle bin again to actually remove the files from the drive.

If this is not the issue, then run the disk utility. Turn your Mac on while holding the Command and R keys until you see the Apple logo. When you see the utility window, select Disk utility. Select your Macs hard drive and verify/repair the disk.

If you've tried all of these steps, and the slow boot tips in the slow boot chapter and you're still stuck, then you might need to take your computer in for repair. If you have a computer-savvy friend, you might want to give them a call at this point as a last resort before spending money at the Apple store. If you do need help from the mothership, schedule an appointment online with your local Apple store.

# 350
# Computer Lag After Update

There is a noticeable phenomenon that can happen right after updating the operating system on a Mac computer. In the first two to four weeks, you may notice the Mac running a little slower than usual. This can be a shock because after all isn't a new operating system supposed to improve the machine? Isn't the computer supposed to run faster afterward? Well, the answer is yes, and no.

This is another area where Mac differs from PC. With a PC we tend to notice a slow down in the performance of the system over time. This is due to the computer's operating method through the use of the system registry. As time goes on the registry becomes more bloated and more internal systems interact with each other causing slowdowns. Sometimes an update on the PC will cause the system to run a little faster if the update repairs one of these conflicts.

Mac is the opposite. Without a system registry, the computer does not slow down with time. On the contrary. With time, the system tends to run faster. The reason for this is that manufacturers continually update the drivers for their monitors and printers and such and push those updates through Apple Update to your computer. So as the saying goes, the system truly does get better with age. When you first do a major update, there may be slowdowns with drivers interacting with other drivers. Also, all of the various applications on your machine will begin to interact with each other. This is happening on your machine and all other Macs around the world simultaneously. Manufacturers begin to learn what issues they have once a new operating system is in the wild in real-time. This is why you will see two or three or sometimes even for updates in the first few weeks after a new operating system releases as new bugs are discovered and worked out.

# 351

## Frozen App Store

Occasionally you may experience your App Store freeze while downloading updates. This can happen from time to time for a number of reasons, many of which are out of your control. What should you do if this happens so you can get your store working again? An application may start to download and then freeze, giving you a message to try again later, or you might get the spinning beach ball of death. What can you do?

The first thing to always try is to quit the App Store and reboot your machine. If this does nothing, try resetting the process by opening Activity Monitor and then double-click the appstoreagent. This will allow you to quit the process and clear the memory.

Try to download the updates again. As a last resort, if this still doesn't work, you might try the hand-grenade approach. Delete the app all together from your machine and re-download it from the App Store. This method downloads a completely fresh version to your computer including all of the latest updates.

# Beta Program

Whenever a new operating system is about to come out Apple allows a select few to be on the beta testing team for it. There are no special requirements to be enrolled in this program other than a willingness to participate and a deep understanding of what you're signing on for. In fact, Apple wants the average everyday computer user as well as the professional enrolled in the program in order to get the widest user range possible. Anyone can sign up for the program by going to **www.beta.apple.com**

As a beta tester, you will have access to Apple OS releases before the general public does and while that's cool, that's not a good reason to be involved in the program. For months prior to the release of this book, I was a beta tester for Big Sur, and before that Catalina. By the time you have this book in your hands, you'll be enjoying a bright shiny new operating system for your Mac, but as I wrote the majority of this chapter, I was drudging through the Catalina beta, a clunky operating system on a Macbook, months away from its readiness and public release.

Beta testers are the test pilots of computers. If you choose to be a beta tester, have a good reason to do so. That reason may be no more complex than wanting to help bring a major product to market for the masses. My reason was to have access to the OS a half year before its release so I could have my book up to date upon its release.

When you're a beta tester you get to see a product developed from its infancy to its final mature state. Because of this by its very nature, you will be dealing with a flawed product. Your job as a beta tester will be to report these flaws and bugs back to the mothership so they can be analyzed, repaired, and perfected. Over the past few months, I have recorded many bugs back to Apple that I found in Catalina. One bug turned out to be a major one that I and ten other people found. This bug would not have been found without the beta program. Now as Catalina is released I do take pride and the fact that I help develop this product in a very small way. My contribution actually changed the face of an operating system and that is the fun and reward of being a beta tester.

If you choose to be a beta tester there are realities that you need to be aware of. First and foremost never put a piece of beta software on a *go-to everyday* machine. In other words, if you are going to beta-test the next operating system for Mac, make sure that you have a second Mac computer that is separate from your day-to-day computers to put the operating system on. These are commonly referred to as mules. You will essentially be taking one of your computers and dedicating the next few months of its life to be little more than a test machine. It will frustrate you, It will crash, it will change sometimes daily. It will be a constant stream of updates and every time you crash or find a bug you will need to fill out a form on a special app on the machine to send to Apple. It is a commitment on your part of time and resources. And through all of this, the only payment you will receive is the satisfaction for a job well done.

# 353
# Product Details

You can find out on the information that you need about your Mac by clicking on the Apple logo and clicking on about this Mac, but what about an iPad? There are times when you will need to know more information about an iPad than is readily available in the General section of system preferences on the iPad. For instance, you may have an iPad and you're wondering if it can be used for sidecar with your iPad Pro. Only an iPad that's running an A8 processor or better can do this. If you look on your iPad, you're not going to find that information in the about section.

There is a website however where you can put in your model number and get all kinds of information about your iPad including your processor. The website is called **everymac.com**. There is a place on the website to enter your model number and it will come back with all of the specifications of an iPad including the processor. To locate this information on your iPad, go to System Preferences. In the General tab click About. Here you will find the model number. Type this number into the website and click *Lookup*. It will give you all of the information that you're looking for.

# 354

# New iPhone

Your Mac plays an important part in setting up a new iPhone, especially if your new phone is replacing an old one. This chapter will assume that you are upgrading from a previous iPhone and it will give you a step-by-step guide to transfer your service and data from one phone to the other.

**Step 1.  What are the plans for the old phone?**

If your planning on selling or giving away your old phone, go to your provider's website to unlock your phone. Your carrier should have a portal page where you can request to have your phone unlocked from the carrier. Do a Google search for *(Your carriers name) phone unlock.* You will find a link for the specific carriers request page. ATT is at **www.att.com/deviceunlock** for example. Your phone will need to be paid off for an unlocked state to be granted. After your phone is unlocked you'll be able to use it with another carrier in most circumstances.

**Step 2.  Unpair Apple Watch.**

If your own an Apple or other smartwatch, unpairing it will write a final backup to your phone.

**Step 3.  Backup.**

Back your phone up to iCloud Drive and make a secondary emergency backup locally to your Mac. Your Mac copy will be your secondary backup if anything goes wrong with your restore from iCloud.

**Step 4.  Set up.**

Turn on your new phone and go through the setup screens.

**Step 5.  Update.**

Download the latest OS to the phone.

**Step6. Restore.**

Plug the iPhone into your Mac. When prompted, restore your phone from the final backup of your previous phone. Like the update, this will likely take some time so be patient.

**Step 7.** Pair your watch.

If you have a watch, now is the time to pair it with the new phone. Choose the previous backup when prompted.

**Step 8.** Activate.

Turn off your old phone at this point and go to your carrier's activation page. You can find it by doing a Google search for *(your carrier) activate phone*. ATT's can be found at **https://www.att.com/checkmyorder/activations/activateDevice.rt** for example. Follow the on-screen directions.

**Step 9. Clean up.**

You'll find that there will be a lot of clean up to do over the next week or so as you go in to launch your old apps. They will need to be individually signed back in to all of their services. The good news is is that all of the really hard stuff, like your contact list and your calendar, will have been done for you.

# 355

# Paste to iPhone

Mac OS gives you the ability to cut and paste between devices. To demonstrate this, I'm going to copy a sentence here on my Mac in Scrivener, and paste it to my iPhone in Notes. Now, I could use almost any app on either device to cut, copy, and paste between. But there are some rules that you must follow for this to work.

First, both devices must have handoff enabled, and be on the same wi-fi network. You must also have Bluetooth enabled on both devices. This technology uses iCloud, so both devices need to be logged into the same iCloud account as well. Note that once you cut or copy an item from one of the devices, it's only available for a short time in iCloud to be copied onto the other. So let's get started!

First, I make sure that both of my devices meet the criteria as stated above. Then I make sure my iPhone is on and awake. Next, I highlight the title of this chapter and use the standard Command C to copy it to the clipboard. On my iPhone I open a new note and use the standard Command V to paste it. If all goes well, I will have magically copied from one device to the other.

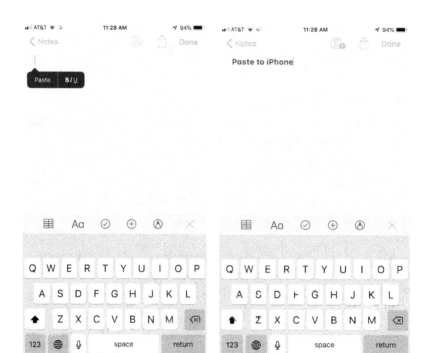

# 356

# Battery Care

Unlike most PCs, mac batteries are not user-replaceable. This has its pros and cons. On the pro side, Mac batteries are some of the most dependable high-end batteries that you will find in any device. Their lifespan is typically many times that of a PC battery. Mac batteries are engineered into the device to give maximum life, taking minimal space, allowing Apple's designers to produce incredibly thin and light devices.

On the con side, when the battery goes, you'll need to take your computer in for a replacement, and if your battery goes dead and you're not around an outlet, you're done until you're able to plug in again.

There are some basic things that you can do to get better life out of your batteries. First, try not to leave your laptop plugged in continually. Also, when you're using your laptop when on battery, go ahead and let it run down to its last 5% before plugging it in for a full charge. These pointers can add years to your batteries life.

How long can you expect a MacBook's battery to last? I've replaced batteries as young as five years old and as old as nine. I would not give replacing a battery a second thought if it begins to show signs of end-of-life past the five-year mark.

To check on the life of the battery on your laptop, click on the Apple logo in your menu bar, press and hold the option key and click on *System Information*. Scroll down and click on *Power*. Here you can check things like your cycle count and the current condition of your battery.

# 357

# Screen Time

In my opinion, Screen Time is an application that will probably not be used by a user unless the user has a specific reason to set it up and use it. I, for example, am the only user of my particular machines and I have no kids in the house that are wasting away on computers all day long.

However, for anyone who wishes to track their computer usage or limit the amount of computer usage for someone in their family, Screen Time gives you the ability to do just that. This application is going to be great for parents who want to police a household computer for instants. You may also wish to use it simply for your own curiosity to know how much time you spend in specific areas on your computer.

# 358

# Clean Install of the Mac OS

There may be a time when you want to completely install a brand new operating system on your Mac, just like when it was new. Perhaps you had a machine set up as a beta machine and now you want to reinstall another operating system. Perhaps your computer is having major issues and you want to start over from scratch. Follow these simple instructions to do a completely fresh OS install on a Mac. Warning! This will completely erase your machine and essentially set it up as a factory fresh computer. You will lose anything stored on it! Back up anything that you care about from the machine before you do this! When you are finished you will have a factory fresh Mac. OK, enough with the disclaimers, here are the directions.

1. Shut down your Mac and then restart it while holding the Command and R keys. This will boot you into your Mac's recovery partition.

2. You will get an option to launch the Disk Utility application so you can wipe out your hard drive. Remember, have everything backed up, you are about to wipe out your hard drive!

3. After erasing the hard drive you will be back at the utility screen where you can load your operating system.

This method will give you a clean installation of macOS, just as if you had bought the machine new. This method comes in handy if you ever sell or give away your machine. You will also need to use this reinstallation method if you ever put a beta operating system on your Mac and then want to get back to a normal state after the public release.

# 359

# Screen Cleaning

Everybody has something that bugs them. Everyone has their set of pet peeves that drive them wild. For me, it's finger prints on my computer screen. If I'm working on my computer around another individual and they point at something on my screen, touching it in the process, I have to calm my compulsion to slap them up side the head.

I read about people complaining to Apple that the Mac had no touch screen before the invention of the sidecar. I would read those complaints and just cringe thinking about how finger printed my screen would be if it were a touch screen. OK, that probably sounds a little on the OCD side, but it has served to make me a bit of an expert when it comes time to clean a computer.

Anyone who has broken the screen on their MacBook can tell you that that is a $500-$600 repair job. What most people don't think about is that you can destroy a screen on a MacBook just as easy by using the wrong type of cleaner on it. MacBook screens are an interesting combination of rugged and delicate. They are one of the most robust computer screens on the market, but they also must be treated properly as they are precision instruments with special coatings and delicate surfaces.

Let's talk about a few of the do's and don'ts. Let's start with the don'ts. Never use an abrasive solvent on your computer screen. You will destroy it. The basic rule of thumb when it comes to the do's, is never use more than you have to too clean your computer screen. This is what I mean by that. If you can get away without using any type of cleaner, that's great. Always use a lint free cloth like a microfiber towel to clean your screen. There are many small microfiber towels out there made for cleaning optics and glasses which work perfect for cleaning a computer screen. If you have particles on your screen or stubborn streaks that won't come off, you're going to need a screen specific cleaner. These can be bought at any office supply store. Spray the cleaner on to the cloth and apply the cloth to the screen. Don't spray the cleaner directly onto the screen.

There's another substance that works great for cleaning your screen and it's absolutely free. It's called water. If you put a little water on your cloth, just enough to make it damp it will make an excellent cleaner as well.

# 360

# Apple Watch

One of the best features of owning multiple Apple products is how the entire Apple ecosystem works together. Every time you buy a new Apple product you get the functionality of that product from a standalone perspective, but you also get new functionality throughout all of your other products.

Apple Watch for instance will bring remote authentication functionality to your Mac. It does this in two specific ways. With both ways, you'll need to have two-factor authentication turned on with your Mac. To turn this feature on you'll need to go to System Settings and click on Login Password. From there you can turn on Apple Watch.

The first thing you'll be able to do with your watch is to use it for logging into your machine. If you walk away from your Mac to grab a coffee and your machine goes into sleep mode, without an Apple Watch you'll be typing the passcode back in every time you sit back down. That can get annoying during the course of a business or school workday. If you have an Apple Watch, the computer will sense it when you are in close proximity and it will unlock your machine for you. You'll get a subtle vibration through your watch on your wrist to let you know that it has unlocked your Mac. Note that this function only works after you've signed into your Mac manually once so you'll still have to enter your passcode by hand when you turn your computer on for the first time on a given day.

The second way that you'll be able to use the watch to unlock your Mac is with download authentication.

# 361

# The Case For Not Updating

What? We should always keep our products updated, right? It's true, I'm normally the guy preaching to my friends to keep all of their products up to date. However, there are a few examples of when you might want to hold off on an update temporarily or permanently.

Catalina was a radical update of the Mac operating system. There were a lot of professionals using the machines to run specific programs that turned out not to be Catalina compatible out of the shoot. I had a recording engineer friend in Nashville Tennessee who's studio ran on an iMac that was running a well-known top professional recording suite. It was his business. Before Catalina was released everyone that had a copy of the software running on their machines got a notification from the manufacturer not to upgrade. Upgrading at that time would have broken the software and brought these businesses to a standstill. In time the software got updated and tested to work with the new OS and all were informed that it was OK to update both the iOS and the software.

When Catalina came out we did not update to it for almost a year at the offices of my business. My wife's computer was running Parallels in order to run QuickBooks. At the time the version of parallels that she was using was not stable under Catalina. There were other issues that caused instability as well as printer drivers incompatibility and such. We waited for a time, and when our research showed that parallels had a good stable version under Catalina and all of our printer drivers had been updated to be compatible with the new system, we finally upgraded. We heard of many horror stories of people that went over to the new system in the first week only to find out that a lot of compatibility was broken with applications that were needed for day-to-day business. Downgrading was not an easy task.

For the most part, updating your machine is a good thing. But if you have a machine that must have specific applications to work under a new system and you are not completely sure that they will, do your research before updating. Your business may depend on it.

# 362

# Bloatware

This lesson is not really a training lesson. It's more of a celebration chapter than anything. Over the past few days, I've been setting up a number of client's Windows 10 PCs to run lighting systems. With each client, I will spend a good portion of the day with the installation because of two factors. First, a new PC will take hours to update its Windows 10 system. This process happens over and over again until your system is finally up to date for that moment. Secondly, every PC comes with a huge amount of bloatware.

Bloatware can be defined as all of the additional programs and third-party apps that are pre-loaded onto a PC at the factory before it heads out the door to you. It's like the sponsors on the side of a NASCAR race car. There are reasons why PCs can be sold so cheaply. One reason is that they are sponsored by vendors who pay a fee to have their products preloaded onto the machines. This bloatware takes up the space that you've paid for on your machine and many run in the background, hogging your valuable resources, slowing down the performance of the PC.

Apple has no such payola system with its product. They take no money from third-party vendors to subsidize the cost of the machine. This is one reason why a Mac costs more than a PC.

I remember the first Mac that I ever set up from the factory. I took it out of the box, plugged it into power, turned it on and it presented me with a few screens that asked for basic information. I answered a couple of questions, and that was it! It welcomed me to the world of Apple, and I was done. My next surprise was to launch the Launchpad app to see only native Apple apps on the machine. That was it, I was totally set up. An incredible experience for someone who was very used to setting up PCs.

# 363
# Alexa

Wait a minute, you can't use Alexa on a Mac. That's an Android device, right? Well, yes and no on both counts. It's true that Amazons talking assistant Alexa has no app for the Mac, however, you can use your Mac to help set up your Alexa and do basic tasks. Many people are unaware that you can do such a thing, but it's actually really easy, and some tasks on the Mac are even easier to use than on the native Alexa application on your phone.

First off, how do you get Alexa on your Mac? You can launch your web browser and log into your Echo devices by going to **alexa.amazon.com** in your web browser. Enter the email and password for your account and you're in! Now you can manage a wide variety of Alexa functions right from your Mac.

The Home screen will present you with a number of options that you can manage on your devices. Pick a task from the menu on the left and you'll be amazed at how many functions you now have control over from your Mac. From your laptop or desktop, you can easily pull up your various lists and edit them from a big screen. Set reminders and alarms from your Mac or edit common ones that you already use.

The Mac can even make Alexa smarter. The Mac is the perfect place to see all of the add on skills that you can add to the Echo devices in your home.

As you add more Echo devices to your stable, you can access Alexa on your Mac to rename devices as you move them about your home. You can also build groups and turn on and off smart devices in various rooms in your home. The possibilities are almost endless.

# 364
# End Of Life

When you buy a PC, its end of life is an assumed inevitability that you will deal within a relatively short about of time. Back in my PC days, the life expectancy of my personal laptops would be at about two years. Occasionally I might squeeze three years out of a product, but they where built cheap, cost next to nothing to replace, and the advancement of Windows kept increasing the demands on the machines to the point that you continually needed the latest and greatest hardware just to keep them running smoothly. When you buy a PC, it's just assumed that you'll be replacing it in a few years.

In the Mac world, I owned seven Apple computers before I experienced a end of life scenario with one of them. The first one to go was an old Mac mini that I had originally purchased seven years prior as a front office machine for my wife. It served as an office machine for three or four years and then was retired from the workplace to serve as a media server in our home for the remainder of its life. The machine had 8GB of RAM and an ultra-slow 1TB optical hard drive. It entered into retirement the first time because the demands of running both Mac OS and Windows at the same time in a work environment became too great for its 8GB workspace. Operating systems continue to increase the demands on every computer, every year, and eventually, your machine will begin to slow down under the new demands.

In retirement, he found new life as a simple media server. He had two jobs really, to play music and stream TV to our home theater. He held up well for us for several years until Catalina came along and stressed the little guy out to the point where he began to freeze and crash constantly under our demands. Eventually, we had to put the poor little guy down. Even then I didn't throw the little guy away. I moved it into the kitchen so my wife could have a machine to view recipes on.

I'll note that this Mini was the cheapest computer that I ever bought from Apple. Its original new cost was just over $500 back in the day. The fact that we got seven years out of it is a testimony to Apple's rock-solid construction. I still have Macs in my arsenal that are going past eight years now, and they're showing no signs of slowing down. These machines were of the $2000 variety so it's no wonder why the $500 unit gave up first.

Apple computers are tanks. Never be afraid to invest as much as you can in an Apple product to get the best you can afford. Your investment will be with you for a very long time.

# 365

# We Made It!

365 Lessons!  We made it!  You made it!  Heck....I made it!  365 lessons seemed like an easy task in the beginning, but two years and two operating system versions later, I've come to appreciate how great the Mac OS really is, and I hope you've done the same.  I've learned a lot along the way and I hope you have enjoyed taking this deep dive journey with me.

Every year the Mac OS will continue to grow change and advance. I will try to keep this book updated to grow and change along with it. Even so, you should be able to pick this book up years down the road and still glean valuable information from it as Apple is quite good about never changing things so much as to make everything else that came before obsolete.  If you've enjoyed this book, you might want to check back on Amazon or my website in a few years to see if new versions of the book are out.  Technology never sleeps.  We are always moving forward.

Thank you for taking this journey with me and I hope you feel like you have mastered your Mac just a little more.  I hope you've discovered some exciting new revelations about what your computer can do along the way.  I hope your computer is of greater value to you today than the day you bought it because of this book.  And for those of you who were comfortable with your computer before you started this book, I hope that now you will consider yourself a MacBook Pro.

# Other Books by Paul Doty

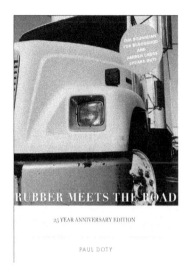

The classic behind the scenes story of Paul's journey as the sound engineer for two of Christian music's biggest groups. 2018 marked the release of the 3rd edition of Rubber Meets the Road. The 25th year anniversary edition brings you up to date with two new chapters and over 200 never before published photographs. Ebook & paperback available now on Amazon.

In our nation's current climate of sexual scandal and negativity, Paul brings a positive focus back with a no-holds-barred candid conversation about sexual intimacy in Christian marriage.  In Sex Positive no topics are off the table as Paul looks at the role intimacy plays in the design and context of marriage.  Ebook & paperback available on Amazon.

Paul returns to his roots with Faith Comes By Hearing. After four decades in the sound reinforcement industry, Paul offers an all-encompassing sound bible for church sound engineers and those who interact with them. The book contains over forty years of wisdom, experience, and information, all presented in a digestible fun read. Faith Comes By Hearing is the fastest way for anyone doing sound to add decades of knowledge to their mixing ability. Ebook & paperback available on Amazon.

The first in The 15 Minute Mac Book Series (Big Sur Edition) explores Apple's Big Sur operating system in 365 easy to digest lessons. Most lessons are no more than two pages in length and broken down into easy to find topics via the content table in the paperback or via the search feature in the eBook. Available on Amazon.

The second in The 15 Minute Mac Book Series (Monterey) continues the tradition with an all new update for the Monterey OS. This update features a forward by Mac guru Peter Alves and features a complete re-write on the previous platform making the book far more than a simple new edition of the first.

Find Paul online at **www.teamservices.pro**